THE JAPANESE ETHOS

Courtesy of Kyōgaku Institute

THE JAPANESE ETHOS
A STUDY OF NATIONAL CHARACTER

YASUOKA MASAHIRO

Honolulu Foundation

Honolulu

Library of Congress Cataloging-in-Publication Data

Yasuoka, Masahiro, 1898-1983 author
  [Nihon seishin no kenkyu. English]
  The Japanese ethos : a study of national character / Yasuoka Masahiro.
    pages cm
  Includes index.
  ISBN 978-0-8248-3623-8 (alk. paper)
  1. Ethics—Japan.   2. National characteristics, Japanese.   3. Japan—Civilization—Phi-
losophy.   I. Title.
  BJ970.Y413 2013
  181'.112--dc23
                          2012031089

This book is printed on acid-free paper
and meets the guidelines for permanence and
durability of the Council on Library Resources.

Designed by Wanda China

Printed by Sheridan Books, Inc.

Contents

Foreword to the First English Translation

The roots of the Japanese ethos and culture describe the process of forming a country from nature created by the gods. Mountains, rivers, plants, trees, and even pieces of rock and stone were created by the gods. The *Kojiki* (*Records of Ancient Matters*), one of the oldest histories of Japan, chronicles these undertakings. The gods also created other gods and gave birth to people, and in so doing, established a characteristic of Japanese moral culture in which humans paid reverence to the gods as a natural part of their daily lives. The essence of the Japanese mind is captured by the words "pure," "cheerful," and "honest." These three words signify cleanliness, purity, happiness, cheerfulness, honesty, and sincerity—qualities describing a Japanese heart and soul that have not changed for over two thousand years.

In addition, Confucianism and Buddhism helped to reinforce the extraordinary spirituality encompassed in the morality and ethics of everyday Japanese life. According to the *Kojiki*, Confucianism was introduced to Japan approximately 1,700 years ago by the scholar Wani (王仁). Wani was invited by the emperor to come to Japan from the kingdom of Paekche (百済), which was located on the Korean Peninsula. Wani, who became a teacher of the crown prince, subsequently visited Japan, bringing with him the *Analects of Confucius* (論語), a record of the words and deeds of Confucius and his disciples, and the *Thousand Characters Classic* (千字文). These events are officially recorded in Confucianist writings. Later, Buddhism came to Japan via mainland China and the Korean Peninsula. Our understanding of these two religions has since deepened through research carried out during missions from Japan, in combination with the additional efforts of foreign students.

With the ancient Japanese Shinto religion as a foundation, Confucianism and Buddhism, introduced from abroad, were assimilated and united to facilitate development of the Japanese spirit, ideology, and culture in daily life. Consequently, it may be said that the combination of Confucianism and Buddhism provided an opportunity to increase the depth and dignity of the Japanese ethos.

Whenever our country has adopted foreign cultures and institutions, it has eliminated those elements of the institutions and ideologies that it considered to be unsuitable or inconsistent with Japanese practice. This reflects the strong principles of the Japanese people—qualities and ideals essential for establishing a nation.

Historically, the introduction and adoption of foreign cultures and institutions in this fashion progressed successfully up until the Edo period, at which time both statesmen and the general public in Japan were astonished at the advanced technology and civilization found in Western countries. They wrongly assumed that everything originating in the West was superior to everything in Japan, based on the false notion that Japan was inferior in all matters, including its traditional philosophy and ideology. By extension of this delusion, the Japanese people also accepted any foreign ideology or philosophy without first analyzing and questioning it.

We have witnessed a rejection of the spirit of the Japanese people, of the historic virtues of dignity, morality, traditional lifestyle, and the exalted national custom of mutual aid and public service. Our blind acceptance of foreign cultures has created confusion in ideology and corruption of spirit, leading to moral deterioration and the decline of the Japanese ethos. Intellectuals sounded warnings about this state of affairs; however, much of the nation took no notice and continued to pursue social success without practicing the ethical and moral lifestyle necessary for cultivating integrity of character. Consequently, moral decay has increased, leading to a dramatic decline in appreciation of historic and traditional lifestyles.

Yasuoka Masahiro was born in Osaka in the middle of the Meiji era. He studied Chinese classics (四書五経 *The Four Books and Five Classics*) from childhood in the tradition of his samurai-descended family. Yasuoka learned swordsmanship and the samurai spirit as captain of his junior high school kendo club (utilizing the Hokushin Ittō discipline; 北辰一刀流), leading it to the tournament championship. Advancing to high school and university, Yasuoka pursued his study of Oriental classics spanning a period of three thousand years. He also mastered the Western classics and modern learning. He was fully absorbed in reading and contemplation by the time he graduated from Daiichi High School and continued on to the University of Tokyo. His study extended to the philosophy and literature of Eastern and Western countries, including philosophy and ideology from original texts in German and English by Tolstoy, Dostoevsky, Nietzsche, Schopenhauer, Wilde, Marx, and Novák. He was also attracted to the writings of Seneca, Pascal, Amiel, Hilty, and Schweitzer. In addition, Yasuoka mastered the classic Oriental texts of Confucianism and Buddhism, and the philosophies of Laozi and Zhuangzi.

From the end of the Taishō period to the beginning of the Shōwa period, many difficult issues existed in politics, the economy, and ideology, both domestically and internationally. These included the extreme impoverishment of rural villages, the intensification of the labor movement, and public insecurity. It was in such times that Yasuoka established Kinkei Gakuin (金鶏学院) for the education of higher-level government officials, emphasizing the Japanese ethos inherited from the historic and traditional spirit of Japan in order to cultivate their personal integrity. Yasuoka also established Nihon Nōshi Gakkō (日本農士学校) to educate rural leaders for the redevelopment of impoverished villages. His approach is embodied in this work, *The Japanese Ethos* (日本精神の研究), which was published in the thirteenth year of Taishō (1924) and was used as a textbook.

The fundamental purpose behind this educational project was to analyze and develop ideas on the essence of civilization and culture, the rise and fall of a nation, and of a people. Yasuoka's intention was to educate his students toward their own realization of the objectives of learning.

Yasuoka Masahiro may be described as a man of virtue, sympathetic, and an activist with an East Asian philosophy. When leaders in politics and business—or anyone with the will to learn, irrespective of age, sex, or status—encounter Yasuoka, they become ardent admirers with an almost religious fervor. A full description of Yasuoka's character, including his warm heart and his personal magnetism, is almost impossible.

Professor Ashworth, Dr. Ridgeway, and others devoted themselves to an accurate translation of his book in spite of it being a difficult classical masterpiece even for contemporary Japanese.

I wish to express my appreciation and respect for their exceptional scholarship and effort. I will be deeply gratified if this book is widely read and it helps contribute to understanding some aspects of the Japanese ethos.

Ohara Toshiaki
Secretary General
Kansai Shiyu Society

Preface to the 1937 Edition

This book is the result of an arduous period in my life. Around the time of my graduation from university, feeling tired and starved in spirit from my concentration on modern Western philosophy and in particular the social sciences, I delved into the ancient wise men of Japan and China; I ruefully studied the rise of communism; and further, convinced of the need to encourage anew the investigation of our Japanese polity and the spirit of the Japanese *Volk*, I engaged in enthusiastic debate with colleagues and through magazine articles, pamphlets, and the media. In the autumn of 1923, I gathered fourteen selections from these writings to form a collection that I entitled *A Study of the Japanese Spirit* [*The Japanese Ethos* in the English edition]; it was published the following March.

At that time, Japan was awash with talk of "democracy" and "internationalism," and Japan and the East were viewed as pitifully inferior, not even worth discussing in comparison to Europe or the United States. Accordingly, works such as *A Study of the Japanese Spirit* were most often coolly dismissed as outdated and misreading the times. Surprisingly, the book attracted a steadily growing number of sympathizers. Particularly from the time of the Manchurian Incident [also known as the Mukden Incident, September 1931], the catchphrase, "Japanese Spirit," suddenly became a widespread topic of discussion, with literary works and essays arguing for a Japanese Spirit appearing one after another. Thanks to this momentum, my book also received a broad welcome, but I myself was dissatisfied with its many shortcomings, and let it remain out of print for a long time. Because a large number of people still enthusiastically wanted the book, a group of them devised a plan resulting in the printing and distribution of a few hundred copies in the spring of 1934, but since then I have adamantly declined to reissue it.

In recent years, however, there has been a resurgence in discussion of the Japanese Spirit, and words and actions in the name of the Japanese Polity or the Imperial Way or "Nipponism" have, in no small numbers, sparked doubts and opposition among thinking people. Many writings have been slanted in their concepts or the materials used, and few have been objective or probing. Perhaps as a result of this, and, as many among our youth are constantly and fervently thirsting after a testimony that records how the activities of pure young souls have brought attention to the wisdom of the ancients, I finally yielded to the urgings of Tsuruta Kyusaku, the head of Gen'ōsha publishers, to have him publish a new, expanded edition.

In this new edition, four chapters from the previous edition have been dropped and five new chapters have been added. The chapters on [Yamaga] Sokō, [Yoshida] Shōin, and [Takasugi] Tōkō all date from immediately after my university graduation, when I immersed myself in the Institute for the Study of Eastern Thought; to keep from falling completely out of sight, I sent my colleagues these materials in pamphlets from that institute. The chapter on Nanshū [Saigō Takamori] is something I provided to the magazine *Japan and the Japanese* in the same period. Only the section on Kusunoki Masashige is relatively recent, as it dates from spring 1935, the result of my strong emotions on the 600th anniversary of Dainankō, as Kusunoki was known.

Last winter, in memory of my departed friends, I published a separate volume through Nippon-seinenkan as an explication of the Japanese Spirit. That volume begins with a consideration of Shinto, and its connections and transitions related to other paths, such as Confucianism, Buddhism, and Christianity, a comparison of Eastern and Western cultures, and nationalism. I would be gratified if the reader took up that volume in parallel with this work.

One last note regarding the calligraphy used in the title of this book: just as was the case for the old edition, Tsuruta Kyusaku, the head of Gen'ōsha publishers, again took up his brush to write the title. That was 1923. It is now 1937. This is interesting in itself, but while there have been great changes in my mental state over this period, there have also been marked changes in how Mr. Tsuruta expresses his calligraphic sensibilities, which indeed is part of our mutual attraction. [Editor's note: Tsuruta's calligraphy is not included in this English edition.]

> Yasuoka Masahiro
> *At Shiroyamakusa-do*
> *On an evening of public concern over*
> *   the inability to form a new cabinet*
> *January 27, 1937*

Acknowledgments

We extend our deepest gratitude, first and foremost of course, to Mr. Masanobu Yasuoka and Mr. Masayasu Yasuoka (grandson and son of the author, respectively), and to the Kyōgaku Institute, copyright holders, and Chichi Publishing Co., Ltd., Japan, which holds publishing rights to the book, *Nihon Seishin no Kenkyū*, by Yasuoka Masahiro.

We also thank Mr. Katsura Arai, Chief and Deputy Director of the Kyōgaku Institute, who revised his Afterword for this English edition, and graciously allowed the use of two photographs of the author: one when he was in his thirties, and one from his later years.

We owe a tremendous debt of gratitude to the members of the Kansai Shiyu Society, especially its Secretary General, Mr. Toshiaki Ohara, whose enthusiastic encouragement was vital in transforming this project from an aspiration to a reality. We are also indebted to Mr. Henry Kawada, who dedicated countless hours to verifying the contents of the entire English translation against the Japanese original. We also thank Mr. Kevin Haseoka for his invaluable role in facilitating the efforts and communication between Japan and Hawai'i.

We sincerely appreciate the University of Hawai'i translation team's extraordinary effort and dedication. The team was led by Prof. David Ashworth, with Dr. William Ridgeway as principal translator, assisted by Tomoko Fukushima, Carl Johnson, and Christopher Smith. Prof. Joel Cohn provided important initial guidance and advice—thank you. Our thanks also to Dr. Yoshiko Dykstra, who rendered a beautiful English translation of a classic Japanese poem.

Special thanks to the bestselling Japanese author, Mr. Ryohei Kamiwatari, who helped this project in many ways, including his introduction and recommendation of the Honolulu Foundation to Mr. Masayasu Yasuoka, Chichi Publishing Co., Ltd., and the Japan Foundation. We thank Ms. Akiko Yamakawa, well-known author and translator, who was kind enough to write a recommendation on our behalf to the Japan Foundation. Heartfelt thanks to Mr. Masanori Minami, renowned Japanese artist, who generously allowed use of his beautiful cherry blossom painting, *To Live*, on the cover.

The editor, Wendell Ishii, worked tirelessly and rigorously to ensure a finished translation worthy of the stature and history of Yasuoka's original. We thank the University of Hawai'i Press, especially its production editor, Ms. Lucille Aono, who lent guidance from the very beginning, and Ms. Wanda China, whose design presents the finished work so well.

We would especially like to thank Mr. Robert Dewitz for his generous support and for his tireless dedication and clear advice. Without his help, we could not have finished the work. Finally, we thank all those, near and far, who contributed their time and energy to this project.

In keeping with the mission of the Honolulu Foundation, it is our sincere hope that this work will help increase understanding and appreciation between Japan and other cultures. The period during which this book was written by Yasuoka was a time of enormous transition for Japan and its tone reflects the perspective of those times. This perspective should not be interpreted by the reader positively or negatively, but rather as one part of understanding the evolution of a society and the cross-cultural relationship that are today so important in our global community.

Honolulu Foundation
*A Hawai'i 501(c)(3) non-profit organization whose mission is
to promote interest in and understanding of Japan by introducing
thoughts and works little-known outside of Japan, especially those
conveying Japanese values and promoting a world with harmony
between all peoples and the environment.*

Translator's Introduction

Yasuoka Masahiro has remained virtually unknown in the West, outside of academia, in large part due to a lack of English translations of his books. The reach of his thought is quite profound, challenging the reader in general and the translator in particular, requiring some understanding of the classics (Japanese and Chinese) of Yōmeigaku (Wang Yangming studies) and Confucian teachings, *character* among other schools of thought.

Since the time of Confucius, the concept of <u>character cultivation</u> has been of primary importance for making one's way in the world, and Yasuoka also pursues this questioning: What is character? What constitutes a person of character? To whom do we look for models? For this reason, Yasuoka will be essential reading not just for understanding Japanese character and the Japanese ethos but also for comprehending Japanese intellectual history.

It is a privilege and honor, therefore, to be associated with the translation of Yasuoka's *Study of the Japanese Ethos* and contributing, in some small way, to bringing his thought to the attention of English readers. Special acknowledgment should be given to my fellow translators at the University of Hawaiʻi at Mānoa, who labored diligently over this difficult text: Professor David Ashworth of the Center for Interpretation and Translation Studies, and his students, Tomoko Fukushima (PhD student in history), Carl Johnson (PhD student in philosophy), and Christopher Smith (PhD student in Japanese literature).

Special thanks are also extended to Henry Kawada, who meticulously examined and commented on the drafts of each chapter as they were completed.

In the words of Cervantes, "translation is the other side of a tapestry," and it is to be hoped that through the work of these translators, only the dense, bright fabric of Yasuoka's tapestry will be shown.

Dr. William Ridgeway
Honolulu, Hawaiʻi
August 2010

A Note on the Text

Asian names are given in the traditional order: surname (family name) first, followed by the given name. In his writing of this book, Yasuoka used many words and phrases in other languages besides his native Japanese (mainly Chinese, English, German, and Latin) which have been retained in the English translation. His copious footnotes, largely biographical in content but some an amplification of matters in the text, have, for the most part, been incorporated into the English translation. Emphasis in italics is Yasuoka's.

1   The Consciousness of the Japanese *Volk*

A mysterious Creator created Nature and clarified Spirit; through this Spirit the Creator simultaneously gave life to the marvels from which Nature was propagated. Through the interpenetration of the physical and the spiritual, the self is consummated. Human character is also something that progresses, through interactions with circumstances and environment. Consequently, difficult circumstances and environment make the test of character all the more significant and fully reveal the value of character.

Now, before our eyes in Japan, citizens, one and all, are unequivocally conscious of being confronted with a terrible crisis. The time is now for Japan, as a nation, to realize a remarkable development of character. The time is now for the Japanese *Volk* to test its spiritual might. Just as the embattled samurai checks his trusty sword, we first must attain a self-resolve.

Exercising self-reflection in this manner, do we have confidence in our ability to deal with the reality of Japan today, at this critical juncture—not as a problem for one country, but to deal with the affairs of Asia or rather international affairs? Taking stock of one's self, how can one remain unfazed?

Seizing upon a resemblance to our present day, I will now recollect the rise and fall of the Tokugawa shogunate. Only during the founding period among the three eras (Ieyasu, Hidetada, Iemitsu, 1603–1651) of that regime was there an overflowing of an ethos of simple robustness. The fall that accompanied the peace after the founding and the relaxation of tensions holds for us, in truth, something that resonates deeply.

In the main, when civilizations peak and human spirituality comes to weaken, the human form invariably collapses, customs become looser, and the slender frame is prized.

In the early days of the shogunate, most women, with the exception of pleasure women working in teahouses, were ashamed to walk through town showing a bare face. At some point, however, the opposite came to be: a woman flirtatiously skirted about town in full cosmetic application. It became fashionable for a man, on the other hand, to hide his face calculatingly beneath a hat woven of rush or some such headwear and to bear two swords, large and small, at his side. Dazai Shundai (1680–1747), an Edo Confucian scholar, viewed this indignantly: "Oh, how many are they who, with an air of moral decadence, avert their eyes away from the public gaze" (*Keizairoku* [経済録], 1729).

In olden times, a man prided himself on a strong sword, but swords of this period came to be decorated on the outside with gold, silver, and mother-of-pearl inlay—even having light whalebone deliberately inserted into the blade. That was not all: Inoue Kinga (1732–1784), an Edo scholar of Chinese classics, observed that the so-called young samurai of recent years considered walking about with two swords to be boorish and left them in the keeping of merchant townspeople as they made their rounds. There were also those who carried one sword. Many of these young samurai, their hearts like a bird fleeing its cage, would visit establishments where *jōruri* ballad dramas were performed—*many of them taking delight in being seen by the townspeople*. Similarly, even the townspeople gradually lost their simple stalwartness. Instead, the norm became slender men with fancy hats covering their eyes, the long sleeves of their scarlet crepe undergarment glimmering in the spring breeze, whipping up their kimono hems lined in red, wearing shiny black-lacquered clogs, skulking along a fence, casting their narrowed gaze downward—such were the tastes and preferences of the day.

Frivolous tastes and preferences of this sort appear to have endured until the demise of the shogunate. Shirakawa Rakuō (1758–1829), for example, gave a detailed description of the customs and morals of the time.

> Men of old confronted the world in an unkempt manner, not even oiling their hair. Not too much time passed before men began oiling their hair until it was as hard as lacquer. Flirtatious men powdered their faces and had a fondness for beautiful clothing. Things changed again such that the style now is for men to oil their hair lightly, leaving their forelocks hanging down in a disorderly fashion, as if they had not tied their hair since the day before. They don't wear beautiful clothes and seem not to care if their sleeves are different lengths. They even seem to have abandoned sensual pleasures altogether. The attitude toward oiling the hair nowadays seems to be that any way is fine so long as it looks inconspicuous.

The public sphere tended more and more toward delicacy in physical terms, as described above, which is also indicative of the decadence of the sensual appetites of society in general. The prevalence of sensual appetites and immorality also speaks of that society's decline and destruction.

It was after the Great Fire of Meireki (1657) that today's Yoshiwara became the pleasure quarter and, in the years to follow, the so-called visits to Yoshiwara became increasingly popular. Visitors, who at first had to suffer the gaze of others, gradually forgot their shame and, singing "Bungo-bushi," "Tanzen-bushi," or other popular ballads of the day, sticking their nose in the air and their hands in their pockets, walked the embankments of Yoshiwara, now priding themselves on being *sui* (chic) and *tsū* (connoisseurs). In the public bathhouses about town, pleasure women called *yuna*, who sold sexual favors to bathhouse customers, proliferated; the trade in licentiousness spread.

These coy pleasure women lined up twenty in number, rinsing off grime, and combing hair. The attractive, alluring women fetched hot water and tea for the customers, exchanging tales of the "floating world." Once a man turned his head toward them and showed his interest, they said a hundred words of coquetry to sway a man's heart. This was called the *yuna buro*, the bathhouse of pleasure women.

This brings to mind a teaching of Tai Gong Wang: "To fool an enemy, offer a man who is fond of gain a gift of money and ensnare him; offer a man who is fond of lovemaking a beautiful woman and ensnare him." Like the oft-related fable of the old fox who ensnares with carnal desires, "Come! Come!" the women say, "Tonight and tomorrow night," making everyone fond of a hot bath. These and other stories are told in *Sozoro monogatari* (Rambling tales). Vassals, retainers, and many a man fell prey to these temptations.

One factor behind the popularity of *yuna* was the prevalence of the infamous *kagema* teahouses—establishments with male prostitutes. These were the iniquitous places of amusement where beautiful youths, actors, and others sold their charms. Yushima and Yoshichō were two of the most abominable of these dens of iniquity. The clientele of such establishments were not unlike what one might expect today: mainly priests, women of good houses, widows, and nuns. At that time, there were many willing to speak out about the depravity of nuns, because of which, the shogunate had to issue strict prohibitions against such licentiousness during the Genbun (1736–1741) and Tenpō (1830–1844) eras.

A life of sexual appetites and the complications of love were increasingly the primary material for *jōruri* ballads, drama, and literature. It goes without saying that mid-ranking samurai were the ones who consequently suffered the most deleterious effects. Sexual decadence always saps men and women of their fundamental vitality. Accordingly, humans fall into a state of effeteness and meanness. Morally, their spirit falls to ruin, and they become economically distressed as well. Even the Tokugawa samurai, who realized peace at great cost after the disarray of the Warring States period—they who were the leading class of citizens forming the backbone of the nation since then—were all lost to the last man.

During the Kyōhō period (1716–1735), the actual state of affairs was surprisingly weak, even as Yoshimune, the eighth Tokugawa shogun, frequently aimed at promoting samurai morale. For example, one man of a great samurai family made a commotion on seeing red trickling down his leg, thinking it was blood, when, in fact, it had resulted from crushing a red berry or something when he fell in the grass while on a falconry expedition. Shogun Ieharu, while in residence at Nishi-nomaru, assembled his samurai in attendance for a round of archery on horseback one day, and broke out in laughter on seeing them all fall from their horses, to say nothing of missing the target. Sugita Genpaku (1733–1817), a doctor of Dutch medicine in the Edo period, also writes in his book, *Yasōdokugo* (An old country man talking to himself), similar accounts on the temperament of samurai at the close of the shogunate.

At that time there was a poem lampooning, with sharp-edged words full of significance, the samurai's behavior:

> All the world's a peaceful place, and you and I can get by quite well, thank you very much, if we just hunker down.

This poem captures the samurai's principle of security first over everything else, their opportunistic and mechanical livelihood, their servility and empty formalities: "That's the way the world is." "Quite right, sir." "Well, what do you know?"—that's all they know.

These samurai had lost their sense of fidelity and had no unshakeable convictions. In other words, they adapted themselves to the current thought and trends, and blindly followed harmony and peace. "That's the way the world is," indeed. They yield easily to a person of power; they lack the spirit to use justice as a shield. They do not have the fortitude of spirit, as Mencius said, of an estimable man of character, "who cannot indulge wealth and rank, and keeps his principles intact through poverty and suffering, and righteously challenges unjust authority and force"; who is unmoved. Just as an object is moved by a force, their living bodies "quite rightly" give in to, without hardship, the things that oppress the self—disregarding wealth and rank, the poor and lowly, authority and force. As for "Well, what do you know?" as far as the fundamental problem is concerned—one's beliefs, one's path in life, what is justice?—they know no way at all to respond. Indeed, "that's all they know."

This is called glossing over the situation. This is called idling one's life away. The destruction of the Tokugawa shogunate and the collapse of the samurai government was, after all, the inevitable result of having invited that glossing over and idling one's life away to hold sway.

The Tokugawa period is not alone in experiencing this particular phenom-enon. Another example can also be clearly seen by going back to the Heian Era (794–1185), in which the collapse of an aberrant civilization is related to destruction of the government of the aristocracy. The life of the aristocracy at the end of the Heian period was almost completely given over to lewd passions and amusements of dissolution and idleness. Their garments and houses were extravagant; bows and swords became mere decoration. As the phrase "one hundred nights of visits" expresses, a man made it his sole mission to court beautiful women; a woman considered it an achievement to make as many gentlemen love her as possible. Adultery, in extreme cases, was committed openly by or among kinsmen who attempted to violate a woman—even a stepmother or a stepdaughter; not uncommonly did connoisseurs calmly carry out such liaisons.

What is more, there was an exceedingly atrocious form of play in the relations between men and women that was overtly popular. It might be referred to as playing "man and wife," in which roles were assumed temporarily, beginning with uttering sweet nothings and culminating in sexual intercourse. People competed for awards in poetry and song vividly portraying this lifestyle of decadent sexual appetites.

During these times, there was also *dengaku*: the rustic, chaotic song and dance of the peasants, that spread through the capital with amazing alacrity. People of all ages, including nobility and townspeople, formed groups and snaked their way through town, dancing wildly, wearing outlandish fashions, and keeping rhythm with flute and drum. "It was humanly impossible to explain the 'bewitching source from which it sprang,'" sighed the astute Ōe Masafusa (1041–1111), a member of the late Heian literati.

The aristocratic class, however, became impoverished. Nowhere to be found in their spirit was the valuable moral sense of being able to sit chastely alone in one's room, the spirit of worship toward the *kami* (gods and Buddhas), the spirit of forgetting the self for the sake of the country, the spirit of having a clear conscience. All that remained was a vile selfishness and hedonism.

The usual state of affairs was infighting as bitter enemies—whether kinsmen or not—over conflicting interests. The Fujiwara's involvement in the internecine strife between the Minamoto and Taira clans is a good example of this. They committed self-destruction, as it were, by their tireless pursuit of pleasure, returning evil for good in an ugly, animalistic way. If one were to reflect quietly on these phenomena, repeated frequently throughout history, indeed, one would think we were looking at the image of the present in a mirror.

The customs and tastes of the present times are too fragile and delicate, are they not? Young men have neither spirit nor pride; they have lost the appearance of the plain and simple, and go to the extremes of the frivolous and superficial. The taste for a virile and splendid demeanor has disappeared, and the current style is the slender, languid line, as depicted in painting and advertisement.

Women, too, have completely lost their *refined taste*; many of them, surprisingly, with heavy makeup and slovenly dressed, can be seen making their way through town, shamelessly and unchastely. Especially of late, as Rakuō observed, they go about with their hair intentionally bound up in a casual style and turning down the hem of their gloves, as Western women are seen to do.

The lives of people today amount to a frenzy of selfishness and a self-indulgent, self-degradation of carnal decadence. Depravities akin to the *kagema* teahouses and *yuna* examples above are widespread. Men and women in mutual embrace dance a crazy dance that, while not winding its way through town as such, has continued to make its way from public and private dance halls into the home. Literature of sexual desire dominates an entire generation. Precisely for this reason, there is nothing to hide the enervation and distress of people today.

While advocating continental expansion, they fear the climate, they fear the natural features, fear the natives. Narrowly confined to a land protected by officials, they neither sweat nor grow within. And what kind of governing of the continent is there?

At the same time, people all hide in the shadow of the herd; losing clear-eyed self-reflection, no one remains with moral courage—it is diminished. Together, they are attached to the vulgar ego, burning with invidious jealousy stubbornly entwined with avarice, making all aspects of society partisan; a lifetime is laid to waste. Should there appear a historian of civilization possessing lucid insight into the life to come, would he or she be able to argue correctly that the present day is Japan's degenerate age?

The degeneration I have described here in our time can be traced to the material civilization that has arisen since the industrial revolution. It goes without saying that the most significant effects of the industrial revolution on human beings were the invention of machinery, development of the division of labor, and the sudden rise of cities of commerce and industry. All these developments were accomplished, necessarily, through the effort of humans to create wealth and convenience in their lives. Still, catastrophe is enfolded in happiness, and happiness in catastrophe—such is the life that must be lived. However much these things have changed life—the invention of machinery, development of the division of labor, the rise of commercial and industrial cities—humans have benefited much from the convenience. However, on the other side of the coin, quite unnoticed, they have fomented an unexpected catastrophe. To begin with, humans have used machines and increased their efficiency; but before long, machines began to use humans. In other words, humans became mechanized.

Moreover, as the division of labor inclined more toward the detailed and complex, humans were transformed into *Teilmenschen* (one person for one particular part), narrowly restricted to performing only one aspect of a job; they could not but become more and more mechanized and commoditized. The growth of modern cities widened the disparity between rich and poor through new economic structures, encroaching on farming communities and destroying a simple and honest way of life. At the same time, the crowding in cities, materialistic stimuli, mechanized labor, and the pressures of modern life naturally eclipsed the space for a mystical, spiritual life, robbing people of individual reflection amid a herd mentality. They sank into a life of mere materialistic desire, weariness, and strife.

Max Nordau (1849–1923), operating, ironically, under the banner of the science of diagnostics and analysis, gleefully drew a scalpel across the pathological psychology of fin de siècle men and women in the circumstances described above, picking apart their hidden tendencies and shortcomings one by one. The most significant plight of the modern man, in my opinion, is attributable to the bankruptcy of character caused by mechanization of the human. Originally, character was a uniform wholeness of man's intellect, emotions, and will. The value of the human must be in the integrated development of intellect, emotion, and will. An anomalous civilization, however, wrongly develops and distorts human character in only one dimension.

In particular, intellectual inclination causes the majority of people to become logical machines, simply following scientific laws. Always observing reality only in a mechanical way, they proudly test superficial explanations on everything. The mechanical view of reality, however, makes men easily lose a taste for the knowledge of life and robs men of sacred ecstasy.

A mechanical view, of course, analyzes the structural elements of things and is a way of seeing in which one reconstructs those things themselves. Therefore, this view is possible when limited only to a mechanical existence of analytically-comprehensive freedom. Conversely, in a life-phenomenon human-character existence that cannot analyze and reconstruct this structural element, this method is certainly not appropriate.

A tree has an existence that is more meaningful than the sum of its parts—roots, branches, trunk, and leaves. A wise man can hear the sounds of the earth through trees, and can realize the silent turn of the seasons. Examining an exceptional work of calligraphy on a scroll, he sees that it is not an enumeration of assembled strokes but rather the totality of its resplendent character or spirit.

However, today's so-called individual of intellect, the *verständliches Einzelwesen*, analyzing and observing a tree by its parts—roots, trunk, branches, leaves—cannot appreciate the life of the tree. Analyzing the strokes in calligraphy, he misses completely the spirit and character of the whole. Seen through those eyes, the family is also a jumble of parent and child, brother and sister, or an assembly of utility. The state, too, is nothing more than a concatenation of the sovereign, the territory, and the people. Heroes and commoners alike lead nothing more than a natural existence that follows the laws of biology. Accordingly, they are animals connected under the laws of nature. The great joy in the sacred ecstasy of life and spirit is no concern of theirs.

People today are unable to bear loneliness without speaking and conversing, all because of such ways of thinking and attitudes toward life.

Along with having a superficial, logical, mechanistic view, people nowadays also have become remarkably sentimental. Unreasonably, they run amok with nervous excitement at problems as slight as a mote of dust in their lives. Afloat amidst dreamlike, beautiful ideas, they argue poems, singing the praises of salvation. And they are a voluminous company, weak in will and poor in execution, lacking the brave spirit of the so-called ascetic and the courage of will to go forth, stamping both feet on the vast earth as they go.

Much of the disordered thought in vogue today has a deep connection with the depravity of reason and the degeneration of emotion and will, as explained above. Take, for example, today's institution of the family and thoughts about its dissolution, wherein each person becomes an ugly, egocentric transformation and, at the same time, the beautiful link of humanity and justice in reciprocity between and among one's family dissolves. The superficial mechanical way of thinking regarding this—namely, that ideas such as the family (husband and wife, parent and child, brother and sister) are an aggregation of utility—began to spread and finally invited the degeneration of the present. The spread of materialist socialistic and anarchist thought, after all, must be called the inevitable result of human moral corruption and a mechanical view.

When a mechanical view becomes a life attitude in all respects, the disappearance of the sacred ecstasy of life, the loss of actual meaning, as mentioned above, automatically ensnares humans into the pitfalls of "skepticism." The most precious, the most noble of all problems for humans—understanding truth, the value of character, the significance of our existence itself—will no longer, nor ever again, burn in that person's heart. All that can be said is that they live only mechanically. In other words, they move materialistically, acting on impulses of the senses. They are nothing more than this.

Pseudo-impartial thought is one manifestation of this. As a result of modern man's observation of the human in a merely biological way, through this logical mechanical view, the great man and the wise man have all reverted to a vulgar, animal-like existence.

Modern man certainly overflows with a sense of the saying, "What could Emperor Shun do that I can't do?". What the people of old called understanding, however, is the exact opposite of what modern man is thinking. Modern man says, "Who is Shun? Is he not also human? Is he not the same human being as we are? As legend has it, Shun (2317–2208 BC) had two wives,[1] and Shun was a man

---

1. [Both wives were daughters of Emperor Yao, who was testing Shun's character in his search for a successor.]

like others who had sexual desire, vanity, and ambition." Modern men scorn the worship of heroes and the glorification of sages as being the slavish, submissive thought of a feudal age.

However, in this way, viewing humans with impartiality *while being lenient on oneself* is nothing more than the wretched play of intellect. True democracy, of course, must be the kind of thought that tries to heighten the sacred mental state of the people as a whole, that forms character, and that recognizes intuition in them. Democracy that is limited only to the external aspects of life, especially a democracy that attempts to deny and leave out the internal aspects of life, is blasphemy against human life that must not be allowed. It would impede human progress.

Nevertheless, the requirement for the deepest, most profound true character cannot be satisfied by the thought of an age such as this—not without searching again for something that can uplift and save the self. But, of course, in an attempt to open the world of peace by one's toil, the emotions will seize up and not respond. This is where religious literature is welcomed; religions of salvation by the other are popular, and bizarre religions that take advantage of the weaknesses of suffering humans run rampant.

Through religious literature, we are able to experience aesthetic contemplation. Momentarily quenching the flames of *kleśa* (polluting thoughts and desires) and selfishness, we can taste ecstasy that is like religious rapture. Yet, is all this nothing more than Rosei's dream—that all life is nothing but a dream? This is fleeting solace for modern men. They speak of religion, avidly reading *The Suffering Buddha, Sufferings of Shinran,* and all the books like *The Monk and The Acolytes.* Under these circumstances, the teachings of salvation through *tariki* (Other Power) are like welcome rain in a drought. No ascetic practices are required. Not being able to argue good and evil, right and wrong, is fine.

> Believe in the one Buddha of Amitabha. Call upon the name of Amitabha: *Namu Amida Butsu.* Then certainly you will be reborn in the Pure Land. Even when the most evil of persons call on the Buddha, they are accepted and never abandoned by the Buddha.

In this teaching, for the modern man whose intellect is already afflicted, emotion and will are corrupted; now unfit to trod the great path of life, it is sufficient to be able to feel great gratitude and reverence.

Lose your self! One must get lost. *Bonnō soku bodai: bonnō* or *kleśa* (earthly desires) are themselves *bodai (bodhi)* or enlightenment. Without losing one's way, there is no understanding of life. One can do whatever evil deeds one wishes. Even the most evil of persons, if he will only call on the Buddha, will be saved. If one confesses and does penance, one is forgiven. Nay, this is the business of charlatans.

This kind of thinking with false morality controls, in particular, the heads of many young men and women.

Impudently, they speak of God in this way. It was the same in olden days: Shinran sighed,

> But the person who purposefully thinks and does what he should not, saying that it is permissible because of the Buddha's wondrous Vow to save the foolish being, does not truly desire to reject the world, nor does he consciously feel that he himself is a being of karmic evil.

Miyamoto Musashi, of the Niten School of swordsmanship, whose life and ideas will be expounded upon later in this book, kept his pledge to "Respect the *kami*: gods and Buddhas, but do not rely on them." Modern man has sullied the *kami* and Buddhas, and relies on them. Therefore, it is easy to understand why invidious, bewitching ascetics take advantage of this and misuse the *kami* and Buddhas to lead fools astray.

In whichever world this takes place, it is a phenomenon one can always see through. Today, too, is no exception. Once a man has absorbed some of the tricks of this method, he shows them off, pretending to be a savior, and takes the title of Great Holy Man or High Priest. No one considers that, in olden days, when even truly great men were offered purple robes or honorary titles, they would be awestruck and reject them. Instead, outrageously assuming the social standing of a monkey wearing a crown, making one's person majestic, he first assumes the personage of the period or becomes a sycophant, indulging in fame and fortune. Even if this were otherwise, the world is swarming with hucksters who, under the pretext of prophecy, try to deceive the public.

I can't help but be disappointed by these things: the prevalence of strange people spouting their beliefs, the popularity of preposterous Other Power religions, the praise of insipid devotional literature, the staggering rampancy of literary arts of sexual desire, the assertion of a superficial mechanistic philosophy, the public performances of hideous music and dance, and the moaning of the demons of avarice.

The true characteristic of the spirit of the Japanese *Volk*, sweeping aside once and for all these iniquitous tendencies, must be—as aptly symbolized in the Three Sacred Treasures (the sword Kusanagi, the mirror Yata no Kagami, and the jewel Yasakani no Magatama)—to endeavor to polish the light of wisdom that emanates purely and brightly from the mirror of the heart, to wield bravely the sword of justice, to embrace virtue like a beautiful jewel, and finally, to accord God and man: "Rise above the whole world to strive with all one's might." Without realizing the spirit of the *Volk*, how can we confront and take heart against new difficulties? This great responsibility, needless to say, lies with the young men of the country.

Young people, think on these things. Furthermore, turn your mind's eye and look upon the various friendly nations of Asia.

For the peoples of Asia, the nation has a sacred existence. Indisputably, it is not the king's private dominion and property; neither is it the power relationship of submission. Nor is it a union of the sovereign, the people, and the land. They assert first, before giving such an external, materialist interpretation, that the nation has a great human character-like existence. They believe that the nation's existence must be the most sacred thing on earth: a nation has high moral ideals, absolute freedom of will, and bears the responsibility to make it so.

However, what are the real conditions of these great articles of faith now? Throughout Asia—clearly, in China, India, Persia—they are persecuted for the sake of materialistic utilitarianism and the complete egoism of aggressive, interfering white nations. There is no time for the parley of calling each other friendly nations; every enemy chokes them and stabs them in the back, self-indulgently trampling on and violating human character.

Are they not all—Turkey, Persia, India, Afghanistan—unnaturally and untimely harmed in this way? And now, from sacred nations they have become pitiful slave nations. Human character is denied, and they are cut off from the light of freedom and God-given justice. Racial equality was not a problem exclusively among white people. It was simply that only men of character could properly obtain equality.

How could an international union regulate justice and freedom? As stated in Article 10 of the Covenant of the League of Nations,

> The Members of the League undertake to respect and preserve, as against external aggression, the territorial integrity and existing political independence of all Members of the League. In case of any such aggression, or in case of any threat or danger of such aggression, the Council shall advise upon the means by which this obligation shall be fulfilled.

This means that the so-called justice and freedom of white nations is not, in the end, illuminating races of color. In Europe, in Egypt, in Asia Minor, the Chinese, Indians, and black people from America and Africa who always stood on the vanguard struggling were, to white people, literally human bullets. Noble human character they were not.

Witnessing the atrocious acts of these nations, the people of the world should have indignantly rejected such states. St. Augustine, writing at the end of the fourth century, held that *civitas terrena*—the earthly city—was *mala necessita*—a necessary evil. Lift up your eyes, wide awake, and witness the reality before you: that Asia, the "land suitable for Mahayana Buddhism," has fallen into a futile, slavish state. Who can look, without crying hot tears, at the noble-minded patriot, the man of virtue, born earnestly in the light of the East, who, because of this, sobs regretfully—body-wracking sobs, feeling the anguish, choked with resentment? Look! Even now, beginning in Turkey in the west, and extending to the natives of Java in the east, a spirit of vehement hostility is rising.

Destiny must not be in vain; the time has come for Asia's compatriots to stand and restore again the solemnity of human character's freedom and glory. Here, I once again think deeply: Is Asia, in its present condition, really prepared with the appropriate consciousness and ability to shoulder the tremendous responsibility that is called for? Near the end of the Trojan War, Ajax prayed for more light that he might see his enemy's face. And now, is there a prayer for the people of Asian countries to clearly recognize the face of the enemy in the brave fight for justice? Unhappily, I cannot yet identify that reality.

Surely, this much is clear just from looking at our country, Japan, a pioneer and a pillar of Asia. In a frenzied state for a time, caused by the precipitous sensual stimuli of European civilization, Japan, China, and India wandered recklessly, impatiently, without acquiring correct consciousness or expending great efforts. Forgetting their own inexhaustible resources, they went from house to house, pot in hand, requesting handouts, but instead of obtaining something, they were made to suffer unbearable fatigue and humiliation. Accordingly, not even knowing their own inexhaustible treasury, much less could they know the treasure house of other families.

In labor problems and social problems, in philosophy, literature, and religion, have the masses not pursued too many other superficialities? At the same time, to what extent have they recognized and been conscious of the ancient ideas of the East—philosophy, literature, religion, politics, economics, and so forth—in all their aspects? The world until now was merely a human stage, *blossmenschlich*— our common humanity. But the world, in the aftermath of the great European War that *sounded alarms* from heaven, had to develop towards *geistiges Leben*—a spiritual life. So long as they attempt to confront the white race with *blossmenschlich*—mere human will—the peoples of Asia are, I must say with great sadness, meaningless and powerless.

On the other hand, sublime meaning is only to be obtained once the peoples of Asia shed *the merely human life (blossmenschlich)* and the existing servitude in Asia, the land suitable to Mahayana Buddhism, and begin to concretely realize the life of *the human spirit (geistiges Leben)*.

In the awe-inspiring words of the philosopher Zhuangzi, "*shi* [samurai of great integrity] must be compassionate and strong-willed. His duty is heavy and the road is long. Making benevolence his personal duty, is it not heavy? Even unto death the burden must be borne; is the road not long?" These are inspiring words that I think the peoples of Asia must understand individually and through personal experience.

Accordingly, the duty of the Japanese people is grave, unparalleled. It must be anticipated completely, with readiness and preparation, as a matter of course. I have no other reason for writing this book. Calmly visiting the ancient moral teachings, personally considering the problems, as if to receive from the masters the beliefs in the essentials of the Way of the Samurai, as a young *bushi* warrior looks forward to battle, I use my modest ability impartially to probe this eventful autumnal time of my country. Through visiting the ancient teachings, a deeper consciousness is reached, and a future that is a more infinitely creative endeavor will open unto us.

2

Foundational Attitudes in World Consciousness

> The movement of heaven is full of power.
>
> *(Yijing 1)*

Today, as civilized European nations pass their apex and hasten down the path of decline, it is as their predecessors lamented. It has become *Der Untergang des Abendlandes* (The Decline of the West) into the twilight of the nations, sinking before the eyes of all. In this circumstance, the *Volk* of Asia especially stand out among those rejoicing at this opportunity—in other words, among the so-called colored races. Our Japan has actually been the impetus behind this sudden rise and, moreover, emphatically remains so.

Yet I believe that the Asian *Volk*, just like present-day Japan, in order to cast off this persecution and establish, in truth, their own independence and freedom, will need resolve and effort that will not come easily, since they have suffered at the hands of the civilized European *Volk* a persecution greater than any experienced in all prior history.

This persecution is the objectification of character—in other words, the mechanization of humanity. Modern man is, for the most part, an object rather than a man. Everywhere the activity of character is hidden in the shadows, and mechanistic activity bustles before one's eyes. That the deepest source of modern man's devastation resides therein is sure to be affirmed by many.

The rising Asian world certainly must not be built upon the aforementioned *attachment to objects*. To the contrary, its entire foundation must rest upon the emergence of a life of character that is entirely different from that above.

With this in mind, there are two culprits that cannot be overlooked. One is bigoted ultranationalism, and the other is superficial worship of foreigners. The latter means forgetting to pay attention to one's true standing in the world and praising the illusion of an unduly hollow concept while being corrupted by vulgar, sentimental, and materialistic feelings. The former is without any depth of interior life, and is therefore proud of lifeless traditions and afflicted by mutual hostility arising from the ensnarement of self-deception. The two are "one beast with two heads," equally blind to introspection and existing in a fruitless practice that never surpasses the materialistic way of life. The youth of rising Asia must not be bound up in either such existence.

Those who are inclined to discuss the Asian rise enthrone shallow Eastern thought against Western thought. Today, when thought has already progressed quite far from the days of yore, the problem is that those who do not possess both a deep understanding of Eastern thought and sufficient comprehension of Western thought are unable to contribute to the discussion. Both are ways of thought that are equally human. One cannot truly elevate the Eastern thought that a rising Asia should embody if one does not first grasp the heart of the questions of human life: their real foundations, human ideals, delving deeply into the particular characteristics of Eastern and Western thought. Otherwise, it is as foolish as saying you caught a tiger when it's actually a cat.

So, I will next briefly touch on the general differences between Eastern and Western thought, and try to cast light on the principal objects of the ideological foundations that the youth of rising Asia should be conscious of, generally known as Confucianism, Daoism, Zen, and Other-Power Buddhism.

What modern man generally gathers as a sign of its nature, out of the flow of Western culture, is clearly that Western thought is biased toward conceptual cognition. Conceptual cognition, of course, opposes conforming to the true conditions of reality and sees reality as separate from its true conditions. To borrow Bergson's words, it tries to fix pure continuity in the form of simultaneous existence. In other words, the world of conceptual cognition is not a fact of reality. On the contrary, the world of conceptual cognition, which is far from true reality, is a mechanical world composed by subjectivity.

Hence, those who think that they grasp reality by possessing mere conceptual cognition are misjudging its essential disposition. Certainly, they are isolated from life and chasing an empty illusion. Necessarily, such persons invite a hollow way of life and an irrefutable, uneasy weariness. I have always believed that the worst forms of sentimentalism, which make one morally incompetent, also have an important relationship to a disproportionately conceptual way of life.

The base on which conceptual cognition stands is the antagonism of subjectivity and objectivity. Undifferentiated pure experience is separated into opposed subjectivity and objectivity, from which cognition and will are developed. In this case, when there is no deepening of consciousness, and empty concepts are given disproportionate run, human nature is seized by a relativistic state, defying the unity that antagonism expects. In this state, the innermost nature of a human being, which desires unity—a heart that yearns for the absolute, chasing infinity— will be distressed by its lack of union with things here and now.

The great Greek humorist Aristophanes tried his hand at giving an amusing speech at the symposium of Agathon [see Plato's *Symposium*]. Long ago, he related, there were three kinds of humans: the all-male, the all-female, and the androgynous. They all possessed great power and, at length, had together boldly pursued an extremely audacious plot to overthrow heaven and take its authority and blessings for themselves.

The gods of heaven, who sensed this, were greatly shocked and driven to anger. As punishment for mankind's outrageous treason, the gods cut their bodies in half, twisted their heads to face outward as an eternal mark of sin, and then banished them. Because of this, each half of mankind searches unsteadily, day and night, for its beloved other half, wandering with craving and longing. Feeling pity for their condition, the gods gave them the bare consolation of putting their sexual organs on the outside to permit them to find some fleeting joy in the embrace of one of their fellow wanderers.

This is truly an appropriate kind of humor for Aristophanes. However, true humor is humor that contains a grave significance behind it. When one earnestly reflects on this story, it actually enchants with its variety of meanings. Modern man, with his bias toward conceptual cognition, is a hollow vagrant isolated from the experience of the concrete harmony of life. He tires of his roaming, but all things are to him as only a distant dream of mere lamentations, wanderings, and regrets. In that, the blessings of life first given by the gods are not preserved.

In this way, the West has naturally brought about its own decline in the spiritual life by moving in the direction of a relativistic differentiation and unifying in the expectation of differentiation, while retreating from the direction of the absolutely universal. In opposition to this, the East has developed its intuition remarkably. It tries to look deeply into unity through differentiation. It tries to grasp the general from deep within specialization through experience. In other words, it tries to grasp reality directly and awaken its perception of a natural life apart from human artifice.

There is a poem that goes

行水の棄てどころなし　虫の声
Gyōzui no / sute dokoro nashi / mushi no koe
Nowhere to throw / the water from my bath / the cries of insects
(Ueshima Onitsura (上島鬼貫) [translation by Donald Keene])

One foreigner translated it as something like, "Where can I pour out the water of this bathtub? After all, everywhere I go the insects are chirping." We cannot, however, feel any poetic inspiration in this. For us, poetry is not intellectual. It's not introspective. It is a real participation in the life of nature. As much as possible, poetry must be a direct outpouring of the life of nature.

"Nowhere to throw the water from my bath; the cries of insects." Once, when I was still a high school student, I made a literal translation of this and showed it to a German instructor. He said, "This is a strange way to write poetry. I don't get the logic behind it at all." This might not have happened if he understood poetry more deeply, but I believe his way of thinking just illustrates the difference between the minds of easterners and westerners.

A real, living unification is at work in being able to grasp, just as it is, the fact of standing still for a while, hesitating to pour out the bathwater, while insects are chirping, and then to write "Nowhere to throw the water from my bath; the cries of insects." There is a pure continuity in this. On the other hand, to order this into the causal relationship of "after all" is already to lose the truth of reality to introspection, to conceptual cognition. Poetic inspiration must not become as cold as the void.

> *Blue Cliff Record*, Case 7:
> A monk asked Hōgen, "I, Echō, ask you, Master. What is Buddha?"
> Hōgen said, "You are Echō."

This is the true state of having attained enlightenment.

Asking, "What is Buddha?" and receiving "Buddha is..." is a scholastically-founded, conceptually-contemplated thought. The inquirer here thoroughly mastered this fact and peered into the state of mind where words and bondage are extinguished. It is not a truly genuine contemplation if one does not come this far. I believe it is clear that philosophy's supreme boundary, ultimately, must attain some kind of religious state.

Eastern thought always portrays a life of fulfillment which results from conformance with this unifying standpoint. The unity of character is preserved. There is no chasing of empty illusions or wandering. The West always bears the sorrow of division, and the East always feels the joy of harmony. Their respective tendencies toward differentiation and unification are important reasons for the flourishing of the natural sciences in the West and the development of religion and morality in the East.

Still, there is a problem here that must be carefully considered. It is a danger that is easy for easterners to fall into. What we must try to grasp is that there are higher and lower levels even within unification. Unification is simultaneously differentiation. Without great differentiation, higher unification will also be absent. Otherwise, when stuck at the lower level of unification, one can become attached to the ego. This is falling into conservative narrow-mindedness, following an arbitrary dogmatism.

Nevertheless, the so-called National Learning (*kokugaku* 国学) and Sinology (*kangaku* 漢学) scholars did fall into the trap of this smaller unification and were unconscious of their need for a "why" [English in original] to deepen and widen themselves. They only took pains to preserve the records of their venerable predecessors' deep intuitions and life experiences; they were unable to clarify the logical process by which those intuitions ought to have been made more penetrating. Similarly, they were unable to produce from the synthetic studies of their predecessors a diversity of objects of inquiry.

This is why the people of today know Confucianism only as far as Confucius and Mencius, and Daoism only as far as Laozi and Zhuangzi. Yet, even if one does arrive at a grasp of their thought, is one able as a result to make a true study of their thinking? This, actually, is the sorrowful truth of the world of Eastern scholarship. Hereafter, there absolutely must be the beginnings of a grand scholastic differentiation and a flourishing of thought in the world of Eastern scholarship.

But here also, with the changes in European affairs, people have recently turned their attention toward Eastern teaching, and it has suddenly become the focus of an inquisitive eye from people who were heretofore indifferent. However, what these people do, relative to the youth of rising Asia, is the equivalent of an aimless ultranationalism, which also warrants deep restraint.

Advancing the reasoning of the New Culture Movement of Wu Yu (吳虞), Chen Duxiu (陳独秀), Hu Shih (胡適), and others, in opposing the traditional spirit of conventional Confucianism, and praising them blindly and sweetly is just as imprudent as plotting to anachronistically promote the revival of traditional Chinese literature in order to eradicate dangerous thought.

Anti-Confucianism, concurrent with a fascination with early Daoist thought, has brought forth a great number of interpretations of Laozi's work, though in my view they are, to an extreme, frivolous, sentimental, and dubious in nature.

A majority of the religious literature that describes Shinran's (1173–1263) dharma gate of the Other-Powered (*tariki*) *nembutsu*, Ryōkan's (1758–1831) immersion in feelings of loneliness and *sabi*, and Tōsui's (1612–1683) praise of a life of poverty conspicuously reveals what is, after all, the same tendency. Of course, beyond such trends, one cannot help but perceive the grave anguish at the heart of the era. However, if we are trying to take advantage of Asia's destiny to rise by clearing up the existing stagnant, cloudy, and decomposing atmosphere, making actual a fresh and spiritual way of life, then sentimental thought, which is incapable of washing its feet of the muck of reality, must be rejected. And, as previously mentioned, such modern discursive thought must have an entirely new foundation. In other words, it must proceed directly on "The Way to Chang'an" (following basic moral principles to enlightenment), under the light of a sharp and clear consciousness.

I believe that the moral determinant for those who are the heroes of this new era, or the losers of past eras, depends upon whether you are an estimable man of character with an overflow of moral consciousness and willpower that marches unwaveringly and at full speed on The Way in your life, or whether you are a pretty little lamb utterly lost in fine details. And in this point, we see that the quintessence of ancient Eastern thought was all in this teaching of an estimable man of character. In the following, for example, I will attempt to make clear the essence of Confucianism, early Daoist thought, and the aforementioned teachings of Other-Powered *nembutsu* Buddhism.

Confucianism is properly a teaching of the whole earth in the conflict of good and evil. If you plant your feet on the ground where good and evil contend, and listen carefully and silently with your heart, there is the absolute command of the supreme being echoing in our truest hearts: "Whatever happens, devote yourself to an unyielding, unbending striving!"

No one can doubt that this mandate from Heaven is the very definition of moral excellence: to ascertain this mandate, to measure and follow it, means to take what is genuinely necessary out of what all men desire and achieve it. The Song Dynasty Neo-Confucians call this, "leaving *human desire* and following *the principle of heaven*," while the Yangming School also calls it "discarding *the physical shell of the self* and achieving what is necessary for the *true self*." This is called The Way (道 Ch. *dao*, Jp. *michi*). The teaching of Confucianism is, in other words, the clarifying of these formal principles and, correspondingly, the explication of what we should concretely do and what kind of feelings we should possess.

Thus, Confucianism is the growth of the core to a most manly life and the establishment of the principles of our life activity. (I believe that the spiritual life that Eucken described as "the development of a concrete core" [*Herausbildung eines festen Kern*] or "attachment to our lives" [*Befestigung unseres Lebens*] carries the same meaning.)

Good and evil are, in the end, the distinguishing of what agrees with The Way from what disagrees with it. Therefore, the ethical teachings of Confucianism are through and through a battle for the conquest of evil. If it objects to me, it is resisting me. (Fichte also claimed that an object [*Gegenstand*] is a resistance [*Widerstand*].) In this, there is a will that cannot stop until all evil is converted. And just so, Confucianism and its schools greatly value courage. They love Kōzen no Ki (浩然の気), a great and magnanimous spirit that permeates heaven and earth.

Master Zengzi (Confucius' disciple, 505–436 BC) said to Zi Xiang,

Do you admire courage? I once heard about supreme courage from the Master. If, on looking within, one finds oneself to be in the wrong, then even though one's adversary is only a common fellow, coarsely clad, one is bound to tremble with fear. But if one finds oneself in the right, one goes forward even against men in the thousands. (*Mencius* 2A.2)

Are there not those who press ahead as though the spirit of the great man has actually leapt up to join him? The Yangming School explained the significance of this as being that fellows of our party must always be "heroes." As Mencius taught, to be an estimable man of character, one must be rooted from the outset in such courage.

Thus are the impenetrable heavens and earth, from which all sentimental, materialistic utilitarians ought to shrink like little lambs. At the same time, we must view this as a state of mind that bigoted ultranationalists and others cannot expect to easily achieve. Where there truly is a man of virtue (君子 Ch. *junzi*, Jp. *kunshi*) who gets the point of Confucianism, demands are placed on the other. For example, it has been reported that Professor Raphael von Koeber was awed before Mr. Nemoto Tsūmei (根本通明), even before a single word had been exchanged between them, and Paul Richard agreed in spirit with Mr. Tōyama Mitsuru (頭山満).

So then, what is the chief provenance of early Daoist thought?

The widely-held idea that those who follow Laozi and Zhuangzi's thought are skeptics is no more than a misinterpretation. It is no doubt founded on the short-sighted view that Laozi and Zhuangzi's use of the words "void" (虚 Ch. *xu*, Jp. *kyo*) and "nothing" (無 Ch. *wu*, Jp. *mu*) has a merely negative significance.

Early Daoist thought opposed the dualistic Confucian view of good and evil, and tried to hold absolutely to the standpoint of a pure monism. It insisted that the profound depths of character lie in pure continuity.

Confucianism acknowledges that there are oppositions to everything, but that opposition is simultaneously the anticipation of unification. Where there's a flower, there's a branch. Where there's a branch, there's a trunk. However, by uniting the flower, the branch, and the trunk into one thing, we first see the tree as a whole and grasp the significance of each part all the more. Each individual thing is certainly not an absolute thing. Therefore, stated another way, every opposition has as its genesis, and develops and diverges from, a single source. The One is the Mother that gives birth to all. "The obscurest [玄 Ch. *xuan*, Jp. *gen*] of the obscure, it is the swinging gateway of the manifold mysteries" (*Daodejing* 1). What Laozi called "玄 牝" (dark female, Ch. *xuanpin*, Jp. *genpin*) thus indicates this.

Calling some things "good" and other things "evil" is certainly not absolute being. The same is true of speaking of "self" and "other." It is together that the absolute develops itself. Because man is attached to the small self of the ego, he eternally suffers from an irresolvable contradiction. But, if he can escape from the relative foundation of self and world into agreement with the absolute, then all is truth. (Deep contemplation is needed here, since this is the most easily misunderstood point.)

Laozi calls this absolute way of life "carrying together without separation" (*Daodejing* 10). Zhuangzi's uniquely unrestrained cognition advocates that in this state one can wander "without doing" (無為 Ch. *wuwei*, Jp. *mui*) in the boundless fields of the natural utopian no-place of being without being. The True Person (真人 Ch. *zhenren*, Jp. *shinjin*) or Achieved Person (至人 Ch. *zhiren*, Jp. *shijin*) in early Daoist thought is thus a symbol of this kind of profound, pure continuity of character, and certainly not a mere representative of skeptical, naturalist, irresponsible greed.

Therefore, early Daoist thought has an extreme abhorrence for egoistic human life. Above all, it abhors a possessive love. It would be an imbecility beyond caricature if someone depicted Laozi feeling sentimental about a love that was madly passionate and jealous.

Confucius once traveled to Zhou because he wished to ask Laozi about standards of conduct. It is said that Laozi told him, "Give up your prideful airs and your manifold desires, get rid of your stiff deportment and lascivious thoughts. All of these do you no good at all." (*Shiji, Laozi Han Fei Liezhuan* 63-2)

A "prideful air" is a capriciousness that breaks a deeply absorbed heart internally and ostentatiously deceives the self. "Manifold desires" needs no explanation. A "stiff deportment" is necessarily sexual, an affectation. "Lascivious thoughts" indulge in the vigorous pursuit of things. One cannot truly grasp the thought of Laozi and Zhuangzi without purging oneself of such things.

In truth, however, this is no simple endeavor. Is it possible that cowards, weaklings, or the small-minded who cannot even face a battle will be able to master the soft teaching of Daoism and win the battle without a fight?

Therefore, the Indian philosophy of Gandhism, or the condition of being "weak like a God," which is popularly called "the principle of nonresistance," is, of course, not something that should be superficially, outwardly exaggerated. Those who follow a script shrieking about humanitarianism are, rather, a pathetic joke.

What then is the chief aim of Other-Powered (*tariki*) *nembutsu* Buddhism?

It goes without saying that the chief aim of Other-Powered *nembutsu* Buddhism lies in believing earnestly in relief by the Absolute Enlightened One. Might not one say that it is the religious version of Daoism's philosophical thought? "Being reborn in paradise" is thus the pure continuity of character. The "*nembutsu* opens up the great path of unobstructed freedom" (*Tannishō* 7). Placing one's faith wholly in the Absolute Enlightened One (i.e., conforming well with unification), "the consequences of karmic evil cannot bear fruit" (ibid.). This certainly does not assent to the ugliness of reality, nor does it grant an unreflective approbation to evil basely relying on the Buddha's relief. It is only through the total-self clinging to Buddha that one can be delivered from evils and karma. Hence, it is called Other-Power and without action. In early Daoism, it is called use without using or doing without doing.

It follows that the practitioner of the *nembutsu* must throw down all of his karmic bonds and cling to the sacred Buddha. He must cast off the small self of the ego and leap into the absolute self. Here is the subtle interplay between self-power and Other-Power. Even the most profoundly evil person will be saved merely by calling on the Buddha. It is not a conceptual question. It is a question of the whole of one's character—of the soul. Does not modern man turn even the sacred Buddha into a concept? Does he not see things mechanically, as if one calls a doctor for treatment while being careless about one's health?

Necessarily, as much as a person can practice the *nembutsu*, he must separate himself from the impure land and sincerely desire rebirth in the Pure Land. Yet, modern adherents of the *nembutsu* have an excessive fondness for the impure land. Did not Shinran himself say so?

> Human beings are such that, maddened by the passions of greed, we desire to possess; led astray by the passion of ignorance, we do what should not even be thought. But the person who purposefully thinks and does what he should not, saying that it is permissible because of the Buddha's wondrous Vow to save the foolish being, does not truly desire to reject the world, nor does he consciously feel that he himself is a being of karmic evil. (*Letters of Shinran*, a translation of the *Mattōshō*, #19)

As a result, can it be easy for an unenlightened person to know the true repugnance of this world or the evils of the body? Those trapped in the views of the unenlightened and those mired in bad karma must have great courage to be saved by the earnest vow of Amida Buddha.

The true worth of the Eastern spirit is clear from the preceding explanation of their systems of thought. It is solemn. Confucianism's combative spirit of self-reflective direct advance, Daoism's nihilistic spirit of carrying together without separation, and Other-Power Buddhism's heart that wholly entrusts itself to the sign of Amida through the *nembutsu*—all of these are irrepressible expressions of the nature of man's deepest and inmost soul, and in them we are able to find true and genuine "freedom."

Searching for freedom—this, in a word, is the object of modern man.

However, ought we to believe that modern man's understanding of its significance is sufficient to bear fruit? Asked about freedom, what does modern man answer: "No external restraints on the self." This has truth up to a point, but next, ask him to explain concretely what he means by no external restraints on the self. His response is as expected: emancipation from all the restraints of political and economic pressure and from conventional religion and morality.

Yet, we must say that this response is quite vague. If, for some reason, we were to claim that freedom is merely having emancipation from external things, then man would be an object and not a person with character.

Restraint is necessarily limited to the surface of a factual object. Seen internally, restraint is submission. Thus, in its true and proper meaning, *emancipation* must simultaneously be a casting off. Based on this signification, I think of "emancipation" as the term for freedom's objective realization as an object and "casting off" as the term for the half of freedom that consists of the subjective realization of character. Thus, the explanation of freedom's significance must differ from modern man's definition of it.

Freedom is the state in which the actions of the self have their origin in the character of the self and not in some regulation by another.

From the perspective of casting off, the character of the self is what determines freedom. From the perspective of emancipation, external objects are what determine freedom.

Said literally, true freedom lies in the complete fusion of personal character and external objects. Yet, modern man is mistaken about the significance of freedom because of a disproportionate emphasis on the portion of freedom's objective side in objects and neglect for its subjective portion in character. This is one symptom of modern materialistic, mechanistic cognition.

As a result, while criticism of the social system becomes ever more exacting, individual consciousness of one's interior life becomes all the more insubstantial. One sees the environment as all-powerful but shuts out any power emerging from character.

They say a student will not be able to study on his own these days if his school's equipment is insufficient and cannot accommodate applicants appropriately. Scholars and educators say that they are neither able to think about studying nor think enthusiastically about education since they are treated so poorly. Because the way of life of the proletariat is threatened with unease, they say there is no time to indulge the heart in mysterious arts or poems about nature. But it's not that there's no time. Something is wrong if proletarians have spare time. When they do have time, they then say those people are not true proletarians. As stated before, this is no more than half of the truth, not the whole of the truth. From a different standpoint, the opposite statement can be made as well. But, to the extent that we consider that the significance of humanity lies more in the existence of character than in the existence of objects, we must say that the perspective of casting off is a more humanistic interpretation.

On this point, Eastern thought is properly human. Modern man may generally reject idealistic Eastern thought as inhuman and unnatural to the degree that it is spiritual. But, if we look comparatively at the inhumanity and unnaturalness of the one rejecting it, we find that we must say that Eastern thought is rather the more human and natural.

Yangist thinkers [followers of Yang Zhu 楊朱, 370–319 BC] propose a theory of "men in flight" (遁人 Ch. *dunren*, also given as 遁民 Ch. *dunmin*) and "men in accord" (順民 Ch. *shunren*). A summary of their thought is as follows:

People find no rest because of four aims: long life, reputation, office, and possessions. Whoever has these four aims dreads death, dreads other men, dreads authority, dreads punishment. I can call him "a man in flight from objects" (*Liezi, Yang Zhu* 16). The force that regulates his way of life lies in external objects.

If, contrary to this, you were to see life and death as facts of nature, why should you yearn for long life? If you are not conceited about honors, why should you yearn for reputation? If you do not want power, why should you yearn for office? If you are not greedy for wealth, why should you yearn for possessions? One who sees this is called "a man in accord with things" (ibid.). This is the central core of life because it is removed from a relativistic standpoint.

That is to say, the so-called men in flight are, according to this school of thought, heteronomously (externally regulated) objectified beings. They vigorously prove Max Stirner correct: "Man, your head is haunted; you have wheels in your head!" They are all being moved about by illusions, for example, by the views of masses, by the power of morality, by a noble lineage, by the spell of gold. In other words, they are all alike as men in desperate flight from the morality of nature.

On the other hand, men in accord are those who adapt in accordance with the morality of nature. They cast off all things and proceed by mastering themselves. Zen teachers and others call this "making yourself master of every situation." Just make yourself the master of every situation, and wherever you stand will be the true place (*Record of Linji* #12).

I believe that, over and above character, this so-called mastery must be the chief substance of freedom. Previously, when I have explained the foundations of Eastern thought, I said that it lies in "the great valiance of an autonomous heart." Because the freedom in this is identical to autonomy (self-regulation), we can conclude that the foundation of Eastern thought actually also lies in "the earnest desire for true and genuine freedom." To illustrate this, let me relate here a remarkable tale of an African-American slave.

In a town in America, a runaway slave was captured and taken before a judge. The judge deliberately softened his voice and asked him,

Judge: Were you unhappy there?
Slave: Oh no. I had a good life there.
Judge: Were you mistreated?
Slave: No. [Old masa and me was the greatest of friends. Fished and hunted together.]
Judge: Did you have good food and housing?

Slave: Sure enough. [Ham and 'taters. Molasses. My little cabin had roses over the door.]

Judge: I don't understand. Why did you run away?

The judge leaned in, and the slave said triumphantly, "Well, Your Honor, the situation is still open down there if you'd like to apply for it."

The judge unconsciously shook his head.[1]

Autonomy, autonomy, yes, that is freedom! Good food, good housing, and good treatment are not elements of freedom. People will not be pacified by just improving the system. There is actually a grave humor in the shaking of the judge's head.

All of Europe and America, in their colonial policies, thought of the freedom of other races as something to be bought with money. Even in Japan today, there are blockheads who say things like, "Maybe India shouldn't be independent. Perhaps the Indians will be happier under the English government than under a government of Indians." The thinking of those who speak this way should be regarded as scornfully as the luxurious happiness of a gold digger with a degenerate old sugar daddy. Certainly, we must say it deserves the mocking scorn of African slaves.

Just as the freedom of the individual lies in his autonomy, the freedom of the state lies in its independence. According to one theory, the foreign word "sovereignty" is said to originate in the medieval French word *"soverein,"* which is a noun indicating the supreme or highest level.

In other words, saying that a state has sovereignty means that the state is an absolute; that there is a being that nothing else can regulate *against the will of the state itself.* From the perspective of external affairs, this is also called "national independence."

Without independence, there is no freedom in a state. Further, freedom, of both the state and the individual, is always the most deeply concealed, the most strongly felt ideal. Whatever conciliatory measure England may make toward India, whatever favor France may show toward Muslims, necessarily they will not, by these measures, long succeed in robbing them of freedom.

The ancients said this. "The Combined Armies can be deprived of their commander, but common peasants cannot be deprived of their purposes" (*Analects* 9.26). In Asia, now that the dawning light of consciousness has overflowed and swept the land, the policies of the European civilized nations toward the East are

---

1. [Traditional joke, as retold in *Emancipating Slaves, Enslaving Freemen*. This is the original story from which the author excerpted his own, shorter version. Bracketed portions omitted by Yasuoka.]

stepping into the twilight. At this moment, Kemal Atatürk, Mahatma Gandhi, and others are rising up; and the ringing of the sunset bells is reaching remotest Europe.

We Japanese—we Japanese who bear the driving force of life of our Asian predecessors and of the rising Asia—what are we doing now as we face such an important time? Seeing that the babes who should be in charge of this difficult time have reached a state of stupefied effeminacy, how can those men of great intellect who understand the exigencies of the time possibly suffer this?

> Oh, what we desire
> Is neither the eyes of a dog of a house in mourning,
> Nor the eyes of a wild beast!
> Let all such ill omens depart;
> We desire only eyes that shine like stars!
> (*Shiji, Kongzi Shijia* 47-25)

3

A Heart That Loves the Eternal Now

Whenever I think about the battle of Sekigahara (1600), the one who most moves my heart is Ōtani Yoshitaka[1] (大谷吉隆, 1559–1600). When Uesugi Kagekatsu (上杉景勝, 1556–1623) conspired with Ishida Mitsunari (石田三成, 1560–1600), causing an incident by building a castle at Aizu, it put the empire into disarray. As Yoshitaka saw this, he was, in short, filled with a deep regret toward what he saw as reckless behavior. He set off from Tsuruga Castle with the express purpose of negotiating between the two sides, but along the way he stopped at Sawayama to discuss it with his good friend, Mitsunari. There, Mitsunari, who always relied heavily on Yoshitaka's discernment, loyalty, and courage, vigorously tried to persuade Yoshitaka to assist him.

But Yoshitaka's judgment was clearly written on his face: Mitsunari's grand plan would, in short, do no more than subject the masses to more meaningless suffering. Yoshitaka's mind was made up, and he earnestly remonstrated with Mitsunari to abandon his plan. Yoshitaka took his troops and went east. Still, Yoshitaka was genuinely concerned about his friend. He dispatched Hiratsuka Tamehiro (平塚為広, 1565?–1600), whom he trusted wholeheartedly, to talk to Mitsunari. Though Tamehiro repeatedly beseeched Mitsunari to change his mind and turn back, Mitsunari would not be deterred. Hearing this, Yoshitaka sank into a deep anguish.

Yoshitaka had long suffered from leprosy, his eyesight was poor, and he was unable to get up on his own. Despite his incurable disease, the late Toyotomi Hideyoshi (豊臣秀吉, 1536–1598) had loved his talents and gave him special treatment. To Yoshitaka, Hideyoshi would always be an unforgettable leader to whom he owed a great debt of gratitude.

Mitsunari had also worked hard beside Yoshitaka, under Hideyoshi, making them old friends. Though Mitsunari's plan had from the start the sense of a great exploit, he would also have to take into account the loyalty and personal support of the old *bushi* who had supported Hideyoshi.

---

1. [Ōtani's given name was Yoshitsugu 吉継.]

Keenly observing the situation, Yoshitaka realized that it was beyond his power to negotiate peacefully between the parties. At any rate, if battle was inescapable, it would be better to devote one's body to the cause of a friend of many years than to greedily extend one's remaining days uselessly. Moreover, though no one could believe that the ultimate outcome of the battle would be Mitsunari's victory, the chief ambition of a *bushi* warrior must never be to live emptily while looking out at the exposed corpse of one's friend. Rather, it must be to willingly give one's life for friendship.

Thus, Yoshitaka resolutely raised his flag. Leading Hiratsuka Tamehiro and others, he went to Mitsunari's aid and, at the end of a severe battle, died honorably as he had wished.

Thereafter, he came to live eternally, tugging at the heartstrings of his countrymen.

For what reason? Is it not because, through him, we are made to reflect on what it should be to "truly live"?

Of course, the will to live that all have is the impetus behind human life. At the same time, however, merely wanting to live does not cross the boundary separating us from animals. The internal demand to start from the question of *how* one should live is born out of human character. Herein lies a world of supreme value permitted only to persons: a world of law, a world of freedom.

A will to merely live is soon seen to become an effort at self-preservation, the maintenance of the species; it desires long life, hoping for immortality without limits. Yet, a new consciousness is born in the effort to possess the self and maintain the species if it once becomes grounded in the internal demand of "how should one live?".

The former is an attachment that is limited in time, always trying to steal a little more time, whether a minute or an hour. But the latter seeks to transcend such finite calculated time and peacefully reside in the Eternal Now.[2] The one is the satisfaction of sensual desires; the other, the mastery through experience of the supreme value: the realization of the ideal.

A life that makes no efforts to realize the ideal, one step at a time, is, as Fichte said, "ceaseless dying." We must say that between the world of character and the world of carnal desire, the significance of life and death has totally different meanings.

Yoshitaka lived eternally by the Great Death (see *Blue Cliff Record*, Case 41, etc.). In contrast to this, Kobayakawa Hideaki (小早川秀秋, 1577–1602), Fukushima Masanori (福島正則, 1561–1624), and others were persons experiencing ceaseless dying. How miserable were the later years of those who were led by vas-

---

2. [Yasuoka renders the latter phrase in both Japanese and English in the original.]

sals following utilitarian calculation (cf. *Hagakure*). In this lies the hidden heart of fidelity and morality in Bushido. If the problem is merely to live, there is no space for questions about Kōzō (行蔵, whether to go forth or retire). The idealistic spirit of the Japanese *Volk* comprises amassing such training in "How should we live?". This question comes to have the same significance as the question, "How should we die?".

For a person to die the splendid death of a hero, it is necessary to find the resolve for death even in everyday life. After all, a splendid death is the embodiment of absolute value—that is, eternal life. Yet, should one be thrown into a sudden confusion in facing death, then the wisdom that emerges from silence extinguishes its light and there will be no means of acquiring supreme value. Only by unceasingly looking upon death is there the opening from which one will be able to arrive at a death that has an immortal value.

I believe the chief provenance of a *bushi* warrior (samurai) lies in having the resolve for death in everyday life. When one is prepared for death, squalid delusions naturally hide their own shadows and human truth (*ningen no makoto*) appears.

As Daidōji Yūzan (大道寺友山, 1639–1730) reported,

> The man who would be a *bushi* warrior considers it his most basic intention to keep death always in mind, day and night, from the time he picks up his chopsticks in celebrating his morning meal on New Year's Day to the evening of the last day of the year. (*Budōshoshinshū* 1)

We must say that anyone wishing to enter the way of the samurai will take these words as apt.

A "prepared mind" is perhaps the most radical of contrivances.

When the great soldier Tokō Tahyōe (都甲太兵衛) of the Kumamoto clan met Miyamoto Musashi (宮本武蔵, 1584–1645), who had honed the solemn freedom of his character by the sword, Musashi saw Tahyōe's extraordinary personality in an instant. Asked by the daimyo to explain his own everyday resolve, Tahyōe briefly shook his head, then at last uttered with great deliberation,

> I would say that I suddenly saw myself as a criminal whose head can be cut off to test a new sword, and I took this realization to heart and so prepared my mind. A man who is like this can be destroyed at any time. In fact, I strengthened my resolve to accept such destruction with a light heart. At first, one who does so is unlikely to forget his insignificance. And yet, precisely because this thought is always with me, I cease to be afraid of it. Eventually, as the contrivance begins to prepare my mind, it becomes perfectly natural, and nothing can withstand it. (From Mori Ōgai's short story, "Tokō Tahyōe")

All of the *geidō* (the practice of arts) in Japan are founded upon this state of mind.

As the death poem of Ōta Dōkan (太田道灌, 1432–1486) says,

> Had I not known
> that I was dead
> already
> I would have mourned
> the loss of my life.
> (Nitobe Inazō, *Bushido: The Soul of Japan*)

At the time when it really matters, one would be thrown into confusion without a prior resolve toward the loss of one's body. There can be no expectation of forming a view of true value in such a case. Take away resoluteness toward death, and there is no true way of living. The school of thought that never tires of physical desires and that finds its reason for living in their satisfaction is what Zhuangzi might call laughing at the dream and wailing at the dawn (*Zhuangzi* 2-12).

The last sayings of Bashō (松尾芭蕉, 1644–1694) are recorded in the *Hanaya Nikki* (花屋日記) and express how deeply he had resolved himself in everyday life:

> The other disciples, among them [Kagami] Shikō (各務支考) and Isshū, whispered something to [Mukai] Kyorai (向井去来), who, grasping their meaning, arranged the master's sickbed and spoke to him: "Of old, many great teachers have left a final verse at the proper time. Should one as skilled as you leave no final words it would surely be spoken of in the world. Your students would take much satisfaction, rather, if you could leave behind one verse of mourning."
>
> The master replied, "Yesterday's verse is today's death verse. Today's verse will be tomorrow's death verse. All the verses I have written through my life, each of them is my death verse. If someone should ask you for my dying verse, you may say that any of the verses I have composed in these long years was my death verse. The *Lotus Sutra* tells us that the authentic characteristic of all dharmas is their cessation. These were the Buddha's final words, and from them has sprung all Buddhism. As for me, every verse I have composed since I originated my own style—typified by 'the old pond / a frog jumps in / the sound of the water'—every verse composed by myself since then is my death verse."

Resoluteness toward death is a shaking off of the nightmare of human existence. It is the sweeping away of a heart that carelessly laughs at life. From this beginning, a shoot of morality begins its steady growth. The ideal shines on reality with an incandescent glow. Thus, a person casts off the fetters of materialistic desire and instead desires to live a moving life.

There is no way for the sincerest heart (*magokoro*) of a human being to truly show itself without sweeping away the heart that carelessly laughs at life. Daidōji Yūzan also said this:

> Being resolved that a man may be alive today but not tomorrow, one will be aware that today may be his last chance to serve his lord and attend to his parents. Thus, when before his lord receiving orders, or looking on his parents with thoughts that it may be for the last time, his concern for them *will be* sincere. (*Budōshoshinshū* 1)

An estimable man of character does not honor public sympathy or pity, because he loves a sincere heart. This is perhaps in common with what Nietzsche attacked in sympathy as slave morality (*Sklavenmoral*). Feelings of careless laughter must be rejected because of love for a sincere heart. Disdaining romantic love is not a negation of it, for love plays many games. The compassion (情け *nasake*) of women will always be different from the compassion of a great man. The compassion of a mother has depths that cannot possibly be sounded by a daughter. I believe there is nothing in this world that can attain the exalted compassion of a master teacher, full of years and virtue, who has exhaustively seen realized human life.

The Japanese are this worldly. That they are a *Volk* possessing a psychology with a mysterious disregard of death is a frequently observed fact, and there is truth of a sort to be found in it. Because one is resolute toward death, one will love this life. Recognizing that one can never know where the dew of this life may be expected to fall from the grass along the way, all the more will one treasure the time before the dew dries (see, for example, Jakuren's poem in *Hyakunin Isshu*, etc.).

Resoluteness toward death that gazes upon death must not be mistaken for despair over it. Giving in to despair when gazing upon death is a madness of secular minds that have not risen above physical desires.

In other words, one draws toward "eternity" in conforming to "now." The fool understands eternity by thinking of a range not limited to minutes or hours, and interprets it spatially. Thus, they think as though once you go past today, tomorrow will be here. Such men live as if in a drunken dream since, to quote Daidōji Yūzan again,

> No matter whether he be of high or low rank, if a man forgets death, he will constantly eat and drink too much, will become involved in lasciviousness, dissoluteness, and all manner of unhealthful activities, and will bring disaster to his viscera and an expected early death. Even if he did live, he would, in the end, become a useless invalid. (*Budōshoshinshū* 1)

In such a picture of time, there is no significance to continuity. The <u>true eternity is in the now.</u> Eternity must be an involution[3] of the now. An eternity like this cannot possibly be understood as being in the phenomenal world of constantly changing birth and cessation. When you cultivate the moral character that can grasp the absolute essence through the phenomena and penetrate the objects, then you can experience eternity.

Those vassals that feared Tokugawa Ieyasu (徳川家康, 1543–1616) out of concern for the future generations of their houses were miserably without comprehension of the significance of eternity. The critics of those who battled on the side of Yoshitaka, out of a so-called foolish concern for the justice of Bushido, and those who ask why the rebels did not follow their original intention of establishing peace for the masses, are necessarily without any taste of the eternity of now. Because they are revoltingly unable to go out beyond the world of objects, they speak with a prejudicial view of morality as hypothetical judgment, as in "if you do this, then that will happen." It is an inexcusably shallow wisdom.

However, one need not wait for me to say that resoluteness toward death does not mean accepting dying in vain like a dog. Resoluteness toward death is having a heart that loves the eternal now. Loving the eternal now is an attempt to embody absolute value. In this, *a wisdom springing from the silent depths must shine forth.* Actions of a samurai of great integrity are an effect of this wisdom, whether he is using discretion to decide when to show himself in the world and when to retire from it, or whether he is choosing where he will die.

The death in battle of Kusunoki Masashige (楠木正成, 1294–1336), Ōtani Yoshitaka's fight for justice, and, more recently, the final days of Saigō Takamori (西郷隆盛, 1828–1877)—all of these, I believe, were of course acting from a deep and grave wisdom. This wisdom is certainly not what passes for understanding in our shallow knowledge in the present age. Kikuchi Taketoki (菊池武時, 1292?–1333) wrote a poem stating that "Hearing the signal arrow's call to battle, God would know what a warrior's heart is aimed directly at" (*Taiheiki, Zoku Hyakunin isshu* 93). Truly, without following the innermost god of our hearts, we cannot correctly understand the actions of such people.

Those who die like Saigō Takamori create the greatest divisions in popular opinion. Indeed, Saigō once planned to retire from public life and farm in Hokkaido because of his hatred for the self-interestedness of the new government. But he gave up the idea at Itagaki Taisuke's (板垣退助, 1837–1919) passionate and sincere remonstration. Iwakura Tomomi (岩倉具視, 1825–1883) had asked Emperor Meiji that Saigō Takamori resign both as chief of the Tokyo Police and as a general of the National Army at the time Saigō returned to his home in southern Satsuma.

---

3. [Yasuoka uses both Japanese (内展) and English for this term.]

However, the emperor had insisted on Saigō Takamori staying as a general of the National Army, while permitting his resignation as police chief, since the capital would not be left defenseless without the latter. When he heard the emperor's words urging him to stay on as a general, Saigō cast his body on the ground and bowed toward the Imperial Palace, overcome by emotion and wordlessly choking back tears. Though it led him into conflict with the government's forces, it is not difficult to sympathize with his predicament.

Those "sages" who judge Saigō as a fool for his temporary emotional lapse are less sagacious than foolish. Never forget that the wisdom induced from the more silent moral character is the deeper.

In this way, when life and death are shining in the light of eternity before one's eyes, suddenly, delusory attachments are scattered; an earnest wish for truth, goodness, and beauty alone shines forth. Nihilistic views of the past, present, and future cease. Immeasurable light and life are added to one's determination toward the now. In mastering this resoluteness, for the first time even our bodies will have a holy existence.

I believe that the cultivated craft of the *bushi* also springs from this. Is it not admirable the way that Kimura Shigenari (木村重成, 1593–1615), before reaching the final front of battle, burned incense in his helmet to be prepared for death as a dignified *bushi* warrior? The way that Ishida Mitsunari, even while looking at his execution grounds, placed a heavy importance on his personal grooming? The hearts of the valiant women who purified their bodies of defilements and, binding their knees, submitted to the blade? In other words, true courtesy also is born here. We must not forget our determination toward truth. Thus, as of old, these things have reverberated with the gentle chimes of the heartstrings of the Japanese *Volk*.

4 | Faith in National Polity

All of the miscalculations and bewilderment that we have experienced stem from our misunderstanding of the fundamentals of human life. Until now, the life that we have made an effort to live is not a creation based on the foundation of human character but just on "the attachment to objects."

Even though we were born in a world free of all obstacles, we block its eternal light, do not grasp life in all of its inexhaustibility, hide in the cocoon of "the material," and continue to work mechanically. Just how significant is this as a way to live? It is just a vain effort to keep things that may be destroyed in a second; just as an unfortunate child who abandoned its parents comes back to its homeland long after a wandering life and sheds tears, humans should also come back to the homeland of their spirit.

Humans have truly been unable to escape the materialistic point of view for a long time. Even human psychological processes were actually thought merely to be secretions of the cerebrum.

Count Soejima Sōkai (副島蒼海, 1828–1905)[1] remarked that "Ancient people explained that humans were better than beasts, but recently humans are not so much different from beasts."

We have been fools like Sun Wukong, the Monkey King: humans build a tiny materialistic world, blindly believe this is the absolute way of the world, and indulge in a life, as the proverb says, "unruly like a horse and fussy like a monkey," proud of their success. But their miscalculations have now been revealed.

While the public madly believes in the universal power of material things, scientists delve deeply to discover the secrets of matter, ultimately losing the ability to discover anything else unique that could be called material; philosophers have conversely reached the point where they realize the absolute power of human character. Humans will no longer be able to face the universe and human life based merely

---

1. [As a politician in the Meiji era, Soejima used the name Soejima Taneomi (副島種臣), reserving "Sōkai" for his calligraphic and academic work.]

on empty materialistic rules. We must become able to understand profoundly the rationale for this.

Viewed thus from the philosophical quest of the highest humans, I have come to realize that it is in Japan that we can see the exalted rationale, not only for the individual lives of each of its constituent people, but also for a country's land itself, as well as the state—something that is without parallel in other nations.

In seeking the origin of my country, what first inspires my piety is the creation myth of Japan. After the beginnings of heaven and earth, the god Izanagi and the goddess Izanami descended to the island of Onokoro. Born first was Ōyashima—the lands of Japan. Then were born the gods of water, trees, and fire. The goddess finally passed away from this world and went to the land of the dead.

Seeing the land of the dead was forbidden, but Izanagi broke the rules and saw uncleanness.

When he rushed back to this world and washed away the uncleanliness, from his eyes and nose were born Amaterasu, Tsukiyomi, and Susanoo.

Needless to say, Amaterasu is the ancestor of the imperial family. Thus, Japan and Amaterasu are siblings. The mythology tells us that first Japan was born, and then Amaterasu was born from the same parent. I am aware of the eternal rationale for this myth.

Scientists may see electricity as the foundation of the world. Philosophers may see it as will and also as consciousness. Everything is an offshoot of a single spiritual origin. It is not a dual existence with different origins of matter and mind. Matter and mind are of one origin, not two.

However, according to my experience, we become aware of mind through matter. Thoughts do not come from matter; matter is the first indication of mind. Right after people are born, they are still physical bodies. Then, complex psychological development begins and noble ideals also are born.

This is made clear through the twelve-karma theory of Buddhism.[2] The six basics (eye, ear, nose, tongue, body, and mind) of a baby start in its mother's womb. This progresses to the four phases of early human development, proceeding from organ to sense to emotion to will.

This also appears in the creation myth of Japan.

Japan is not just a material substance.

When searching for its true nature, I discover the Japanese people's religious faith. The lands of Japan were born as a necessary prerequisite to eternally enhance our blazing ideal spirit, which is represented by Amaterasu. Japan has a holy mission to make the ideal come true. If I were to use a Buddhist term to explain this, it is certainly the "land suitable for Mahayana Buddhism."

---

2. [i.e., the twelvefold chain of dependent co-arising]

If Japan were mere material substance for us, then if we gave Kyushu to England or Hokkaido was taken by Russia, it would be the result of people's absent-mindedness or incompetence. However, owing to the great significance of the founding of our country, if even just a part of Japan were seized by another country, this would be a great sin of the people and should be atoned for by death.

I see a great tragic, yet brave resolve in Emperor Kameyama, who laid down his life to supplicate the gods to save Japan from crisis when the Mongols attacked. For this very reason, he is a true emperor of Japan.

Look at the pitiful German Emperor Wilhelm II. He pushed his entire nation to the edge of annihilation. The ugliness of him stealing the remainder of his life by living in a foreign country, without any sign of past glory, is something that a true Japanese will never be able to understand.

If we expect to have a brilliant future for our nation, we must become conscious of the meaning of the sublime character of the nation. Even in the case of an individual, when a person comes to recognize that he is standing under the sublime power of heaven and earth, only then he can finally feel his own importance. It is precisely because our flesh and bone is dependent upon our ancestors that it is our duty not to harm ourselves. This is the origin of filial piety.

A man with determination should take care of himself. If one thinks that when his life is secure, it does not matter which country rules our nation, this is the same vulgarity as that of a prostitute.

According to the myth, Susanoo, the brother of Amaterasu, came down to the land of Japan first. When Ninigi came down upon the imperial order of Amaterasu, Ōkuninushi, the descendant of Susanoo, ruled the country. Ōkuninushi behaved himself and gave up his reign, knowing that the heavenly Amaterasu's grandson had arrived.

When Ninigi came down to the land, Amaterasu conferred upon him the Three Sacred Treasures of the Imperial House. About the mirror, Amaterasu said, "This mirror—you should worship as if in my very presence." As this suggests, Amaterasu showed the dignified virtue of wisdom. Susanoo symbolizes bravery, as many scholars agree. We should not understand the mirror, Amaterasu's wisdom, as a simple wisdom.

Amaterasu's wisdom means the fundamental abyss of self-awakening. With the illumination of self-awakening, all the values of one's character are enhanced. The bravery of Susanoo becomes perfect and righteous with Amaterasu's dignified virtue. Bravery without righteousness will foment a war in which one ends up as a traitor.

The descendants of Susanoo, often against the will of Amaterasu, took possession of Japan and ruled it; but the country regained a just reign by the advent of a heavenly grandchild.

This shows the change from power-oriented rule to rule by virtue, and we established the foundations of a self-awareness living there throughout the land. After the enthronement of Emperor Jimmu, he gave the imperial order: "The spirits of our imperial ancestors, reflecting their radiance down from Heaven, illuminate and assist me. I ought to worship this and develop filial duty." He ordered the construction of the ceremonial site at Mt. Tomi and worshiped the mirror. This is how he demonstrated his action of filial duty as the first emperor. The more we reflect on the founding of our country, the more we are deeply touched.

Amaterasu, the ancestor of the Imperial House, constitutes the foundation of the character of Japan. Japan achieved self-examination through Amaterasu and acquired an everlasting internal existence through the advent of the heavenly grandchild. On this point, Japan was not, from the outset, a mechanistic entity ruled by foreign principles but a virtuous subject acting through the power residing within itself.

Japan (Ōyashima) originally belonged to the same god as Amaterasu, and if it were not for Amaterasu's dignity and virtue, Japan would have ended up as a wasteland for eons. It tried to achieve new development by virtue of Amaterasu's dignity and by reflecting deeply on itself. It thus became exactly what Amaterasu's heavenly parent wanted it to be. That is to say, as a result of Amaterasu's self-reflection, an imperial state was born.

We should realize that the true nature of emperors, who are the descendants of Amaterasu, resides in this point. An emperor's rule signifies a life of self-awareness. The political world (the nation in its true sense) exists through the emperor's dignity and virtue.

Politics means to rule properly—the written word means "regulate (rectify) the distorted and disordered"—and it holds moral significance. A political world—the state is a world of morals—signifies none other than character. Character refers to the natural growth of the self. This creates moral consciousness out of chaos, recognizing good as good and bad as bad.

Thus, "Emperor" is Self in its deepest and most profound meaning. It creates a government from a chaotic society, "suppresses disorder, and makes things right." Therefore, by its nature, a government should be equal to a conscience in a person. On the other hand, the common people symbolize ordinary human desires.

Thereupon, when the education of the people develops, if the manifestation of their individual wills reaches a high level of freedom, which will not impair the development of overall harmony (true freedom is not something granted from the outside but which exists within each individual self), governance gradually becomes simplified, attaining the emergence of a society in which actions are free and "under the unification of the king." On the other hand, the lower the morals of the people are, the normative/restrictive force of a government cannot help but become stronger.

However, molding enlightenment into a state of unconditioned spontaneity is a never-ending ideal, and realistically, it has to be a constant moral improvement based on the conflict between good and evil. Hence, a government constantly has a relative existence, literally possessing the property of regulatory control.

An emperor, though, exists on a dimension different from this. As mentioned above, he is a creator without limits. He transcends good and evil, and, at the same time, he possesses the great virtue to treat good as good and evil as evil. We should distinguish here a deep philosophical principle of social revolution that can be seen only in Japan.

It is easy to figure out that corruption in government will lead to revolution. Many people think that revolution is a terrible, wicked thing, but a minor revolution is the enforcement of official discipline in the fundamental sense. In a case when the decadence of a state reaches its utmost level, though, revolution is nothing other than the emergence of life as an action that a state necessarily must take as the sole means for renewal (*Wiedergeburt*[3]). This is an act of self-rectification, just as "Christ was reborn following after Adam, who had the nature of a viper."

Hence, since an ordinary country lacks, in its way of life, a leader of the highest stature such as an emperor who manifests/expresses a creative, independent self, higher than any government, revolution is the means for bringing down a government or a ruler in power. That is, the self of a deepest and most profound nature has not yet revealed itself in the structure of the government. It is only our emperor who reveals this. From this it is clear that among all nations, Japan is the only state with the highest virtue.

Thus, in Japan, the revolution must come from the emperor.

When people can hardly be saved because of the decadence in their lives, just as what boldly advances a new life is the energizing of the creative free self deep within one—when a state faces great danger from the decadence of its government, it is the imperial virtue that revitalizes society by carrying out a revolution. It is the august virtue of the emperor that does this.

In Japan, a revolution means punishment from Heaven because a government went against Providence. In Japan, a revolution foolishly attempting an act so blasphemous as to draw one's bow against the banner of the emperor himself is bound to end in failure.

It was just such people as Hōjō Yoshitoki (1163–1224, the regent for the Kamakura shogunate) who were able to comprehend this principle. According to the *Masukagami*, when Hōjō Yasutoki (1183–1242, the first son of Yoshitoki) went to war as commander-in-chief of the Kanto Forces in 1212, in the midst of everything he took the trouble to turn back. Yasutoki asked his father, "This is not

---

3. [Yasuoka uses both German and Japanese for this term.]

in our plan, but if the emperor with his palanquin, with his banner, were to appear in battle himself, what should we do? I ran back by myself to ask this matter."

Yoshitoki answered, "Good question! About this issue, we never take up arms against our emperor. In that case, you take off your helmet, cut off the bowstring, and leave your fate up to the emperor."

After dealing with the rebellion of Hōjō Tokiyuki in 1335, Ashikaga Takauji (1305–1358, first Ashikaga shogun) finally rose in revolt. At that time, he never declared that he was against Emperor Godaigo. Probably, he did not have in mind revolt against the emperor in any real sense. He was fighting against Nitta Yoshisada (1301?–1338, supporter of Emperor Godaigo in the Nanboku-chō period).

The Japanese never even dream of taking the throne away from an emperor. Such is the vilest of suicidal acts.

Thus, to make a distinction between revolution in foreign countries and in Japan, we avoid the term "revolution" and instead use "reformation" or "restoration."

Therefore, an emperor is an eternal creator. He is the ultimate unifier. He is the nation itself. In this sense, he can use the phrase, "I am the nation." In contrast to the invisible gods people worship morning and night, the emperor is a truly a god in human form. To develop ideals endlessly and carry out constant improvements is the nature of an emperor.

I think these improvements and ideals should well be the subject of research for "emperor training"—in other words, education for leaders.

When I think of Japan and emperors, my earnest wish is that we may expand upon the wisdom and virtues of Emperor Meiji, which I first observed as a child.

Emperor Meiji showed modern Japanese what the real heavenly virtues were. In the Charter Oath (五箇条の御誓文, *Gokajō no Goseimon*)[4] of 1868, he said,

> Our nation is on the verge of a great change. I myself take the lead. I swear by heaven and earth to stand up and set such great national policies as to make the whole nation secure. The people also must make efforts to bring their minds together to follow this trend.

These are noble words, an embodiment of the heavenly virtue of the Japanese Reformation. The life of the emperor was, above all, a quest for the ideal and for development of Japan's national character. His great awareness of himself in his noble life makes us admire him all the more. People who live for an ideal should search for the ideal within themselves and examine this through their own wisdom.

Emperor Meiji's life simultaneously represents perfect virtue and courage. At the same time, his poems are brimming with his deep self-awareness and intuition,

---

4. [More literally, the Oath in Five Articles.]

free-flowing and dignified, unlike those of anyone else. They are natural, monumental works, seamless, without any trace of artificial poem-making devices.

> From the time of its origin, surely the prosperity of our Land of Reed Plains came from the protection of the gods.
> Since the time the pillars of the palace were built by our remote ancestors, Japan has never shaken.
> The Japanese cleanse their minds, scooping up the pure waters of Isuzu River.

Thus, his poems resonate in our hearts as a national belief. When that strong faith becomes a solemn prayer,

> The pillars of the nation remain unshaken. I pray more fervently for the prosperity of Japan.
> I pray that my people will be forever happy. Please protect my reign, Great God of Ise.

Thus is his faith reflected in such poems. This has resulted in profound self-examination and self-awareness.

> Whenever I view ancient sources, my thoughts are of how my country has been.
> I have seen my country undergo unprecedented development. This all comes from the guidance of the gods.
> A great force, powerful enough to penetrate mountains, is born from the Yamato spirit of Japan.

I cannot but be deeply moved precisely because the grand, ideal spirit of Emperor Meiji has such deep roots. Only a master could compose poems with such profound ideals.

> I would search through things of antiquity of the God of Ise and rule on modern affairs.
> I hope my mind has no shortcomings; like the moon shining on this world.
> A light green sky is perfectly clear. If only my mind were the size of this sky!
> I hope my spirit rises as high as the peak of Mount Fuji in the clear sky.
> Like the bracing rays of the morning sun, rising ever higher, I hope for a mind like the rising sun.

We can truly see that the character of his body is dignified, like a ceremonial tripod, and the spirit in the emperor is like the rising sun.

When we seek his emotions in his poems, we discover how noble they are.

Though I dream mountains and water every summer for playing peacefully, there is no summer when I have time to do so.

For his people, he devoted himself earnestly to state affairs. He always held "mountain and water," which means nature, in his mind. When the palace caught fire in May of 1872, he moved into Akasaka Imperial Palace once, but construction and modification of the palace was not completed. He went to Hakone on August third, but soon returned to Tokyo on the thirty-first. This was his first and last summering.

When I read his feelings during the time of the Russo-Japanese War,
If we consider all people around the world are our brothers, how can such troubles occur?

True, great bravery only comes from such a selfless personality. "A great force, powerful enough to penetrate mountains" also springs from the Japanese spirit (*Yamato damashii*).

Emperor Shōmu gave the following poem to Fujiwara Fusasaki when he was appointed *sestudoshi*, a military officer:

Brave warriors, please do not be negligent of your duties along the journey, brave warriors.

Creating this poem demonstrates the high spirit of the emperor's mind. How serious is his anguish over such an unsolvable dilemma compared to our small problems of morality? I think that we can never fully understand his noble state.

His poem reads,

I spent my summer nights in disturbed sleep because I have so many thoughts about my reign.

And the poem of Emperor Kōmei:

Wrapped in the cold of blackest winter nights, what I think about are my people.
To no avail, and again to no avail, I worry for my people, being unable to rely on things in the plains of Musashino.

When we reflect on such poems, even today we can still feel their passion.

Since the beginning of the nation, Japan has been a country illuminated with the ideal spirit. The lands also carry self-awareness as being the domain of the

Gods. The Three Sacred Treasures of the Imperial House are the eternal symbols of great spirits. The emperor manifests very deeply the character of Japan. Simply by virtue of being born in Japan, does it not make us feel unending reverence and awe?

By examining the Japanese national spirit and gaining insight into the real nature of Japan, I feel a breathtaking solemnity, and my heart races, like "following a flying dragon and dancing in the sky." At the same time, I realize that the first priority is not intellectual pursuit, but that the best kind of study is in internalizing the discipline of great virtue. I am ashamed to admit to my previous childish learning.

5 Cultivating Character
On Yamaga Sokō (山鹿素行, 1622–1685)

Since ancient days, it has been commonplace to hear, as well as say, that character must be cultivated, yet this problem is forever acute. The present age has nearly fallen into critical condition due to the abuses of mechanized civilization, so the biting poignancy of this voice conveys a feeling of tragic sorrow for the delusions of the human world unchanged from myriad ages past.

Efforts that overlook the cultivation of character are necessarily ill-fated. Be that as it may, the practical realization of character cultivation begins in having suffered such an ill fate. This awakens one to a realization of the importance of character cultivation, which previously had only been grasped intellectually. Thus, the voice that says character must be cultivated arises ever anew. But we have not yet made clear what kind of person character cultivation will create.

The demand for character cultivation must not be simply a system of thought. It must not be what the literati embraced in the past—and to be sure, now as well—a dreamlike, empty theorizing that does not tread upon steadfast realities. Rather, character cultivation must be an ideal demand that penetrates reality as an embodied and earnest seeking of the truth.

According to the desire for a living ideal, the Japanese should have possessed a grand ability that ought to be acclaimed. For example, the ancients took pleasure in contemplating the pains of their hearts in *budō* (武道, the way of martial arts) and the various *geidō* (芸道, the way of art) of old. I, for one, hold more dear the Japan of our ancestors—which possessed the souls of Shinran (親鸞, 1173–1263, a Japanese Buddhist monk), and Dōgen (道元, 1200–1253, a Japanese Zen Buddhist), or even heroes such as Miyamoto Musashi (宮本武蔵, 1584–1645), who would not rely on the gods themselves for the sake of kendo (剣道, the way of the sword)—rather than a modern ethnic culture that possesses multitudes of smooth-tongued promoters of freedom and humanitarianism.

How noble indeed is the ideal that each manifest his own way—the farmer as a farmer, the carpenter as a carpenter, the samurai warrior as a samurai warrior—rather than the capitalist (or so-called cultural) ideal that cannot succeed in love without gold, embellishments, and flattery, let alone making one's way in the world. The former leads a life of purity, whereas the latter makes sport of the turbulent rivers of consciousness. On the basis of such an ideal of truth, we must advance at full speed toward the ideal about which Yoshida Shōin (吉田松陰, 1830–1859) said, "Knowing full well the fate that awaited me, the Yamato [Japan/Japanese] spirit urged me to do what had to be done."

Is it not the case that a faith that casts off the self found in the radically unenlightened and karmically sinful viewpoint is essential even for Pure Land's Other-Powered Original Vow? What about the chief provenance of Zen? Does it not require an unrepeatable Great Determination to hurl oneself off a cliff and resurrect again? And, of course, there is no need to explain here how this applies to *budō* above all others. As Kikuchi Taketoki (菊池武時, 1292–1333) said, "Hearing the signal arrow's call to battle, God would know what a warrior's heart is aimed directly at." Even the gentlest love would be meaningless (a mere play) unless it is of a nature similar to those expressed in the ancient poem that says, "My love, do not worry over things; neither fire nor flood will ever separate us" (*Man'yōshū* 万葉集 4.506).

In his theory of *budō*, Yamaga Sokō also emphasized establishing one's fundamental principles first. He took as the fundamental principles of *budō* three articles: directing one's will toward the Way, knowing one's duty, and being focused and working hard toward your resolution. A *shi* (士 Jp. samurai, Ch. *shi*) is one who, as Mencius so fittingly put it, has a constant heart even if lacking a constant livelihood (*Mencius* 1A7; 3A3). In other words, they are men who live not by things, but by purity of spirit. Such a person is not a subject possessed by [Schopenhauer's] *Wille zum Leben*: an avaricious will to live, controlled by desire [original in German and in Japanese], but a subject with *Wille zum Kulturleben*[1]: a naturally nourished will to live sublimely [same as above].

Today, there is no one who does not cry out for the reformation of society. However, the majority of social reform theorists argue every possible reform except the reform of oneself. Their reforms do not go beyond Eucken's so-called attachment to objects. By necessity, such an approach will never bring about happiness.

For many people, mentioning Yamaga Sokō immediately brings to mind Ōishi Yoshio (大石良雄, 1659–1703) and the "Forty-seven Rōnin." Truly, there is something of the depth of Yamaga Sokō's scholarship of moral education in these warriors of conviction who offered up their lives, realizing that "Though a myriad of mountains is not heavy, obligation to one's lord is; though one hair is not light, one's life is." For the sake of the integrity of *budō*, and in grateful obligation to

---

1. [In the original, Yasuoka uses Japanese as well as German to express both *Wille zum Leben* and *Wille zum Kulturleben*.]

their lord, this generation of heroic souls cast off all pains and difficulties to avenge themselves on their bitterest enemy. Surely, this could only have been because of Yamaga Sokō's cultivation of their character.

Sokō was an exquisitely Japanese samurai: his excellence of reason was like a torch illuminating the quintessence of all scholarship, his efforts directly and skillfully arrived at the ground of things, and his character was dignified as the teacher of royal and noble great men. He was born to Yamaga Sadatomo (山鹿貞以) in the year 1622 as a descendent of the distinguished Yamaga family of Chikuzen.

Sadatomo was originally the retainer of the Kameyama-Seki House in Ise, but he received a stipend of 250 *koku* of rice[2] from Go-Shirakawa's Marquis Machino Nagato for a period of ten or so years. During this period, he took as his wife an adopted daughter of the Machino House, whose father Seki Echigo-no-Kami was entitled to 10,000 *koku* as guardian of the Echigo Barrier of the Inawashiro area. On the twenty-fifth day of the eighth month in the eighth year of Genna (1622), Sokō was born in Machino Nagato-no-Kami's residence on the grounds of Shirakawa Castle when Machino was chief retainer to Gamō Tadasato (蒲生忠郷, 1602–1627).

In his *Haisho Zampitsu* (配所残筆, Last testament in exile), Sokō himself claims that his father made him learn to read at age six, but as a "dull student," it took until around the age of eight for him to practically master the *Four Books* and the *Five Classics* and various other literary works, which does not sound like the work of a dull student at all.

And so, at age nine, he entered into the school of the great Confucian of that time, Hayashi Razan (林羅山, 1583–1657), and caused the master to be unusually moved by his recitation of the unpunctuated Chinese of the preface to the *Analects* and poems by Huang Shangu (黄山谷, 1045–1105). From then on, thanks to his brilliant teacher and his natural talents, he progressed rapidly. By age fourteen, he was proficient in Chinese literature and poetry, and as a youth of age fifteen or sixteen, he was already giving lectures interpreting the *Analects* and *Mencius* for dignified samurai. His genius was so surprising to the intellectuals of those days that, at age eleven, Lord Horio, the governor of Yamashiro, offered him a 200 *koku* stipend to enter his service, but his father would not allow him to take it. His father was also quite wise.

Thus, he demonstrated his unusual genius in Confucianism. At fifteen, he quickly mastered the teachings of Obata Kagenori (小幡景憲, 1572–1663), an authority on martial studies, and Kagenori's student, Hōjō Ujinaga (北条氏長, 1609–1670). Having mastered their secret teachings, at age twenty-one, he was

2. [1 *koku* (石) was historically defined as the quantity of rice adequate to feed one person for one year.]

pronounced without peer among all the students. The famous Yamaga School of Martial Studies actually came out of his teacher's instructions, yet it was flavored with his own particular originality.

In addition to this, from around the age of seventeen, he learned *shindō* (神道), first from Kōyū, then from Hirota Tansai. He also studied poetry, so that by the time he was twenty his genius was actually showing itself in surprisingly deep scholarship.

This young genius was offered positions with generous stipends by Tokugawa Yorinobu, governor of Kishū; Abe Tadaaki, governor of Bungo; and Matsudaira Toshitsune, governor of Chikuzen, among others. But, as ever, his father, who wished for greater accomplishments for his son, refused to allow him to accept any of the offers. When Sokō was twenty-five, Matsudaira Sadatsuna—already a venerable sixty years old, governor of Kuwana, and one of the foremost lovers of learning in his own right—summoned Sokō as his teacher. Tanba, the high steward of the Left in Kyoto and daimyo of Nihommatsu, also summoned him and was deeply impressed by his lectures on martial studies, Laozi, and Zhuangzi. We should also know his aspirations.

Already his reputation had reached the ear of Tokugawa Iemitsu (徳川家光, 1604–1651, the third Tokugawa shogun), who secretly dispatched a page to study him. Iemitsu's innermost intention was to hire Sokō for himself, yet this great shogun was to pass away from this world before being able to find an appointment for such a heroic genius as Yamaga. That both Miyamoto Musashi and Yamaga Sokō passed by unnoticed in the space of Iemitsu's lifetime (though, of course, Iemitsu died before the latter) really was a most regrettable, incomparable loss.

And so, at age thirty-one, as fate would have it, Sokō accepted an offer from Asano Naganao (浅野長直, 1610–1672), daimyo of Akō Domain and grandfather of Asano Naganori, the lord of the Forty-seven Rōnin. He received a stipend of 1,000 *koku* and was treated with the courtesy due to a visiting teacher rather than that due a vassal. We must say that for someone of his rank to be treated in such a manner was really unprecedented. Yamaga Sokō was also aware of this favorable treatment, and after nine years of sharing with his lord from his vast stock of knowledge, he resigned his position.

After leaving Akō, Sokō one day related his thoughts to his former lord. It being a time of peace, there appeared to be no way for him to repay his great debt to his lord, so in its place he believed that he could plant a seed that was sure to bear fruit by cultivating the roots of ethical conduct in the hearts of his lord's vassals. His own scholarship and virtue for those nine years of his life must have been greatly fulfilling.

When he returned to Edo, feudal lords and great noblemen from across the country, with their hearts set on the way of learning, thronged to his school. *Tales of Past Worthies* (先哲叢談 *Sentetsu Sōdan*) records four thousand of their number. Their famous and honorable ranks constituted a kingdom outside of the shogunate. Yet, for the shogunate at any rate, to have someone outside of the government found such a dignified school and receive this kind of respect from across the social ranks was just the same as if he had established a hostile state hidden in their midst. Yui Shōsetsu (由井正雪, 1605–1651) had achieved similar fame as a scholar before being put to death for treason. Thus, Sokō began to glow with the light of suspicion in the eyes of the shogunate. As his studies were not inconsiderable, other scholars fanned the flames with their jealous reactions.

It was his *Essentials of the Sages' Teachings* (聖教要録 *Seikyō Yōroku*, 1665) that became the unexpected opportunity for these jealousies to explode. *Essentials of the Sages' Teachings* is an outline of the view of Confucianism he had already espoused when he reached age forty. Before that, it had come about that Confucianism was divided into two opposed interpretations: the so-called Zhu Xi School and the Wang Yangming School. The Zhu Xi School was always strongly tinted by its close connection to the ruling powers, and Wang Yangming's school was seen as a heresy against Confucius' teachings by the Zhu Xi school.

Sokō held that, seen from the point of view of the sages, the Wang School and the Zhu Xi School certainly could not both arrive at true teachings. In the eyes of the public, this was a seriously treacherous argument to make for someone like Sokō, who was a product of the Zhu Xi School lead by Hayashi Razan.

He held that the aim of the way of the sages lay in becoming a man of character. That is, their objective was to teach the way to become a man of character. If becoming a man of character is not the sort of thing that one can do by reading texts, it is also not a mere system of thought. The teaching of the sages must be a force that moves men's lives always in the direction of a fresh and vital reality, since it is in reality that a wide-eyed and earnest desire for the ideal results, on a small scale, in the training of a single body, and on a large scale, in the pacification and governing of the world.

The reason that Confucius is generally regarded among men as the wisest of all the sages is that his scholarship—that is, the system of Confucianism that is surely an outpouring of the societal discord that afflicted the heart and inner life of Confucius himself—is based on an incomparably solemn ideal that he firmly established in reality.

The explication of an empty system of thought by a Confucian who is not himself illuminated inside by his teachings, and does not himself suffer along with the world's sufferings, cannot possibly be something that succeeds in the teachings of the ancient sages. The sin of the scholar is to separate scholarship from life and to take truth as quite apart from reality. Sokō wrote, "The way of the Duke of Zhou and Confucius has become lost to opinion, the world misled, and the people confused," with great sorrow. For the vulgar Confucians, statements like this were most grave, and all the more so because of their soundness. And so, for the shogunate as well, Sokō's teachings had to be called a seriously dangerous way of thinking.

Generally, when the faction of the powerful should think a system of thought dangerous, there is nothing so frightening for them as a brave man whose heroic soul is too thoroughly devoted to accommodate or compromise, who takes an action self-consciously to prostrate both himself and the world equally before the impartial moral law.

One can offer something to all other schools of thought, blunting the tip of their spears. But, only in the case of an estimable man of character, so long as he should resist all cajoling, does his spear become sharper. When thoughts like those of Sokō call the world's noble great men into action, it can only make the shogunate government authorities shudder at the unexpected menace.

As a result, in the autumn of his forty-fifth year, on the third day of the tenth month of the sixth year of Kanbun (1666), he was summoned out of the blue by Hōjō Ujinaga, ōmetsuke (central inspector of the shogunate; the same Hōjō who had previously taught martial studies to Sokō under Obata Kagenori). Ujinaga, hidden behind his role in the government, was among those who viewed the Yamaga School's rise with jealousy.

Thus, his once-prospering destiny had come to ruin in the course of a single day. On the ninth, he was escorted under heavy guard to exile in Akō Domain. However, to be swept off to Akō was, for him, a pleasure. Here was the land in which he had once instructed heroic souls and served the feudal lord, who, along with the whole clan, held deep respect for Sokō, now as ever. After he arrived in Akō on the twenty-fourth day of the tenth month, the kindhearted treatment he received from its lord made him feel obliged rather than distraught. Among the vassals, Ōishi Yoshio's uncle, [Ōishi] Tanomo Yoshishige (大石頼母良重, 1619–1683) took special care of him. Yoshio was eight years old at the time.

Reconsidering his life in exile in Akō Domain on the basis of these virtues, it was probably an unusual blessing. Here he was, gifted with an unforeseen surplus of time, which made it possible for him to truly read, meditate, and write at leisure. *Actual Facts about the Central Realm* (中朝事実 Chūchō Jijitsu), *Records of the Warrior Clans* (武家事記 Buke Jiki), *Questions from Children in My Exile* (謫居童問 Takkyo Dōmon), and *Last Testament in Exile* (配所残筆) were all written at this time. There, he spent ten years of his life. And so, in the third year of Enpō (1675), while commemorating the twenty-fifth anniversary of Tokugawa Iemitsu's passing, he was finally allowed to return to Edo in the eighth month.

He was already entering his fifty-fourth year. In the ten years of his absence, there had been a remarkable decline in the culture. After returning to Edo, his school became just as prosperous as before, but his prior sharpness would never reveal itself in the public square again. He had already thoroughly polished his virtue in obscurity, and so on October 23, 1685, at sixty-three years of age, this heroic soul also went to its eternal rest.

The theory of Shidō (士道, the way of the samurai) is the greatest accomplishment of his blessed era.

A theory of Shidō is a theory of character cultivation. How ought we to cultivate character? What state of mind is achieved by cultivating character? On fundamental questions such as these, his instructions to his disciples were extremely penetrating, scrupulous, realistic, elegant, and clear. Above all, his teaching that "the ways of the heart [心術 shinjutsu] must be made clear" is what awakens us from our slumber.

The "heart" (shin) in "ways of the heart" refers to our character, and the "ways" (jutsu) refers to its function: a "path" (Jp. michi, Ch. dao). In other words, because the ways of the heart are various acts of character, lunatics and the feebleminded are outside of the theory. The discussion of the ways of the heart begins with a person whose character is prepared to accept absolute responsibility for action. When a man of character is rooted in his foundation, one can cultivate the extraordinarily delicate ways of the heart, as all the trees and grasses are rooted in the nourishing earth, and natural beauty is developed from there. So long as his foundation is broad and deep, the charming excellence of the ways of the heart will be infinite.

The new man is raised in a modern, materialistic, and mechanistic civilization in which law, economics, literature, and philosophy seem quite richly cultivated. Yet, all of this stops at the level of the ears and mouth. At the level of the heart, he is all the more desolate. On the other hand, the only one who can properly establish the foundation is the shi (士: samurai of great integrity), and the ways of the heart must be made clear. The mountains and rivers in the landscape of the heart must be bathed in the surpassing excellence of infinite light.

To do so, in his theory of the way of the heart, Sokō discussed how to cultivate the spirit: distinguished magnanimity, resolve, compassion, personality, conscience, and self-interest. He also explained being secure in one's fate, purity, uprightness, and adamancy.

I. Cultivating Spirit

Concerning the heart and spirit (気 Jp. ki, Ch. qi), just like Mencius, Sokō teaches that the fundamental form of the heart is found in the spirit. In other words, the will is the heart's fundamental form, and even the existence of the body takes its urgency from the will. When the spirit is still, the heart is also still; when the spirit moves, the heart moves also. Because the heart follows the spirit, and the body in turn is seriously affected by the heart, one must "train the body and pre-serve the heart by cultivating the spirit." Mencius also explains,

> I am good at cultivating my Kōzen no Ki: a great and magnanimous spirit. It is a spirit that is supremely great and supremely unyielding. If one cultivates it with uprightness and does not fail to nourish it, it will fill up the space between Heaven and Earth. (2A2)

The real life of human beings is necessarily a system of desires. The pattern of our lives becomes diversified through a process in which our various superficial desires begin to govern in place of our most fundamental desires. This is because some live life like rats, scurrying after crumbs, while others roar through life like dragons and tigers. When our activity of will—that is, our spirit—directs the ferocity of its dragons and tigers with uprightness toward the heavens, the clouds swirl in the sky and mist comes out from the earth. Those who are good at cultivating their Kōzen no Ki spirits are like this.

II. Conscience and Self-Interest

Shi must next differentiate the conscience and self-interest. Sokō emphasizes,

> The means by which an estimable man of character preserves his heart lays solely in demarcation between conscience and self-interest (義利 *giri*). The difference between a man of virtue and a petty person, a true king and a tyrant, all lies within the differ-ence between conscience (義 *gi*) and self-interest (利 *ri*). One may ask how we should speak of conscience. If, in self-reflection, one finds something shameful, one then acts so as to be satisfied with oneself thereafter; this may be called conscience. One may ask how we ought to speak of self-interestedness. If, in one's internal desires, one is self-contented, and one idly follows them, this may be called self-interested.

Our lives are already a system of desires. Thus, it naturally follows that the desires themselves must be legitimate. Now, as one reflects long and hard on one-self, going deeper and deeper into one's innermost core, there will surely be some-thing that one finds fearfully shameful. When one carefully pursues this, one is mysteriously able to realize a deeper satisfaction from within oneself. Conscience is something like this. Conscience is, in other words, none other than the legitimate heir of one's various desires. Opposed to this is self-interest, which is the satisfac-tion of impulsive desires, moment-by-moment, without self-reflection, while cov-eting the pleasurable. In the case of self-interest, without fear there would be no shame, so there would be no permanent blessedness. To extend the metaphor from before, without the dragons and tigers of our nature, we would be no more than rats timidly sniffing from the entrance of our rathole.

Mencius also explained his Kōzen no Ki by saying,

> It is a *spirit* that harmonizes conscience with the Way. Without these it starves. It is naturally produced by accumulated conscience. It cannot be obtained by force or intentionally. If one's actions leave one's heart unsatisfied, it will starve.

Though one may try to separate conscience from the Way, they are not two different things. In our lives, the fundamental principle without which we cannot live is the Way, and the determination that unites our various desires as a way is the conscience. Thus, the accumulation of conscience can never stop making us more beautiful, more true, more holy, and more good. This is the reason for cultivating Kōzen no Ki. Since it truly is produced by the accumulation of conscience, even if it is set to the shape of morality, it is not something that can be obtained otherwise.

III. Resolve

In this way, a samurai must distinguish between conscience and self-interest, and cultivate his spirit. And what drives the spirit is the will (志 *kokorozashi*).

The same meaning lies in the spirit of the will as in the desires of an object-oriented idea. Thus, Mencius also teaches that the will is the teacher of the spirit. The spirit of the will, or "resolve" (志気 *shiki*), is actually a name showing that the remarkable progress of the spirit is driven by the will. It may also be called the Geist of the ideal.

Those who honor their Kōzen no Ki must, therefore, be lofty in resolve. Sokō explains resolve in the following manner:

> Resolve can be called that which shows the integrity of spirit of the will of an estimable man of character. One who would be great, even an estimable man, if he set his will on something small, will, through his studies and actions, achieve small things, lacking greatness. The resolve of Zengzi and Mencius was such that when they willed the Way, they considered it insufficient to accomplish as many great deeds as Guan Zhong and Yanzi did for their clan. If one is content with small successes and one does not achieve integrity of spirit, one will never know greater function than instrumental awareness and will always be trapped in the negligible. The ancient vassals tried to make their ruler follow the instructions of Yao and Shun. Should one of them fail to achieve that, he would be ashamed of himself.

When serving your father, you should do it as devotedly as Zengzi took care of his father; ancient men held themselves to a high standard and would not be satisfied with small accomplishments. No one with an elevated resolve will ever find themselves guilty of small accomplishments and small self-interest. When Emperor Yao offered Xu You control of the empire, he washed his ears out in the River Ying. A nest-dwelling hermit saw this and thereafter refused to let his cows drink from the river, illustrating that a hermit of noble character would be ashamed to be tainted by politics. Fan Li floated off in the five lakes, rejecting the honors of Yue's victory. When Huizi felt that Zhungzi was to deprive Huizi of the role of prime minister of Liang and threatened Zhungzi, Zhungzi compared it to the soaring phoenix being threatened by an owl, which was afraid of the phoenix getting his prey—a rotten mouse. When Yan Zi Ling was offered three of the highest positions in the government, he refused to accept the offer and to give up his life at Mount Jiang and went fishing instead. All of these followed the path of the sages. Even if some ill fate should befall them, whatever happened, they never allowed their will to set itself on self-interest. Even if it would allow one to be a great instrument of the empire, one should never choose personal ease. Striving to express one's integrity of spirit must truly be called the condition of the estimable man of character. To dust his clothes of the corruptions of materialism upon a thousand-foot mountain, or to wash his feet of the mud of worldly desires in ten thousand miles of river, is what the heart of an estimable man must embody. If, however, one should stray from the path of the sages and solely respects the elevated integrity of one's spirit, one will honor heretical ideas of emptiness and void, treat the world as rubbish, think of the empire as chaff, and then one can only lead a reclusive life. Therefore, we must clarify the reason and the justice of these matters exactingly.

Generally speaking, those so-called gentlemen or men of virtue do not have such resolve. They believe that not to do anything, right or wrong, is the ultimate goodness. They are as excited as if they had done the gravest and most serious good by supporting a cart on a hill by removing a stone from the wayside. While quite deplorable, it cannot be helped, even should such gentlemen and beneficent men be subject to the contempt of the evil men of vulgar background who are rampant in the world. The truth is that a man of virtue must be a daring figure in the world. A sage must be a heroic man.

IV. Magnanimity

If your resolve is already lofty, then without being particular about each small affair or small goodness, you will prosper. In his teachings about magnanimity, Sokō says,

Shi should be one who is broadly magnanimous, having a heart that freely takes up the great affairs of the world; otherwise, one would be narrow-minded. Just as one cannot know the full limits of the winding Yangtze River, or just as the great Mount Tai contains innumerable birds and beasts, grass and trees, so too when the heart is free, even while containing the myriad affairs of the world within it, this can be called magnanimity. It bears the weight of the starry heavens on its back, letting the birds fly freely, and can be entrusted with the depths of the murky oceans, where fish swim freely. One who lacks such magnanimity cannot be said to have the heart of an estimable man of character.

The *History of the Later Han* (後漢書 *Hou Han Shu*) records the great Confucian scholar Guo Tai (AD 128–169) as saying, "Magnanimity is like a flood wave covering a thousand acres. Though it is cleansed, it's not clear. Though it mixes, it won't be muddy. It is altogether immeasurable." Before he was killed, Zhou Yi of the Jin dynasty once told Wang Dao, "There is hollow in here (pointing to his belly as a metaphor of his capacious magnanimity), it could hold hundreds of those of high stature, whose magnanimity is, itself, already thought to be great," which demonstrated the magnanimity of each.

If one does not have such character, one's abilities will never be strong. Ability allows one to calmly arrange the myriad things in this world, to ply the four seas with a smile on one's face, to bear the weight of the earth, to fill in the width of the ocean, to fill up the heavens without limit, to illuminate everything with the light of the sun and the moon. Such actions are all the result of natural ability. As such, were you to establish yourself in the middle of the world and pacify the people of the four seas, this would be no ground for boasting. Should you handle great affairs and show your integrity to all the tribes of the world, you would not think of your own greatness.

Thus one must cultivate the abilities of one's spirit if one would be great and magnanimous and not narrowly weighted down by particulars. For this reason, it can be said that possessing magnanimity is essential.

When one cannot cultivate one's spirit enough, and becomes narrow, and fails to establish oneself as the definition of an estimable man of character, one allows the heart to be controlled by likes and dislikes, self-interest and self-injury; and thus one's spirit acts blindly and the truth is lost. When a person rushes toward things, the spirit moves blindly and is lost. In moving blindly, intelligence is hidden and everything done is without reason. Moreover, there will be no magnanimity in this.

An estimable man of character sees things from the perspective of the great affairs of life and death. Facing the danger of an unsheathed sword, he draws a blade and shows the adamancy of his principles. Meeting with a great affair, he makes an important decision with courtesy. Raising not his voice, he leaves the world to the peace of Mount Tai. The great purpose of all the civil and military affairs exists within magnanimity.

V. Being Secure in One's Fate

Being clear about one's integrity, broadening one's resolve, and expanding one's magnanimity; in other words, such a state is emancipation from mental slavery and a heteronomous life, driven by various impulses to blind and rash action. In other words, true freedom establishes the self. A free and established self is nothing other than a single point of subsistent awareness within creation. Here, for the first time, true wisdom is born, and one can know and be secure in one's fate.

Knowing and being secure in one's fate is not simply a matter of not caring what happens and steeling oneself for whatever may come about. It is about making yourself the master of every situation, so that wherever you stand is the true place (*The Record of Linji* #12). Therefore, one who knows and is secure in one's fate will, to the contrary, overturn his so-called destiny. Whatever happens is eternal destiny, and it is a matter of one's own actions. To the contrary, the vulgar, who chase after self-interest and fame like mad dogs, are, for all time, slaves to destiny.

"In general, the first step to establishing oneself in the world of men is to seize the time. The second is to be born to an outstanding house. The third is to have integrity of spirit suitable for one's person and one's time. To be fulfilled with these three steps, then…" you will be able to succeed in life.

However, how much can one desire to succeed in the world? Is success in this world really everything? Where is there something to be truly honored? People do not think of such questions but are hasty to make a name for themselves. Success to such people is no more than pleasing the self and flattering the flesh. The blind and rash actions taken for success in the world deprive human beings of their self-rule and make them like slaves in all things, employing cunning only for servility. Destiny is for heaven to lead men of blind action to prison, down to their graves. Destiny for such persons is to get their prison rations but not their freedom. Being secure in one's fate removes the iron bars of the cell.

VI. Purity

Being secure in one's fate comes from self-satisfaction and not depending on anything else. That is, it comes from purity. Therefore, *shi* must have a natural purity.

VII. Uprightness

The meaning of the virtue of purity is refraining from chasing after external objects. Seen internally, this is uprightness. One might say that, "The pine does not bend to heaven; the orchid is fragrant when no one is around. Such is the uprightness of an estimable man of character." If one were to have a Zen dialogue on *Gewissen* (conscience), would it not say something like this?

VIII. Adamancy

What establishes the fundamentals of the way of *shi* and remains unmoved from there is called adamancy. Gō (剛) means unbending and adamantine. Sō (操) means a will to preserve one's principles in one's heart without the slightest change. As Saigō Takamori (西郷隆盛) also said, adamancy is the ability to see things to the end even at the cost of one's life, to leave aside fame or self-interest. Without this, one can never be a great instrument of the world.

IX. Inherent Attributes

But one must not mistake "stubbornness" for adamancy. The definition of an estimable man of character is not "someone who always carries out the instructions of the devil on his shoulder." As Sokō writes,

An estimable man of character who has established adamancy may appear to be evidence of the vulgarity of culture. However, that is not his inherent nature. As the moon rises above the hibiscus tree and the wind blows around the willow, an estimable man of character ought to have an elegance that is not found in the vulgar state of the world, but one that illuminates others with its refined personality like a crystal jewel. Huang Shangu described the refinement of Zhou Dunyi (1017–1073) by saying, "His heart was carefree like the clear moon or a cool breeze." For such a person, elegance is in his very bones. Everything about the person is natural. Vulgarity shows itself in a vulgar makeup, and nobility shows itself in a noble makeup. The wild crane knows no vulgarity in its nature, and the verdant pine contains the essence of the timbers for roof and crossbeam. After Mencius had an audience with the hegemon king of Liang, he spoke to others saying, "When I looked up at him, he did not seem like a ruler of people. When I approached him, I did not see anything awe-inspiring in his personality" (1A6). When an estimable man of character is not properly cultivated, he might focus solely upon his bearing, his clothing, his dwelling, his attitude in eating and drinking, even his language and behavior; the effect will be but one of crudeness. The uncultivated think such is the carriage of an estimable man of character. This has been greatly misunderstood.

That an estimable man of character looks noble, gentle, and amiable does not mean that he loses himself in a weak personality. An estimable man of character has an elegance without the slightest thing hidden or the slightest bit of vulgarity or clumsiness. It may be likened to storing autumn rains in a quartz receptacle or putting clear ice in a crystal cup. He does not flatter inside and does not bend outside. Whatever may come, his spirit extends to all things: when the hawk flies, it is to the heavens; and when the fish dives, it is into the abyss. It is like when the moon comes to the hibiscus tree and the wind calls to the willows. If such were not his inherent attributes, then how could he not be tainted by the windblown dust? Consider this carefully.

X. Compassion

So far in the discussion of the cultivation of an estimable man of character, a kind of "refinement," "warmth," and "depth" too graceful for words has been associated with *shi*. To borrow Sokō's words,

The integrity of spirit in the magnanimous breadth of an estimable man of character naturally results in a warm compassion. The word "compassion" has a suggestion of tolerance to it. Internally, it encompasses virtue and is filled with light. Externally, it is free of harshness. Those who are short on talent and wisdom establish their intelligence through narrowly instrumental means, showing off before others and boasting to the world. To the contrary, because the condition of the magnanimous is eminent among all things, they do not strive for success or boast of their fame, nor do they have a spirit of resentful striving. Their temperance displays itself in the color of their faces, showing them to have the form of benevolent men of virtue. When they call to those around them, it is like the warm sun of springtime, and they ably achieve their aims.

When an estimable man of character is compassionate, he is skillful in his affection, saving people and helping things. It is as though it causes him bodily pain to see the world too divided and disturbed. Therefore, with gladness, he opens the storehouse, empties his rice pot, disburses treasures, and uses his fortunes for the salvation of all. Such are the accomplishments of the compassionate. A golden mountain settled in a dank green swamp will sink to the bottom and the light of its beauty be swallowed up. One who lacks such compassion cannot be an estimable man of character. The ancients reacted as one would to an empty abandoned boat, and they wouldn't get angry about it (*Zhuangzi* 20). In the same way, one must connect to all things with a deep warmth.

Seen from this point of view, when the fundaments of Shidō are established and a healthy spirit has been cultivated, we, who are like a grain of rice floating on the vast blue sea, will be truly enlightened to the Great Mystery of the Cosmos.

The microcosmos is the macrocosmos. Shidō goes beyond the cloistered interior of the self and changes each of the hundred thousand worlds into its whole body. One must understand that the veritable reality created through this cultivation of character holds profound mysteries.

The Way of the Patriot (1)
On Yoshida Shōin

Zhuge Liang (Kongming) left his hermitage with the tripartite (Longzhong) plan and departed this world.

Jiabiao went to the capital (Luoyang) by himself, and helped the people, but where can we find those men of character here? Even though I consider Guangao as my mentor, I lack his just cause.

I look up to Lu Lian for resolve, but I lack the talent to deal with national crises.

Reading books was to no avail. Thirty years of studying esoteric matters.

Twenty-one times with fierce determination I tried, but could not upset the schemes of traitors.

People disparage me as a crazy, obstinate person, and people in my hometown do not accept me.

I gave myself to Japan (and I am ready to die). For me, death and life always have had the same value.

Only the utmost sincerity has moved things since ancient times.

How can I not admire and follow the wisest of them?

When I read the above poem of Master Shōin, silently and aloud by myself, I feel a white glow inside my body: "Zhuge Liang left his hermitage with the tripartite (Longzhong) plan and departed this world."

Shōin made a poem: "Knowing full well the fate that awaited me, the Yamato spirit urged me on to do what had to be done."

Shōin committed his life to the turbulent period before the Meiji Restoration and was influenced by Zhuge Kongming (諸葛孔明, 181–234), who left his life in a hermitage in Nanyang where he was not seeking notoriety, embraced the tripartite (Longzhong) plan, and plunged into the stream of events. This poem seems to grieve for Zhuge Kongming, but it reveals Shōin's true, passionate feelings all the more.

"Where is Jiabiao, who entered the capital to settle a national crisis?" Few

upright people ever lay down their lives for a noble cause so bravely. Shōin admired
Guangao and respected Lu Lian.

What does "a just cause" mean? It means an everlasting value worth risking
one's life for. Shōin's courage to enter the middle of the crisis by himself—and his
brave resolution to risk his life for an everlasting value—inspired even weak men
to take a stand for many years to come.

He was already passionate by nature, and his determination made him even
more willing to tackle life with greater earnestness. He admired ancient wise men,
sought what he called "study of nonpractical matters" with the innocent pure heart
of youth, dedicated his life to his country, was indifferent to life or death, and could
move the country with his true heart and devotion.

Shōin said, "We cannot reach the heights of ancient men; still, I dare to follow ancient wise men." As Shōin admired ancient men, I sighed with admiration,
looking upon him: "We are much inferior to you; still I dare to follow your model."

As long as we are Japanese, we have the honor to serve gods both inside of
ourselves and outside—which is the emperor. The rules of "conjugation of internal
and external," "union of subject and object," and "agreement of mind and matter" are
clearly proved in Japan. Shōin was a consummate patriot who lived for this honor
throughout his life.

This is a letter from Shōin at Shōkasonjuku[1] to the Ikkō sect Buddhist monk,
Mokurin, in the eighth month of the third year of Ansei (1856):

> I am mending my ways, so listen carefully. I am a retainer of the Mōri House. Hence,
> I strive to serve the Mōri House day and night. The Mōri House is a vassal of the
> emperor. Thus, it is forever devoted to the emperor. When we serve our lord, we are a
> faithful servant to the emperor at the same time.
>
> However, many times over the past six hundred years, the Mōri House failed to
> serve emperors faithfully. We know this is a deadly sin. My intention is to make the
> Mōri House atone for this sin. Nevertheless, neither can I write a letter to the lord,
> nor speak freely, because I am a captive. All I can do is discuss and research this matter
> with father, brothers, and relatives, flex myself like a worm, and crouch like a turtle
> until my time comes.
>
> "My time" means that once I am pardoned, I will be able to meet men of integrity
> from throughout Japan. Once I am enabled to confer with such, I will plan with them
> and help the chief retainers of my lord realize the sins of the past six hundred years
> and the virtues of loyal service. I will make my lord know the sin, inform other lords of

---

1. [Students at Shōkasonjuku comprised a wide range of people from Chōshū in the Edo era—
not only samurai, but also commoners.]

the lack of morality, and all the previous sins of the Tokugawa shogunate, and thereby make the lords become faithful servants of the emperor.

If I do not succeed in this and the government orders my beheading, then so be it. If I die in captivity, I will make sure to leave at least one man of upright character who will carry my will for future generations. If my wish passes on to posterity, there will be a chance my wish will come true. This is what I mean in my letter of this morning when I say, "a true heart makes people move"; I pray that you understand [this].

(*Yasuoka's note:* "I punctuated and transliterated each sentence to make the difficult, old, epistolary style easier to understand. Similarly below.")

His resolve is moving and plaintively powerful, is it not? He described the fundamental principle of his study in *Shōkasonjuku Ki* (Rules of the Shōkasonjuku, 1856):

To begin with, as people, what we should most respect are "the obligations between a lord and vassal." As an individual state, the principle that we must consider most is differentiating between truly civilized countries that embody some holy or inviolate principles and uncivilized countries lacking such virtue. Time is now most pressing for Japan. The obligations of lords and vassals have not been taught for more than six hundred years. Not only have we failed in our obligations as a people, but recently we fail to differentiate between civilized and barbaric countries. People here are concerned only with economy and peace. We were born in a divine country and enjoy the emperor's patronage, yet we forget our obligations as vassals and grow ignorant of the differences between Japan and other, uncivilized countries. Where is the true reason for learning (for the sake of knowledge) and for being a true human in this situation?

As previously explained, the obligation between a lord and vassal is to unify one's internal and external gods, and to serve an emperor. There is nothing to live for if we have nothing to honor. If a country has something holy that cannot be violated, that is a true country, a civilized nation. If people live a life only of pleasure—greedy, ill-mannered, and without shame—that is an uncivilized country, a barbaric nation. They have nothing that merits honor.

As long as we do not know the clear difference between a civilized country and a barbaric one, we have neither progress nor culture. The tasks of being a human, not an animal, and the need for learning, are what make this justification clear. Only when we distinguish these differences can we be considered as true humans and *shi* (samurai of great integrity).

Shōin's *Shōkasonjuku* was the ultimate place of training for *shi*. It was the place to build an everlasting foundation for creating a true culture. Let us examine his "Seven Rules for *Shi*":

1. When you are born as a human, you should know how humans differ from the birds and the beasts. There are the Five Paths to follow. Above all, "the way of a lord and vassal" and "the way of a father and son" are most important. Thus, the very reason a human is a human is rooted in loyalty and filial piety.
2. Because we were born in an imperial country, we should know that our country is a noble one in this world. We live in a country where there is an unbroken line of emperors, a young man takes the hereditary status of a family, a lord takes care of his people, and people succeed in their ancestral occupations. Each person is devoted to his master and inherits his father's will. A lord becomes one with his people, and loyalty and filial piety should be one. This is a characteristic unique to Japan.
3. In the way of *shi*, there is nothing greater than a righteous conscience. It achieves action through courage. Bravery increases as righteous conscience grows.
4. The actions of *shi* should be simple, faithful, and honest. It is shameful to deceive others to keep up appearances. Fairness, justice, and openness all come from these attitudes.
5. If one neither knows ancient nor modern events, nor has the wisest men as mentors, he is a vulgar man. A man of virtue reads books and makes them his friends.
6. Qualifications to be a virtuous and excellent man involve having admirable teachers and good friends. Thus, a man of virtue has selected his relationships carefully.
7. Saying "Do until death" seems simple, but the meaning is deep. For a person who has a strong will, who perseveres, is decisive, and sticks to his opinion without yielding, these words of Confucius encapsulate all.

Here, we can see the characteristics of an everlasting, creative life. Once the foundations of support for the emperor are settled, Japan and the Japanese will be free from all obstacles.

Those who cherish ideals admire sages and always aim to study, by themselves, deeply and decisively. Shōin's passion for sages, garnered from books, truly makes him appear to have fallen in love with them. He is a good example of "a fancy for virtue is like a desire for love." In this, I deem him more noble than any other gifted person.

An appetite for food and a desire for sensual pleasures are still only the basest of human attributes. It is only when a person reveres virtue that he attains humanity at its highest level. Now, we who live at the close of the century, rush about satisfying our meanest needs, unable to appreciate true virtue. Even though we can love talent, we cannot comprehend virtue.

Needless to say, virtue is a creative dynamic that is intrinsic to life, and a talent is an attribute that functions to support virtue. Thus, when we love talent but do not understand virtue, it often brings "skillful deception and overstatement of appearance" but lacks the "simplicity and honesty" of virtue. If one happens to cherish a virtue and seemingly respects a sage, he always treats a subject intellectually; it is a similar attitude to a natural scientist observing things. With this attitude, even if one studies books deeply, one will never be able to reach a higher spiritual level.

On this point, the path that we yearn for should abandon such an intellectual approach; try to experience human character yourself as much as possible, put respect in first place, became a devout believer, and maintain what Shōin called "resolve." In this manner, if we compare ourselves to Shōin, then we could not bear the shame of our own lack of zeal for learning, which would prompt us to earnestly devote every moment of life to learning.

By examining Shōin's life of hardship and drifting about, and by scrutinizing his writings during such a difficult time, we cannot help but be amazed by his tireless zeal. During his Kyushu tour, while exiled to northern Japan, and in prison, he devoted every moment to reading and writing. On top of this, his pure heart, like that of a child's, was racing from the beginning to the end of his experience.

In a letter from Nagasaki on the sixth day of the eleventh month of the third year of Kaei (1850), Shōin, twenty-one years old, wrote,

> Ancient people said, "How do Confucian scholars and civil servants get to know their work in a proper, timely manner? An excellent person knows the proper actions at the proper time." The aspirations of an upright man (士大夫) are not to be either a Confucian scholar's or a civil servant's. Needless to say, he wants to be a person of excellence. However, if one neither reads, nor knows things about all ages, and if what he says does not match what he does, he is sure to be an ordinary civil servant; and if he only reads books, he is but a mere Confucian scholar. Neither are the actions of an excellent person.
>
> Therefore, I want to understand for myself the main points of being an excellent person. I should concentrate on clarifying the nature of our national polity, scrutinize the trends of the times, cultivate mastery of the *shi* mind, make a living, and evaluate the accomplishments of the masters, both ancient and modern. I should be able to avoid becoming a mere Confucian scholar or a civil servant by probing deeply into the factors that affect political turmoil, as well as the rise and fall of nations, and by applying my energy to master thousands of books.
>
> However, when an upright man has a job at a government office, it is inevita-

bly difficult to bury himself in reading books. Thus, he must focus his reading on what is essential. I am not sufficiently experienced or well-informed to know what these essential readings are. Yet, I believe that one should always keep by one's side books about how to lead Imperial Japan upon the right path and books about wise men's words, deeds, and biographies. Besides these books, I will list several books for you that I admire as my mentors. They are books from the Han, Tang, and Sung dynasties.

出師前後表 (諸葛亮)   *Chu shi qianhou biao* (Zhuge Liang)[2]
上高宗封事 (胡澹庵)   *Shang gao zong feng shi* (Hu Dan'an)
争臣論 (韓文侯)   *Zheng chen lun* (Han Wen Hou)
与韓愈論史書 (柳々州)   *Yu hanyu lun shishu* (Liu Liuzhou)
上范司諫書 (歐陽公)   *Shang fan si dong shu* (Ouyang gong) [Ouyang Xiu 歐
                            陽脩]
与高司諫書 (歐陽公)   *Yu gaosi dong shu* (Ouyang gong) [Ouyang Xiu 歐陽脩]
桐葉封弟弁 (柳)   *Tong ye feng di bian* (Liu) [Liu Zongyuan 柳宗元]
審勢審敵 (蘇老泉)   *Shen shi shen di* (Su Laoquan)
送石昌言北使引 (蘇老泉)   *Song shi changyan bei shi yin* (Su Laoquan)
策略五 (蘇東坡)   *Celüe wu* (Su Dongpo) [Su Shi 蘇軾]
待漏院記 (王元)   *Dai lou yuan ji* (Wang Yuan)
相臣論 (明李魏叔子)   *Xiang chen lun* (Ming Li Wei Shuzi) [Wei Xi 魏禧]
上宰相第三書 (韓)   *Shang zaixiang di san shu* (Han) [Han Tuizhi 韓退之]
至言 (漢賈山)   *Zhiyan* (Han Jiashan)
拔本塞源論 (明王陽明与某人書今偶其、名ヲ失ス伝習録中ニ収)   *Baben saiyuan
                            lun* (Ming Wang Yangming or someone else is the
                            author. The name escapes me at the moment, but it
                            appears in *Chuanxilu*.)
諫官題名記 (司馬温公)   *Dong guan timing ji* (Sima Wengong) [Sima Guang 司
                            馬光]
管仲論 (老泉)   *Guanzhong lun* (Su Laoquan)
岳養老記 [岳陽樓記?] (范希文)   *Yueyang lao ji* [*Yueyang lou ji?*] (Fan Xiwen) [Fan
                            Zhongyan 范仲淹]

There are about twenty books, all told.

There should be more books like those that are worthwhile reading. I just wrote down the ones I could think of right now. Please select some books from my list and study them. In the meantime, I made a daily schedule, picking three to five books from the list, to read aloud four or five times per day. If I were to have a job at a government

---

2. [No standard English titles corresponding to these Chinese volumes have been identified.]

office, I secretly and in vain hope, this cultivation of a good spirit would become tremendously important. Disregarding my useless actions and reckless remarks, I would open my humble heart widely and return the kindnesses of my friends.

Shōin made admissions to his brother in a letter from Edo in the fifth month of the fourth year of Kaei (1851), saying that "the reasons why my situation is uncertain are given below," and confessing, "I could not learn anything so far. I know only a few Chinese characters. I am totally agitated. What should I do?" He lamented the limitlessness of what he wanted to study, and asked his brother's advice "to settle his mind."

In a letter to his uncle on the thirteenth day of the first month in the sixth year of Ansei (1859), he wrote,

> I have too much time in prison. I tried to read, but, on the contrary, it only exacerbated my pain because there are too many books, making me busier. The other day, I read *Ni mingshi liechuan* (擬明史列伝) by Wang Dunweng [Wang Wan 汪琬] from the Qing period. The passion and grandeur of the minds of the Ming people touched my heart. There is a world of difference between them and the recent, irresolute Japanese. I surmise that the Japanese samurai of old were like them, and my regret is so deep that I have written a poem: "As I read ancient books, I think of many things. I wish I could have been born in such a time instead of the present…."
>
> The Tokugawa shogunate fears the Americans, and they could not refuse the establishment of a legation in Edo.
>
> The domain governments are afraid of the Tokugawa shogunate, so [they] do not criticize the decision, that is made against the will of the emperor. The men are afraid of their domain governments, so nobody gives up an official position and sacrifices his life to make things right.
>
> What will happen in the future? The obedient attitude of Ashikaga Takauji toward the emperor should be revived; yet, we cannot imagine that a person like Toyotomi Hideyoshi will appear.[3] Even a person equal to Hōjō Tokimune will not come forth.[4] There is no other choice but to be controlled by the United States of America in the end.

We can feel the strong emotion he experienced in his readings in prison. Unlike scholars' bookish explanations, *Kōmōsakki* was a great book showing Shōin's understanding of the mind of Mengzi as Shōin defined it.

In the book, Shōin states

---

3. [Toyotomi Hideyoshi led campaigns abroad.]
4. [Hōjō Tokimune dealt with the Mongol invasion from China.]

I especially cherish reading about ancient matters, such as ancient loyal retainers, dutiful children, and faithful passionate women. From the time that I wake up in the morning until I sleep at night, I keep reading silently and aloud. I cry with emotion, my heart leaps up for joy, and I cannot stop. There is no other treasure for me equivalent to this.

He also writes, "If one does not read thousands of books, how can he become renowned over the centuries?" On the sign at Shōkasonjuku he posted the phrase, "If one neither knows ancient nor modern events, nor has the wisest men as mentors, he is just a vulgar man. A man of virtue reads books and makes them his friends." This is in the "Seven Rules for *Shi.*"

He recommended readings to his apprentices with just such determination and passion. In a letter to Nomura Wasaku (later, Nomura Yasushi) in the fourth month of the sixth year of Ansei (1859), he states,

Wasaku, why do you not read *The Art of War* of Sunzi? I found greatness in *The Art of War*. (I am ashamed to say it, but I have no experience with such great skills. Still, I am very good at talking and writing about it.) I have written comments in this book. However, if you just read through it, you will never understand its importance or its depth. You should copy a set of *The Art of War* without any comments or marks. A direct approach leads you to reach the important points, and read such books as *Kokujikai*[5] of Ogyū Sorai. After you can understand *The Art of War* clearly, without commentaries or marks, take a look at my commentaries.

Here and there in his letter, we can sense his passion to share the value of reading because of the great pleasure he experienced. For beings like him, books afford spiritual nourishment. Reading for one's job, social life, or titillation is a waste.

His sincerity and passion by no means would allow him to tolerate the life of a coward poised constantly on the verge of death.

He exclaimed that "passing one's life as an ordinary person is like a living death. To die and yet to live—this is heroic."

It was his wish to emit an immortal ray of light into the transience of life, to cut himself off from the temptations of the floating world and live in the eternal present.

Hence, he never forgot his determination to grapple with his most worthy opponents and to die after accomplishing some great feat. According to his ambition, neither death nor life matters at all.

He discussed this in a letter to Shinagawa Yajirō and others in the sixth year of Ansei (1859):

---

5. [Possibly *Sonshi Kokujikai* (孫子國字解).]

Just saying "I cannot gain spiritual realization about death and life" sounds so foolish, so I would like to explain, in detail, what I mean. If we say it is a pity to die at age seventeen or eighteen, death at thirty is also sad. Even if we reach the age of eighty, ninety, or even one hundred years, there is no way to say that we have lived long enough. Insects in a field, or in water, have only a half year of life. Yet this is not a short life for them.

An evergreen tree lives for hundreds of years, but that does not mean it lives long. Compared with eternal heaven and earth, these trees are just like flies. People like Boyi never die: he lived on through the Zhou, Han, Tang, Sung, Ming, and even the Qing dynasty. He remains among us still. If he had not starved to death at Mount Xishan out of a sense of obligation to Jiang Ziya, even then if he had lived to one hundred years old, his life would be short.

If we lived longer, could we expect satisfaction? Do you have any specific goals for the future? Both Urashima and Takenouchi died already. A human lives only fifty years. Since ancient times, it is very rare to live seventy years. If, before we die, we do not do something that makes us proud, we cannot rest in peace.

From now on, I will not respond to the current "Revere the emperor and expel the barbarians" people at all, but I have nothing to be ashamed of with respect to ancient wise men.

If you and I have courage, we feel embarrassed with ancients. Modern people are troublesome. What can we enjoy in this life? Nothing. Such is the despicable conduct of mediocre people. When they are shameless, some would-be Confucians shout even while tapping their bookrests.

Confucius said, "A person with high aspirations and benevolence would rather kill themselves to accomplish perfect virtue." Or Mencius said, "Give up one's life but choose obligation."

Some can live a whole life without knowing such noise. You are one of them.

His motivation for learning came from a similar determination. He wanted to arouse a dying Japan. Everything he did—trying to go abroad even against the law, developing a plot to take down the Tokugawa shogunate, and lying in ambush for Manabe Akikatsu—was to open Japan's eyes to harsh realities. He was enraged in his letter to Nomura Wasaku (fourth month of the sixth year of Ansei, 1859):

I let the public think I am a drunken fool. That is fine. Some people are not able to understand anything—not angry at all, no tears, and no guts. Instead of dealing seriously with these people, we should just mollify them and do our own business instead. These days, I think only of such plans. What do you think? I beg your advice.

He flew into a passion in his letter to Masuno Tokumin (same as above, 1859):

Where is the moral fiber of Japan today? I am embarrassed to say it, but it lies only with the emperor, a few noble people, my lord, and me. I should serve my lord; a few noble people should assist the emperor and kill all of the wicked people. If not, the collapse of Japan is inevitable.

If he had not known a way to nourish his mind with books of ancient sages, his passion would easily have taken his life away.

He gave "The Nature Theory" to his beloved and respected pupil, Irie Sanzō, in the fourth month of the sixth year of Ansei (1859). This expresses his anguish well, and it touches us deeply:

I have been so angry that I no longer become upset with anything. I will no longer be offended by anything. Yet, if I am, forgive me, as it is a natural thing to happen.

The Nature Theory
Sanzō, stop being angry.
Is Shōin afraid to die?
Can't he make up his mind?
Is his learning improving?
Is he forgetting loyalty?

However people may judge me, I remain in a natural state. I neither seek nor refuse death. While I am in prison, I do what I can do there. Regardless of the time or the motivation I have, I will do whatever I can, even if I have to end up in prison or face the scaffold.
[Middle part omitted]
From now on, when people give me gentle words, I will answer gently. When they are upset, I close my eyes. When they are angry, I keep my silence. They merit neither words nor disdain.

Thus, while he aspired to great accomplishments, he also developed a firm understanding of the term "respect" (敬 kei) to deepen his resolve. He said,

The word kei (respect) is noted [as meaning] "focus all of one's mind on one's lord, touching on nothing else," and Confucian (Cheng-Chu) scholars explain it as outstanding service [to the lord], but kei is "preparation." In Bushido it refers to "resolve."

By nature, he disfavored violent words or raising his voice. As he states in his Ryūkonroku, which he wrote before going to prison, "My nature is not violent or intense. I want to follow the rules of society and cherish human feelings."

He was quite a soft-spoken person and of delicate health. We can sense his deep compassion.

In a letter to a friend, sent from Noyama Prison in the second month of the sixth year of Ansei (1859), he wrote,

> People who take complacency for granted become speechless in the face of adversity. People who seem emboldened become dismayed when the situation needs them. We should consider Mencius' statement that a great and magnanimous spirit should be nourished naturally. It creates a problem when we push against its nature. When people sent Sase Hachijūrō[6] off, some of his friends drew their swords. Also, Takasugi Shinsaku killed a spy in Edo. From such things, I know that the spirits of friends are failing. I think of death and life all the time. If I die on the block, my blood is redder than yours. However, I hardly ever talk except when there is need to speak. Whenever I say something, I am as gentle and peaceful as a good woman. This is the origin of a strong spirit. We cannot have such an excellent spirit without speaking softly and respectfully, and behaving carefully. We should remember the dignity of Zhang Liang in undertaking an attack on the first emperor of the Qin dynasty, though he was otherwise very gentle.
>
> I haven't had a slice of meat or taken a drop of alcohol since the twenty-fifth of the last month. By so doing, the power of my spirit increases. I cut off contact with my friends, and they have done the same. However, I would like to say this for our long-standing friendship. These are not empty words. They are from the truth of practice and words of ancient sages, so do not take them lightly.

Hot-blooded impetuosity is harmful. Rage also brings evil effects. Shōin warns that these emotions are dangerous. In his letter to Takasugi Shinsaku (高杉晋作, 1839–1867) from the jail in Edo are many passages that prompt serious self-reflection.

> I have been in a jail since last winter, the twenty-fifth of the twelfth month, and my learning has progressed much. I have two manuscripts that I wrote by May. I asked Yajirō to keep them secretly. In these two manuscripts are the reasons why, even if I die, I have no regrets. Please read these sometime later.
>
> You asked me, "How should an estimable man die?" I have a new idea about death since last winter. Li Zhi's (1527–1602) *Fenshu* (1590) helped me improve my thoughts substantially. The theory is quite long, so I summarize it: We should neither favor death nor despise it. If there is no Way, and the mind is at ease, that is where to die.

---

6. [Maebara Issei (1834–1876), a former student of Shōin.]

There are those whose body comes into this world with their mind dead. There are others whose body dies but whose spirit lives on. To live with a deadened mind is of no value. There is no loss for those who die if their spirit continues on. It is remarkable that a person has great resourcefulness and yet endures shame. (Such as when Mingxujie helped Yangjisheng.) One who has no self-cravings or self-interest is not hindered from enjoying life (an example of this is that Wen Tianxiang did not die at Yashan, and he lived at Yanyu for four years.) If there is promise of immortality after death, you may die at any time. If there is promise that while alive you can accomplish great things, you should live forever.

In my view, one puts life and death aside and says what needs to be said.

You asked me how you should live today. When I was in my hometown, you asked me the same question. Thus, I had already answered what I thought, but I am in such a situation that I asked Sanzō to keep the books secretly. It is a grand and far-reaching plan. First of all, when you finish your study, you had better follow your parents' wishes about marriage and employment. If you can serve your lord as a close attendant, please dedicate yourself to the lord and gain his trust. Then, you can discuss true principles and justice.

You will encounter some failures at this time. After that, you should apologize, finish your study, and become a person who doesn't consider your own fame or interest and would avoid conflict. Ten years later, the day will come when you can show your devotion.

Even in the worst case, you would be a person whose name will be long remembered. Seita, Genzui, and Sanzō should not act hastily as I did. I had a lord who understood me well. This is the case. You three should make plans with good men and earn a good reputation during the next ten years. This I told them.

Develop the qualifications to argue logically and correctly, carry them out, and you are sure to fail. When you fail, withdraw quietly and study and learn about virtue. At least if you do that, your name will become known.

How many people would not be really ashamed of themselves when they read this?

I respect a masterless samurai in this sense who does not serve a government.

The samurai who is out in the world, his path is all the more noble.

He also sent a letter to Irie Sanzō (on the twentieth day of the third month in the sixth year of Ansei, 1859) and said,

When things must be done, only the common people can succeed. Wearing fancy clothes, eating good food, having a beautiful woman, and playing with a child is the salaried samurai's business. He has no time for supporting "Revere the Emperor and Expel the Barbarians."

If, unfortunately, I am to die, I would like to entrust at least two concerned people to stand up and carry on these principles.

I read his *Ryūkonroku*, and I imagine the end of the self-composed patriot. I cannot help thinking about how profound his thoughts were.

Readiness for death—emancipation from life and death, moreover—this shows wholehearted seriousness, and totally erases any sense of seeking entertainment. When people become earnest, a quiet, honest sentiment reveals itself. People become tenderhearted. This is not the indulgent sympathy that Nietzsche criticized severely. This is a path of affection. In the code of the samurai, it is called "the compassion of the samurai."

As Shōin himself said, he was truly "a man of compassion" in this sense. He sorely missed his family, longed for friends whom he admired, cared for his lord and emperor, and was concerned for Japan; he found everything in his own passion. On top of this, he sensed how much he would let his parents down by virtue of the choices he had to make.

Reading his letters and poems, we feel for his heart and cannot suppress our tears.

He was born on the fourth day of the eighth month of the first year of Tenpō (1830). He was the second son of the Sugi family at Matsumoto Village in the eastern suburb of Hagi of the Chōshū domain. (Yoshida is his uncle's family name, and that uncle adopted him later.) He had six brothers and sisters. His elder brother was Umetarō, the next is Shōin himself, next to him is Chiyo (she came to be called Yoshi and later married into the Kodama family), Hisa (she married into the Odamura family), Tsuya (she was also called Yoshi), Fumi (later called Miwa and married into the Kusaka family), and the youngest was Toshisaburō, who was a mute. Shōin always felt pity for his handicap. When Shōin made a tour through Kyushu, he visited Kato Kiyomasa's temple to pray for Toshisaburō.

When he was sent to prison in Edo, he composed a parting poem for his elder brother:

> Visitors have departed the prison, and the night is deeply quiet
> Endless sorrow and grief come back to me again
> I hurt my parents' wishes and heart in layers of thousands of miles
> Thinking of my country, I have done nothing in thirty years
> Yet I, the crazy stubborn little brother, brag.
> My big brother and my friends allow me to sing loudly
> My brothers grieve over going through hardship together, difficult to persuade me
>   not to sing
> The plum blossoms are completely gone
> And the leaves are ever greener.

The unmitigated anguish and sorrow of this poem touches my heart. I cannot read it lightly.

The long letter from Noyama prison to his little sister Chiyo on the third day of the twelfth month in the first year of Ansei (1854) and the letter to her before he was sent to Edo in the fourth month of the sixth year of Ansei (1859) should be passed to young Japanese women from generation to generation. He preached knowledge and the conduct of women in detail in the first letter, and in the second, he explained the true meaning of Buddhism in an easily understood way, affectionately and logically. This must be the tender compassion of an estimable man of character, which moves us to tears.

(First letter)
The date of the letter is the twenty-seventh day of November. I received it with the three oranges and a piece of dried bonito last night. The light is dim in the prison, but I can recognize most things. When I imagined what you were thinking, I could not stop shedding tears. I lay down, pulled the quilt over my head, and wept, but I was unable to bear the sorrow. So, I got up and kept looking at the letter. I was choked with tears and finally fell asleep, only to soon wake up again. Since then, I could not get to sleep all night long, and I recalled so many things.

Thanks to our father and mother, I have enough clothing to keep me warm and have plenty of food. Not only that, I have abundant writing brushes, paper, and books. I live in comfort, and the cold weather does not get me down. So, please rest your mind. Your mother-in-law passed away, so you must now take care of everything to the best of your ability. In addition to this, your father-in-law is quite old, so you should be dutiful and take especially good care of him.

Manko is getting bigger each day, so you must put your heart into raising her. How is the old lady of Akaana? She is quite old, so you should be considerate to her as well.

They say that such aging people are family treasures. We cannot exchange them with gold or jewels. From a young age, you knew how to handle things very well. Also, because I feel you are very close to me, and because I read your letter(s), I have told you much, including unnecessary matters.

[Remainder omitted]

He also discussed child education in detail.

About child education, we need not give explanations to children under the age of ten. The only way to teach is *by getting them to sense what is right.* Sages long ago had a theory of "prenatal influence on the unborn child." As soon as a mother starts to carry a child, she should watch all of her behavior and do things correctly. Then, a newborn child will become a better person with a good demeanor. Ignorant people do not comprehend why the mother of an unborn child, who can neither see, hear, nor speak, needs to have a sense of rightness. This is because they do not know the theory, so they do not understand.

Human beings construct [a sense of] form by receiving the correct ki from Heaven and Earth and construct their minds by receiving proper principles from Heaven and Earth, because this is the way [lit. "tool"] by which we acquire them by ourselves without studying or being taught what is right. Thus, if a mother behaves righteously, there is no doubt her children will act properly. This is termed "We sense right from what is naturally acquired."

Needless to say, when a baby is born and becomes able to see, hear, and speak, it can understand what is natural.

Shōin related to her such knowledge about being a mother and taught the significance of ancestor worship and Shintoism, quoting Sugawara no Michizane's poem to teach the simplicity of following the right path: "If our spirits fit the way of nature, the gods make our wishes come true even without praying." He thus explained the Way straightforwardly and gave detailed instructions as to harmonious kinship.

Also, he wished to take misfortune only upon himself, and he prayed for his kinsmen's peace and happiness. When his sister sent sacred rice with the wishes of Kannon (the Goddess of Mercy), he wrote:

> (Second letter)
> Here is a theory. The *I Ching* detests what people called "perfect." We have seven siblings; I am a criminal, Yoshi passed away already, and Toshi is a mute. This seems humiliating, but the other four siblings are doing very well. Especially the elder brother, you, and Hisa, who married into the Odamura family, and have two children each. We cannot complain about this.
> We should compare ourselves with other families having six or seven siblings. Many are not faring as well as we are. As a close example, some of the siblings in the family you married into—and the Takasu family—are ungraceful. So, if our parents can think this way—I, Yoshi, and Toshi, if the three of us take on misfortune instead of our parents and other siblings—then can they rest their minds? In addition to this, the Sugi family is well off; this might be more trouble than my situation.

As I said before, if I die in a prison, I am a kind of immortal person, so I can have happiness with other notables later. On the other hand, with respect to the Sugis, both our father and elder brother hold official positions now, so everything is going well. If the children think this is how things have been always and they do not believe what they were told about how our parents worked hard day and night at the mountain house, then, when we think ahead to fifty or seventy years from now, it seems we have much to be concerned about.

We had many guests at last year's Boys Festival. People rejoice at this as a happy situation. However, I was so deeply worried about the future, I went into hiding in the training room, weeping continuously in private, without anyone knowing about it.

If Kotarō is not like our father, his grandfather, the Sugi family will be in trouble. Among our siblings, you are the last one to remember the struggles of our parents in the past. Even Hisa does not recall much about our life at the mountain house. Needless to say, Fumi, who married into the Kusaka family, does not remember. Thus, it is more important you should teach our siblings "comfort begets adversity" and "happiness causes disaster," rather than praying to Kannon about me.

Also, I am practicing filial duty even in my unhappiness. When even just one of the siblings is not doing well, the others naturally are compassionate and practice filial duty. The siblings become closer to each other. From now on, I will bear all of the misfortunes of this world instead of my siblings. So my dear siblings, please take care of our parents for me.

If this happens, all my siblings will do well. This will lead to the happiness of our parents, and if children follow their parents, in the end this is good for the coming generations. There is no happiness greater than this. Please understand what I am saying. Also, please show this letter to Hisa and Fumi.

Shōin put all of his heart into the letter. A society should be immersed in such sincerity; otherwise, there is no true reform or revolution for society. Any movement stemming from the discontentedness of individualism is nothing but the destruction and overthrow of the existing order. This is simply "appeal to force by force." Why do poets of sentimentality foolishly hesitate? An idealistic and romantic blue flower is blooming right in the hearts of fighters for a noble cause.

I regret that in these times we have taken the ground out from under these warriors of high ideals engaged in a noble cause (*shishi* 志士).

We are deeply infatuated with money and crazed for power. There is greed, debauchery, slyness, and obsequiousness. Easy-living people and their followers judge people only by worldly measures. There is wholehearted hatred.

Empty-spirited, low-class men have burning, jealous eyes, and with their arms outstretched, scheme for the distribution of wealth and usurpation of power. On the other hand, they have tried to fabricate a misrepresented worldview by manipulating coldhearted theories. The world today is full of lazy, empty, idle people who do neither good nor bad. There is no way to be rescued from this situation except by *shishi*.

After all, *shishi* is an appellation for a man who lives for an ideal in its correct sense. It is a title for people who are not living by avaricious will controlled by desire (*Wille zum Leben*) but by a will nourished to live naturally and sublimely (*Wille zum Kulturleben*).[7] The world of humans, whose duty/mission is to generate and nurture everything, ultimately will see no progress if it lacks the properly cultivated spirit of the *shishi*.

First of all, we must be *shishi* in its true meaning. Like Yajirō, whom Shōin scolded, we are embarrassed in front of the ancient wise men. This world is disgraceful. What should we do about ourselves and this world?

---

7. [In the original, Yasuoka expresses these concepts in both German and Japanese.]

7 | The Way of the Patriot (2)
On Takasugi Tōkō (高杉東行, 1839–1867)

When Namba Daisuke, in great trepidation, shot at the prince regent at Tora-no-Mon Gate, Professor Nunami Keion (1877–1927; Japanese scholar) became indignant upon hearing the news, and wrote the following indictment of society:

Think of nothing else,
Just that it was a shot at Tora-no-Mon Gate.
Before blaming Daisuke,
We must first blame ourselves.
The cabinet soon collapsed.
Yet the blame rests not with the prime minister, or on the cabinet, but on we the people, on us.
The blame is on the people, who let the tyrannical "newspapers" say whatever they want without any criticism or punishment.
Worshipping a piece of wood is not a superstition. Seeking and following a role model outside of oneself rather than within is a superstition.
It is not narrow-minded to respect old things because they are old. It is narrow-minded to think highly of new things just because they are new.
A great way lasts for ages
Its essence never changes
A trend is merely its surface appearance.
It is only when such a trend takes the unchanging as its essence
That it becomes a great way and progress ensues
Things to be protected must always exist within—somewhere neither in heaven nor on earth.
I say to do away with convention. Yes—with convention.
Abandon the convention of listening to experts.
Arise, arise, people of Japan.

Make into your bitter enemies
Those people who think it is a new idea—
To hate Japan,
To ignore history,
To be bookworms,
To practice adultery,
And even to commit high treason.
They are the mortal enemies.
Crush their amateurish "enlightenment."
Make clear your judgments about what is good and evil or right and wrong.
Realize that the reason why humans exist in this world is to destroy evil and eliminate
     wrongdoing.
Kick into the ditch those scholars who are intoxicated by unlimitedly vacuous theo-
     ries, and who idolize westerners.
Strike trendy people who become engrossed in superficial beauty, and scholars who
     play with words in whatever situation.
All politicians who seek fame and wealth but pretend to seek justice are my enemies.
All teachers who only give knowledge without cultivating minds, and students who
     attend only for their future livelihood are also my enemies.
Wave torches! Wave spears in all directions!
Leave meditation to your spare time. For now your intuition is enough. Stop thinking
     like a philosopher. Follow what you believe.
Close your books. Give up on talent and schemes.
People should all be like Toyotomi Hideyoshi. We do not need anyone like Tokugawa
     Ieyasu. Do not follow Fukuzawa Yukichi, who taught at Keio University at Mita
     even as fighting was going on at Ueno.
The shots at Tora-no-Mon Gate. Misfortune meant misfortune in the extreme. Yet
     the bullet proved to be a great force to change bad luck to good luck, as it could
     not hit the prince. It even made the prince greater than before. And it has made
     Japan even greater.
Have no doubts. The ultimate judges are at the beck and call of we, the vassals. The
     coming of the messiah and of the bodhisattva Maitreya are prophecies telling us
     to rise up.
The commands of our ancestors echo like thunder in the blue sky.
March and follow their orders.
There are many devils. And the more there are, the stronger the gods become.
Trample on the demons, cut off evil, maintain your cool, and march in rank.
Flutter the Imperial Japanese flag in the wind, beat on the Imperial Japanese drum,
     and march in dignity.

Reciting this statement, how can we keep ourselves from being ashamed and
enraged? We lost our spirit by fiddling with "science" and "thought,"[1] bringing devastation to our pure hearts. By continuing to talk nonsense, by being dallied with
streams of opinions, we bring ourselves and the world ever closer to direct confrontation with danger.

If, somehow, you have time to devote to "civilization," look first in the mirror
at yourself to see whether you have the dignity of an estimable man of character. If
you have an inclination to plea for the privileged classes, give proof of the real value
of such people. If you envy and study communist Russia, you should plot skillfully
against the government. In such situations, it is of no value for me or others to say
anything. I do not think that Professor Keion's written appeal reflects indignation
at all. We accept his invective. That is how much today's society has slackened and
become muddled.

Are there no *shishi* in Japan today who would passionately annihilate this
strange influence on society?

I know well that there are many *shishi* who feel deeply moved to say, "I am
here!" to remedy this situation even today.

Takasugi Tōkō himself said,

> I roamed about in all directions carrying my sword and books. In the east, I met up
> with such men in Mito and Sendai. In the west, I made vows of death with men of
> Kōchi and Kumamoto. I believe that I am good enough to build a foundation to serve
> our country.
>
> We met at such places as great mansions in the mountains or high places close to
> water, or, if not, at restaurants or tea shops. We met and discussed our true opinions
> about the country. When we warm up, we start drinking, sing sad poems, and drink
> more. We throw away much money, like trash, for such parties. We are unimpressed
> by the capital city. Our singing voices harmonized with koto and samisen, knowing
> nothing about cherry blossoms, sunsets, or a moonrise over the eastern mountains.
>
> Good or bad, we said harsh things because we were drunk. Yet, there were reasons
> for what we said. Upon our first meeting, the errors of the government upset us. We
> grieved that there were no inspiring men in our country. We swore aggressively—we
> would keep the true spirit of the Empire even at the risk of our own lives.
>
> In my heart, I think that I will serve Japan with my death. We should not think
> that we will live tomorrow. How can we make plans like people who vacillate and fear
> their fate? We cannot. How can we follow conflicting rules and pretend we are men of
> virtue? We cannot. Even though today people criticize us for indulging in poems and

1. [Yasuoka uses both English and Japanese for these two terms.]

drinking, if we move the whole country with our deaths, everyone will know our great ambition and loyalty. There is no question in my mind.

Since I was jailed, I sat all day long. When I happened to learn the passage, "If I find the Way in the morning, I have no regret to die in the evening,"[2] I cherished it day and night. One day, these transitory dreams vanished into a revelation. Thus, I understood that the source of what I considered pleasures were frivolous and unreliable and bravado threats, and not the origin of sincere pleasures.

Heroes and outstanding characters of history put their death aside, making it the first priority to follow the right Way. If we were to put death aside, how could we make such poems and become drunk, not being certain that we would be alive the following day? Such drunkards cannot put aside thoughts of death, and they cannot deny threats with false bravado. One threat made with bravado means the mistake of that day. A mistake of one day means not only a mistake of that day but also the committing of mistakes for life. It is not the mistake of just a single day. Drinking sake a lot, speaking ill of civil servants, and calling Confucian scholars "fake men of virtue," we still cannot call such people extreme.

The most extreme people let their feelings momentarily give in to anger and by a slip of the tongue leave a bad name for later generations. The harm is immeasurable. When I look back on my past, and whenever I think of how I was, sweat runs down my back and I feel a fever of fear.

My late teacher, Yoshida Shōin, said,

I met people, when I traveled east, who indulged in composing poems and drinking. I think there are not only a few people like Akagaki Genzō of the Forty-Seven Rōnin. However, it was fine because he was Genzō. People who follow the way of Genzō are shallow thinkers. They are not qualified enough to talk about important subjects.

When I think of this, I am so ashamed for ignoring my late teacher's lessons. But now, I do not have time to regret my past actions. An ancient saying goes, "Corrected mistakes make no mistakes." I swear to my late teacher that I will immediately rectify my mistakes, get out from jail as soon as possible, gain and maintain composure, and remain so until the end of my life. I will not drink at all, nor listen to any koto and samisen. My mind is truly delighted. Flowers and grasses from the window of my jail, and the curly stone on my desk, resemble a brush painting by Higashiyama Bokusui. I wrote this under the northern window of Noyama Jail on the first day of the sixth month in 1864. (*Yūshitsuki*)

---

2. [From the *Analects*.]

It was in his twenty-sixth year when Tōkō was imprisoned at Noyama Prison in Hagi on the twenty-ninth day of the third month for escaping from his home province. He wrote the passage above in the summer, on the first day of the sixth month. This is his earnest confession to himself.

People imagine Tōkō Takasugi Shinsaku as an aggressive person, filled with righteous indignation, who composed tragic poems of anger and grief, loved sake and women, and overawed people by his presence. However, this is only his outward appearance. Indeed, he was always passionate through his life (of only twenty-nine years). Yet his passion was not like that of "a foolish man," as his mentor Yoshida Shōin called it. His youthful ardor reflects the heartfelt pain of his conscience.

When we see him from a distance, he is an outstanding, independent-minded man who is free from restrictions. And if we come close to him, he is a very modest person and seems to be a devout seeker after truth who carries deep sorrow in his heart. This is what makes people his followers. People who see Tōkō from a distance and, imitating him, overindulge in playing, drinking, and loving are the people who continually behave however they please, as he described.

Shōin remonstrated, "If you have guts, you must feel ashamed compared to the ancients. Modern people are noisy. What can we enjoy in this world—nothing."

When Tōkō was admitted to the Meirinkan School[3] in Hagi in 1857, he was nineteen years old. There were some true academics at Meirinkan, such as Yamagata Hanshichi, Ogura Shōzō, and Hirata Shin'emon. However, most were stereotypical, conventional scholars. But for Takasugi, who was intuitive by nature and had broad interests, such education was of little interest. Here is a poem he composed:

> I do not bend myself to elevate my name in the world
> I have nothing to hide, and I view things with innocence.
> Even though the hidden meaning of
> Confucian texts are taught at Meirinkan,
> How many ethical people exist there?

Typically, those in scholarly circles are small-minded and petty. This is what a man of virtue is ashamed of. (See the record of "East Han Dynasty, Guanghe Period of Emperor Ling of Han.") They teach "moral politics." It depends on the works of ancient wise men. What spirited and passionate young men seek in such books is for inspiration to feed idealistic spirits. Thus, a mentor should be an upright man who embodies those ideas.

Historical investigation and interpretation of the words without guidance

---

3. [The Meirinkan School was the Hagi clan's school for samurai.]

from such mentors is no way for young men to learn. Hence many great men did not like to study books alone. But disliking book learning was a mistake for an estimable man of character. This is a fault, like ignorant scholars trying to feed a hungry man by drawing him a picture of a rice cake.

Moreover, it was in an age of great urgency. Just as Buddhist chants do nothing for the totally corrupted, the learning and experiences of varied persons, such as Confucian scholars and vulgar people, were of no value to the society of the period.

It was clear that the only urgent need of society at that time—to rescue it from social agony—was a wholehearted, ideal spirit.

A blazing character that abolishes all ingratiating compromises and works methodically to bring back to life those who are drowning in the waters is needed to save such a society.

"When the reign of Your Highness is in peaceful times," it is fine for bookworms like those who are unable to apply what they have read. An estimable man of character in such times wants to learn of the spirits of great men. If Shinsaku, who was a high-spirited, estimable man of character, had been caught among Confucians and ordinary people, he would have gone mad.

Fortunately, the heavens suddenly delivered a great, spirited man to open an admirable school. Needless to say, that was the Shōkasonjuku of Yoshida Shōin. This great forerunner and natural educator schemed to go abroad at a time when Japan was under the threat of foreign powers, and there were tumultuous arguments about what should be done. He wanted to grasp the situation in foreign countries, even though it was against the national laws. His scheme was discovered, and he was sent to Noyama Prison in Chōshū Domain on the twenty-fourth day of the tenth month in the first year of Ansei (1854). He was then released and ordered to remain at home in the twelfth month of the following year. In 1856, the domain of Chōshū, with special consideration, allowed him to teach his family's hereditary learning.

"Knowing full well the fate that awaited me, the Yamato spirit urged me on to do what had to be done."

Whether or not the heavens knew of his passionate Yamato spirit, which he lamented, they oppressed him from all sides. This made both him and his students all the more determined. Thus, Shōkasonjuku reemerged as a school for great men.

As Shōin wrote in his *Shōkasonjuku Ki* (1856),

To begin with, as people, what we should most respect are "the obligations between a lord and vassal." As an individual state, the principle that we must consider most is differentiating between truly civilized countries that embody some holy or inviolate principles and uncivilized countries lacking such virtue. Time is now most pressing for Japan. The obligations of lords and vassals have not been taught for more than six hundred years. Not only have we failed in our obligations as a people, but recently we fail to differentiate between civilized and uncivilized countries. People here are concerned only with economy and peace. We were born in a divine country and enjoy the emperor's patronage, yet we forget our obligations as vassals and grow ignorant of the differences between Japan and other, uncivilized countries. Where is the true reason for learning (for the sake of knowledge) and for being a true human in this situation?

To think that the obligations between lord and vassal constitute a relationship based on a class system is a plebian view. Obligations between lord and vassal, in other words, mean serving something holy and inviolable.

Would not a life be most satisfying and of most value if one such as I were to humbly sacrifice this body and soul, which is full of impurities, before someone who deserves the utmost respect?

To the citizens of Japan, the Japanese emperor is truly sacred and inviolable. There are many sovereign and subject relationships in this world that are defined by contract, as well as those that force respect upon subjects. But where else in the world, besides Japan, is there a country in which a passionate reverence exists between the people and their emperor?

What is the meaning of *kai no ben?*[4] When we use this term to discuss nations, the point of the argument is nothing other than the self-examination by individuals of their morality.

We live a life of virtue only when we come to the realization that we must be brave men in search of the ideal, without being slaves to worldly passions and desires. This is human life in its true sense. Today's brutish misconceptions are shameless, and consider it humanistic to seek desire. This is not humanistic but only animalistic.

A true humanistic life comes with self-esteem. An animalistic life brings disgrace to the people themselves. This is very clear when we see people today. To talk about civilized and barbaric countries, about a nation, means understanding the ethical mission of a nation, and we naturally respect our country. It is regrettable that this has been abolished and may not be taught today.

When we see records of Shōkasonjuku, it is clear that Shōin's teaching was for the enhancement of state principles. Thus, he set down for his students "Seven Rules for *Shi*."

Be it an individual or a nation, when its destiny is in great danger, a divine opportunity naturally arises. If one fails to make the best of this chance, it is difficult to recover.

Also, with regard to the decline of the Tokugawa shogunate, wouldn't a

---

4. [*Kai no ben* (華夷の弁, conflict between civilized and uncivilized countries)]

well-versed expert, on seeing the sudden emergence of the Tanuma[5] era following Yoshimune,[6] know immediately what would come next?

Subsequently, Matsudaira Sadanobu[7] carried out the Kansei Reforms, but he did not achieve his desired results, and the country increasingly fell into a state of neglect and decadence.

Thereupon, Mizuno Tadakuni,[8] who was deeply worried over such trends, made drastic changes. These ended in complete failure, which brought him down. There was no way of dealing with the internal troubles of the Tokugawa shogunate. At this point, foreign powers suddenly pressured the government. In this way, the situation became so violent that finally no one could prevent the veritable hell brought about by politicians such as Ii Naosuke[9] in 1858. Even though there were reformers like Matsudaira and Mizuno, true reform did not occur. What would be the future of a society without such reformers? In the seventh month of the fifth year of Ansei (1858), Takasugi left the domain of Chōshū and went to the east. This was his first opportunity to keep company with men of integrity throughout Japan. He went to Edo, joined the famous Ōhashi School (founded by Ōhashi Totsuan, 1816–1862), studied at Shōheikō,[10] and held discussions with men from the domain of Mito, reputed to be the home of many men of integrity. However, he had difficulty finding any men of integrity appearing to have high ideals engaged in a noble cause.

The situation of the society was still underdeveloped. He said in a letter to his mentor Shōin,

> There is nothing special about each domain today. For everywhere in the whole country is the same, everybody draws in their arms and feels weak at the knees. Like a dog, like a fox, if somebody would start, then they would take short steps to do something good. This is all. Other than that, I have nothing to report about the situation of unifying the country.

Takasugi left Edo on the seventeenth day of the tenth month of the sixth year of Ansei (1859) and returned to Hagi. While he was on his way home, Shōin, who was imprisoned at Denmachō in Edo because of the Oppressions of Bogo

---

5. [Tanuma Okitsugu, 1719–1788; chief senior counselor of the Tokugawa shogunate]
6. [Tokugawa Yoshimune, 1684–1751; eighth shogun of the Tokugawa shogunate]
7. [Matsudaira Sadanobu, 1759–1829; chief senior counselor of the Tokugawa shogunate]
8. [Mizuno Tadakuni, 1794–1851; chief advisor to the twelfth Tokugawa shogun]
9. [Ii Naosuke, 1815–1860; feudal lord and statesman responsible for Japan's signing of the first treaty of commerce with the United States]
10. [The official school of the Tokugawa shogunate, headed by the Hayashi family]

(1858)—but supposedly not also under a death sentence—was executed on the twenty-seventh day of the same month by order of Ii Naosuke.

The grief of Shōin's pupils, including Takasugi, was unbearable to observe. He wrote of his endless sorrow in a letter to Sufu Masanosuke on the sixteenth day of the following month, "I sorely miss my mentor and deplore his death day and night. My grief over his death is extreme." The hatred borne by men of integrity against the Tokugawa shogunate reached its peak.

As expected, the Tairō (Grand Elder), Ii Naosuke, was decapitated by swords of resentment outside the Sakurada Gate of Edo Castle in the third month of the first year of Man'en (1860). The power of the Tokugawa shogunate diminished day by day. The voice of the people, calling "Revere the emperor and expel the Tokugawa shogunate," grew louder and louder. Thus, the shogunate contrived a plan as a last resort: arrange a marriage between Princess Kazu, the sister of Emperor Kōmei, and the shogun Tokugawa Iemochi (1846–1866, the fourteenth Tokugawa shogun), to frustrate the overthrow of the shogunate. There was no way men of integrity could ignore this movement. The arguments increased in intensity.

At this time, Nagai Uta of the Chōshū Domain took the role of bringing court nobles and samurai together. He did this with the view of opening Japan to the world.

Nagai was very utilitarian, with a bent for politics. Shōin had met a tragic end, to be frank, because his ideology aimed at achieving a breakthrough in the deadlock by overthrowing the shogunate. This did not accord with the Nagai faction's compromise plan to establish the Chōshū Domain as the central power.

Men of integrity, such as Takasugi, naturally accused Nagai of being a despicable crook. When the Chōshū Domain made great efforts to bring together court nobles and samurai, following Nagai's plan, Takasugi strongly opposed it, as the plan was makeshift and would impoverish the Chōshū Domain. Finally, he developed a plan to eliminate Nagai.

Katsura Kogorō[11] learned of this and was greatly concerned. Katsura accepted Takasugi's wish to go abroad and arranged to send him to China with shogunate emissaries. Takasugi readily agreed, and travelled to Nagasaki in the second year of Bunkyū (1862), then to Shanghai with the emissaries in the fourth month, and returned in the seventh month.

While such things were happening, the anti-foreigner movement heated up at the court. Nagai Uta was ordered to commit seppuku following the revelation of his plan for a policy of overseas expansion. The position of the Chōshū Domain

---

11. [Katsura Kogorō, 1833–1877, later known as Kido Kōin; a Japanese statesman during the late Tokugawa shogunate and the Meiji Restoration]

later changed into exclusionism, yet they made efforts to bring court nobles and samurai together, in order to compete with the rival Satsuma Domain. When Takasugi came back to Japan, he went to Edo through Kyoto, and fiercely argued that its plan would do more harm than good.

Takasugi foresaw the collapse of the Tokugawa shogunate. Thus, this was a time for the Chōshū Domain to retreat, given the circumstances, and nurture its spirit. If it truly wanted to do something, it would do better by gathering troops loyal to the emperor and destroying the shogunate. If it were yet premature to do so, it would be important to conserve its forces for overthrowing the shogunate. He stated this to his lord's heir, Mōri Sadahiro, but it was not easy to realize. Thus, he escaped the domain and headed to Mito.

Thereafter, he met repeatedly with his colleagues to work out an exclusionist plan, but to no avail. He revealed his spirit occasionally, such as when he set fire to the English Embassy at Gotenyama.

Meanwhile, he was secretly called to Kyoto by his lord in the third month of the third year of Bunkyū (1863). He explained to the authorities of his domain that it was important to build up strength for overthrowing the shogunate. However, even Sufu Masanosuke said, "If we work on the court and other domains to take away the power of the shogunate, the shogunate will collapse naturally. Your theory of overthrowing the shogunate is ten years too early." Hence, Takasugi requested, "If so, I would like to have ten years rest," and he became a monk, taking the name Tōkō. It is interesting to see how his temperament changed so fluently.

His poem states,

> I yearn for a person who goes to the west [implying Saigyō].
> Yet I go to the east [where the shogunate is]
> Only god knows what I am determined to do.

He became a monk, but was not following the dharma. He never shed tears of joy. He caused trouble by venting his anger outrageously. The domain did not know what to do with him in this situation, so they ordered someone to ask him to come back to Chōshū. Then, we do not know why, but he accepted this offer and lived secretly in Matsumoto of Hagi.

In Kyoto meanwhile, the emperor's carriage paid an official visit to Iwashimizu in the fourth month of the same year, and the deadline for the expulsion of foreigners was set for the tenth day of the fifth month. On that day, the Chōshū Domain drove away the American ships, and then French and Dutch ships as well. However, French battleships arrived soon after, and the soldiers on garrison duty at Shimonoseki were savagely attacked. Thus, the lords—father (Mōri Takachika) and son (Mōri Sadahiro)—were greatly concerned, so the domain decided to reappoint Takasugi. He accepted. He felt that the regular soldiers of the Mōri Domain were not capable enough, so his initial action was to gather volunteers to organize a *kihei-tai* (irregular militia).

Even though the Chōshū Domain became involved in the movement to expel foreigners, other domains gave no help. Only a patriot of the Kurume Domain, Maki Izumi, strongly advocated the idea of the emperor directly governing the country. Izumi's plan was to foment a national consensus by announcing the direct governance of the country by the emperor, drawing the shogunate into conflict, and, seeing that the shogunate would not follow the emperor, destroy it in a single stroke.

Maki Izumi skillfully offered this to the Chōshū Domain. The domain totally agreed with him and forwarded his plan. In the eighth month of the same year, the emperor issued an imperial order to advance to Yamato, visit Emperor Jimmu's grave, the Kasuga Shrine, and other places, and establish a military council for exclusionism.

The Guard of Kyoto, the Aizu Domain, was greatly surprised.

This was a serious situation for the shogunate. They had to somehow manage to cancel this imperial order. Thus, with much thought, they asked for help from the Satsuma Domain to drive out the Chōshū Domain, dismiss the Chōshū Domain from the guards of Sakaimachi Gate, and order the seven aristocrats, including Sanjō Sanetomi and Higashikuze Tsūki, to be confined to their houses. This turned the tide completely.

Thus, the lord and son of the Chōshū Domain were falsely charged, and returned to their domain. The seven aristocrats fled from Kyoto to Chōshū at the same time. The Chōshū samurai started a furious action, leading soldiers to Kyoto to exonerate the lord and aristocrats. Lord Sanjō and others also requested that the irregular militia go to Kyoto. However, Sufu Masanosuke, taking cautionary measures, did not accede to this. Takasugi was one of the councilors of the Chōshū Domain. He also thought that it was not the time to make an all-out effort which would end in exhaustion, agreed with Sufu, and made efforts to restrain the men from acting rashly.

Because of the unfavorable situation in Kyoto, the movement for vindication was growing more intense. Finally, it was decided that the leader of mobile forces, Kurushima Matabei, would personally lead them to wipe out the shogunate forces surrounding the emperor. In the first month of the first year of Genji (1864), Takasugi went to Miyaichi in Suō, where the mobile forces were camped, and by the order of the domain, sought to block Kurushima's departure for Kyoto. However, Kurushima, who was in a rage, did not listen to Takasugi. Takasugi lost his temper as he was insulted by Kurushima's accusation that Takasugi was only concerned about his promotion within the domain. Short-tempered Takasugi did not report on his mission and ran off to Osaka, where Kusaka Gisuke and others were staying.

The Chōshū Domain was greatly troubled by his actions, especially since the attack movement was growing. At the earnest request of the son of the lord, Takasugi was forced to come back to Chōshū. As a warning to others, he was held at Noyama Prison. This was the twenty-ninth day of the third month. He was twenty-six at the time.

An estimable man of character becomes the master of any situation. At a time when conditions have suddenly gone mad and the mind of a man of integrity becomes dazed, Takasugi, who, in prison, should have been bemoaning his fate in vain, was able to display his true self.

In the preface to his prison journal, he wrote,

> At the beginning of my incarceration, I regretted my past, thought about the future, and sitting in silence, blamed myself through self-examination. I became like a dead tree, my mind like cold ash, and just waited for death. So, I thought that as I was already imprisoned, I couldn't determine when I would die, so why should I reflect upon it, blaming myself, and waiting for death to come. One day I had an insight and said, "If I find the Way in the morning, I will have no regrets dying in the evening." This is the way of sages. Why should I follow the way of petty Zen monks? Thus, I borrowed books from guards, read them, was moved by them, shed tears that wet my clothing, and gripped myself with patriotic indignation. The feeling would go away, and then come back: my thoughts would never reach the end. Becoming like a dead person, before knowing the Way, is not the way of a human.
>
> Thus, if I find the Way in the morning, I will have no regrets dying in the evening. Immeasurable joy with eternal and spiritual peace. I uttered what my mind felt.
>
> That is what I felt compelled to do. I, Seikai Ikkyōsei[12] Tōkō, wrote this in the fourth month, under the south window of the second building in the northern section of Noyama Prison.

It is only when people are first proud of themselves and then become disappointed that they finally can taste the meaning of life. When we read the poems that he composed in prison, their words and phrases touch our hearts deeply.

> The first day of the fourth month
> I think only about my country, and nothing of myself.
> I stumble, and become resident of a dark chamber.

---

12. [Lit., a crazy person in the western sea]

Why ponder right or wrong about such problems, small as dust?
I face the gracious deity from the bottom of my heart.

The eighth day, more than sixty books read.
In a daze, I am ashamed of my past.
With a mind to the future I sit in silence.
I sometimes read ancient texts.
My original thoughts have not yet died out.

The eleventh day, more than thirty books read.
Let the demands of the times determine when to live and when to die.
Pay no heed to the debates of others about right or wrong.
I remember what the late Master Shōin said.
I think of the past and shed tears profusely.

Day sixteen, fifty books read.
The night falls deeply, and the neighbors are quiet.
A short candle projects a chilling light between the cracks in the wall.
Unending sadness and unending bitterness.
I think of my lord, I think of my father, and I quietly shed tears.

Day twenty-six, fifty books read.
The lights are out, people are sleeping.
The night is already deep.
A lonely prisoner goes to bed, mind beginning to meditate.
I close my eyes and open them vacantly
Thus, enlightening the mind of before life and after death.

The fifth month, second day, fifty books read.
The sun is now about to set in the dark chamber.
The returning crows cry in the distant sky.
Some of their voices now fade amidst the clouds.
I sit alone in prison.

Day eight, fifty books read.
Last night's scant rain clears in the morning.
In back and front of the building, sparrows cry noisily.
I think of my father with a bamboo stick.
He would call out to my sister and walk in the rice fields.

Day nine, ninety books read.

I just nap in my cell.

I dream.

When I wake up, it is so empty and sad.

Truly, a prison is like a mountain village.

It is quite like days and nights of old.

In this way, he also looked over Shōin's manuscripts with deep emotion.

While he was in prison, the Chōshū Domain decided to proceed to Kyoto to prove its innocence, with soldiers such as Fukuhara Echigo, Kurushima Matabei, Maki Izumi-no-Kami, and Kusaka Gisuke. Soon after, the son of Lord Mōri Sadahiro also went to Sanuki. However, this exacerbated the situation between the Chōshū Domain and the Tokugawa shogunate, and they finally began to fight. As a result, the Chōshū Domain met with a crushing defeat. Many soldiers died, including Kurushima, Kusaka, and Terajima. Maki Izumi-no-Kami performed seppuku at Mount Tennō.

The shogunate did not let this opportunity slip away. They roused the army and went on an expedition against the Chōshū Domain. Their excuse was that the Chōshū army had attacked the Imperial Palace. At the same time, a combined fleet from England, the United States, France, and Holland attacked Shimonoseki.

In a panic, Chōshū made a temporary peace with those countries while working on a plan to deal with the shogunate.

After more than eighty days in prison, Tōkō was released and was confined to his house. However, he was suddenly called up on the fifth day of the eighth month, and ordered to go to Shimonoseki. This problem (the fighting against the foreigners) was solved in the middle of the eighth month, after many twists and turns. On the other hand, the problem of the expedition of the shogunate against Chōshū remained.

Even though it was on the decline, the shogunate retained power. It ordered more than thirty domains to join its side, and was approaching the border of the Chōshū Domain, with Owari Keishō as expedition leader. This alarmed most people in the Chōshū Domain, who held conventional views, and they advocated obeisance to the shogunate. On the other hand, people such as Tōkō maintained their opinion that Chōshū should fight the shogunate army to retain the moral high ground in a just cause. Ultimately, the conventional view prevailed, so the Chōshū Domain apologized and was forgiven. Tōkō escaped to Chikuzen (modern Fukuoka Prefecture).

However, there were many hot-blooded men in the Chōshū Domain. Tōkō left Chōshū once, but, while undergoing many hardships, he contrived and carried out a plot. On the first month of the first year of Keiō (1865), he counterattacked the conventional supporters of the domain and swept them away, unifying opinion in the domain, and built up defenses on its borders. Finally, his desire to overthrow the shogunate became a possibility. The situation had changed. Satsuma and Chōshū became allies. The battle between Chōshū and the shogunate reopened in the sixth month of the second year of Keiō (1866). Tōkō became commander-in-chief of the Chōshū army upon its entrance to Kyushu and fought bravely. Even with all its military power, the shogunate was unable to defeat even the Chōshū Domain by itself. By this victory, the balance of power was now in question.

Acceding to the pessimism of the old domain retainers, who said it might take as much as ten years to overthrow the shogunate, he became a monk, taking the name Tōkō. However, after only three years, the overthrow of the shogunate became a realistic goal. We can easily imagine his joy. However, he contracted tuberculosis and was forced to withdraw from the milieu of social unrest at the age of twenty-eight.

> Since I became the owner of a grass-thatched hut
> The hustle and bustle of the world does not bother me.
> I should not pursue passion and power
> As a matter of course, I should rest my body and mind.
> Humans can live only one hundred years.
> I am sick and lie down alone.
> Under a faint light
> I learn the depths of reading more and more.

In such a way, this great and respected man passed away at Shimonoseki on the fourteenth day of the fourth month of the third year of Keiō (1867), before the Meiji Restoration. He bore no resentment, but how uncertain life is!

I did not write in enough detail in this chapter about his great exploits and achievements to show the magnitude of his talent and ability. I would like to leave such issues for another occasion. I pray that men with high ideals engaged in a noble cause—and men of great integrity—understand his spirit, which seemed fraught with resentment and emotion on its surface but reflected his sincere concern for Japan's situation and drove him to keep seeking a proper course of action. They should remember Tōkō for this, rather than his reputation for nightlife and drinking. I also hope that men of integrity can take Tōkō's deeds and spirit, and meditate on them, with a waft of incense in the air, on a quiet night, under a limpid light.

The layout of Shōkasonjuku (Shōin's training academy) is given below.

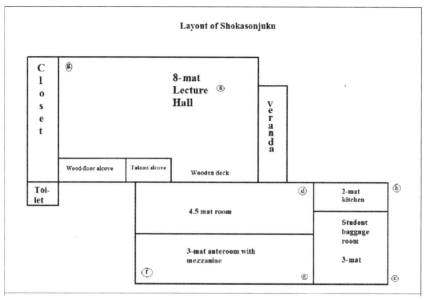

Layout of Shokasonjukn

Key:

a: Original building lecture hall   d–e: Lounge (anteroom)

b: Kitchen (now entrance)   f: Covered mezzanine, where Master Shōin occasionally would retreat

c: Storage for boarders' baggage   g: Former entryway

Areas b–f were added after expansion.

Chronology of Shōkasonjuku

Establishment in Tenpō 13 (1842); approximately 8 years until Kaei 2 (1849):
> The Tamaki period: Time of Tamaki Bunnoshin [founder, headmaster, and Shōin's uncle]; Shōin [attends] from age thirteen to age twenty.

The seven months from the fifth to twelfth month of Kaei 5 (1852):
> The Sugi period: Master Shōin participated in teaching, under headmaster Sugi.

After Kaei 6 (1853); the twelfth month of Ansei 2 (1855) to the eleventh month of Ansei 4 (1857):
> The Kubo period: Kubo Gorōzaemon Hisanari [headmaster and another of Shōin's uncles]; Master Shōin taught at the school located at the Sugi residence for about two years.

Eleventh month of Ansei 4 (1857); permission granted to teach hereditary knowledge, seventh month of Ansei 5 (1858); [until] twelfth month of Ansei 5:
> Approximately one year [teaching] term for Master Shōin.

8

The Way of the Patriot (3)
On Takahashi Deishū (高橋泥舟, 1835–1903)

People must always stand upon their deepest inner selves. And only when, standing in that position, they demonstrate their own sincerity can they lead a life that is valuable to society. This position is crucial for demonstrating the strength of one's inner self and is a moral precondition for social progress.

Therefore we must consider in what position we should stand, in order to be in accordance with our inner selves. If we were to take a certain position as standard, it goes without saying that we must either stand in that position and "go forth," or retreat from it and "retire."

The *Analects* tells us, "If you have use for it, practice it. If not, retire it,"[1] but of course the question of whether to go forth or retire is a subject of serious debate in the lives of *shi* who value the deepest inner self. Disregarding the question of whether to go forth or retire is essentially failing to reflect on oneself. It is a blurring of self-awareness. I must say it is a deadly act, which makes *shi* lose their moral footing. I think the Bushido spirit, which addresses this question seriously, is truly noble.

The resolute desire to form one's character around the decision to go forth or retire is called fidelity to principle. Therefore, adherence to principle is a categorical imperative for *shi*. Whenever we discuss the Japanese spirit, we must not neglect this aspect of it. Now more than ever, with the maturation of materialistic culture, when the dramatic disruption of people's sense of when to go forth and when to retire proceeds apace with the corruption of the human heart, when there is no place to display fidelity to principle, is discussing this not a way for humans to reflect upon themselves?

When I think of this, I cannot help but feel deep respect for Takahashi Deishū, a high official during the Edo period and a pioneer during the Bakumatsu.[2]

Once, the "three Shūs" (Kaishū, Tesshū, and Deishū) of the Bakumatsu were famous. Now, there are many who would be hard pressed to even put their three

---

1. [*Analects*, chapters 7–10]
2. [Bakumatsu: the final years of the Tokugawa shogunate, 1853–1867]

names together. Many probably still know Katsu Kaishū (1823–1899). Yamaoka Tesshū (1836–1888) has still not been forgotten. But the name of Takahashi Deishū is becoming completely obscured. Sometimes, I meet someone who knows about him, but they do not know anything more than "that master of the spear."

Why does Kaishū alone remain famous, while Deishū is being forgotten? If you are thinking that Deishū's accomplishments must fall far short of Kaishū's, that would be a truly unforgivable misapprehension. I have no hesitation in declaring that while Kaishū may have been extraordinary, he never exceeded petty greatness.

Certainly he possessed an insight into the affairs of the time, a manly will, and resourcefulness. However, wasn't everything he did mere scheming? Look at the ostentatious sarcasm and ridicule that poured from his lips. Even worse is his unabashedly self-promoting manifesto. It is as if the lack of grace in his character is reflected in his personality. In his brilliant, eloquent manner, he mocks and belittles people far more often than is normal.

Sima Guang[3] argued sternly, "People who have more talent than virtue are called petty men. People who have more virtue than talent are called men of virtue," and this is quite apt. Kaishū was indeed a petty man, however great.

On the other hand, Deishū was a thoroughly sincere person. He had true feeling. People with true feeling often lead inspiring lives. Since antiquity, the thing that great people should not lack is that true feeling, that inspiration. When I read the letter that Butsuin sent to his good friend Su Dongpo (Su Shi 蘇軾, 1037–1101) that declares "The Buddha too was only a man of flesh and blood," I am as moved today as I was in the past.

Deishū had resolved to lay down his life and mastered the mysteries of *budō*. Relying only on his single spear, he managed to receive the junior fifth court rank (*jūgoi*) and become the governor of Ise (a ceremonial title). Later, he grew concerned about the state of affairs in the nation and devoted himself totally to settling the shogunal government's internal disorder. But then, perhaps out of loyalty to his shogun, Yoshinobu,[4] he simply abandoned what should have been a bright future and never looked back. His entire life is permeated with truly inspiring sentiments. People who make him out to be some kind of eccentric hermit are no better than blind donkeys who cannot describe the Way in front of them. If Deishū had not been around during the Bakumatsu, it is certain there would have been such a collapse that even Kaishū would have despaired. The twenty-three domains of Tōhoku were in quite a state of ferment. Who knows if the shogun Yoshinobu would have declared his submission to the emperor?

Speaking of which, Kaishū must be very grateful to Deishū. And what a

---

3. [Sima Guang, 1019–1086; Chinese historian, scholar, and high chancellor of the Song Dynasty]

4. [1837–1913; the last Tokugawa shogun]

schemer Kaishū was! Taking advantage of Deishū's retirement, whenever he met someone who happened to talk about him, Kaishū would, in his eloquent way, mock him so smoothly that one couldn't tell if he was praising or criticizing Deishū. Why do educated men of virtue regard him as an upright person? Nevertheless, the world knows of Kaishū and not of Deishū. We cannot help but feel, in a corner of our hearts, shame toward our predecessors for this. (At present, my thoughts about Kaishū have changed quite a bit, but I will not discuss that here.)

What kind of relationship did Deishū and Tesshū have? Tesshū did not originally have the name Yamaoka but rather Ono. And Deishū's was not Takahashi, it was Yamaoka. Deishū was called Kenzaburō (Sei'ichi after the Restoration) Masa'akira. He was born on the seventeenth day of the second month of the sixth year of Tenpō (1835), the second son of Yamaoka Ichiro Uemon Masakuni, a shogunal flag bearer. He was Ki'ichirō Masa'akira's younger brother, but when he was seventeen he left and became the heir of the caretaker of Ninomaru Castle, Takahashi Ren'nosuke Kanezane, to whom he was related on his mother's side. Tesshū, or rather Ono Tetsutarō, was Deishū's student.

(Ki'ichirō) Masa'akira (Deishū's older brother) died on the twenty-seventh day of the seventh month of the second year of Ansei (1855). Deishū, regretting having been cut off from the Yamaoka family's inheritance, appealed to his student Ono Tetsutarō, to whom he was close. Deishū had his younger sister Fusako marry Tetsutarō and had him inherit the Yamaoka house. Accordingly, while Deishū and Tesshū are teacher and student, they are also brothers-in-law. Without knowing this, it is impossible to understand the friendship between them.

Yamaoka Ki'ichirō Seizan (Deishū's older brother) died at the young age of twenty-seven, but at the time, he was a genius who had been called a master of the spear, with no rival in the entire country. I understand that he also had a good-natured and upstanding character—truly a model samurai. Somewhere in Dr. Nakamura Masanao's (1832–1891, Meiji era educator) writings it is recorded that when Seizan was practicing his spear techniques throughout the day and night, as soon as he saw the day break, he jumped up and, determined to keep going, tied a rope tightly around his stomach, and through this wretched device, was able to keep practicing his spear swing with great vigor. In truth, no matter which path one is aiming at, without that level of effort, it is difficult to make progress.

The nerves of modern people are becoming frayed. Because of the onslaught of colors, the cacophony of sounds, and the endless labor that comes with modern civilization, our nerves are always being stimulated at the periphery, making us constantly twitch, giving rise to a weariness that one cannot easily recover from. And while on the surface it seems as if our senses are sharp, in reality our nerves have been weakened considerably and no longer behave as we want them to. If you look around, everyone's eyes are flitting to and fro. When people walk through the city, they stagger around. This is evidence that they have not established steadfast, immovable hearts within themselves. Accordingly, what people say is also incoherent. Whether in calligraphy or art, there is no room at all for the display of correct behavior and quality of character. If people don't have a steadfast, immovable place within themselves, they will become degenerate.

In truth, when we look at ourselves, do we not find that we are terribly lonely? Are we not desolate? The only way to escape the loneliness and desolation that eats away at our souls is to settle the nervousness in our hearts. Because one of the main foci of *budō* is the firming up of people's souls, I think it is truly ideal for this purpose.

I think people who have learned swordsmanship will remember: Because our spirit lacks unity, when we take up a sword and face an opponent we do not know where to direct our gaze. Although we try to advance, our legs do not move as we command them. Although we try to strike, our swords swing and don't hit the target. Thus, to train your heart and mind, for sword and body to become one and come and go like the wind, is truly the essence of *budō* through vigorous penance. And this art has value precisely because it reveals this unified self under the sword of one's opponent.

No matter which discipline one pursues, if one cannot build up the resolve to lay down one's life, no progress can be made. For example, people who wish to excel in Zen must have the resolve to come back to life, even after flinging themselves into a bottomless chasm. Most people, like timid kittens, are frightened by this and shrink away. Our glorious *budō* takes people and puts them under the sword. When breathing is synchronized and two souls are focused on each other, existing in the tensioned instant of pure no-self, there is nothing I love more. The idea that it is about taking up weapons and going around bloodthirstily making trouble is laughably narrow minded.

Deishū followed his older brother Seizan and underwent training that the people of today cannot even imagine. When Seizan died in the seventh month of the second year of Ansei (1855), Deishū had just turned twenty-one. We can see how deep his feelings were from his grief at that time. Overcome with sorrow, neither food nor drink passed his lips, and he brooded so much that it was thought he had lost his mind. Once, he almost managed to commit seppuku, but apparently his servants were able to stop him through their combined efforts. However, even after the funeral, whenever he thought of his brother, new tears would flow, and he could never forget him. At some point during this time, he decided to follow in his brother's footsteps and began teaching students.

It was one night in the second month two years later, and no one knows whether it was a dream or reality, but his older brother Ki'ichirō, whom Deishū had been unable to forget for years, appeared and spoke to him. Although this is well known among proponents of building character through kendo, my pen seems eager to write it here as well, so I will quote from Abe Masahito's *Collected Works of Deishū*:[5]

> "It has already been three years since I passed from the world. I ascended to the heavenly realm where there is no end of pleasure, but my love for you is earnest and you have been constantly on my mind. Therefore, I have come. I wanted to come and see whether you had made any progress in your skill with the spear."
>
> Deishū said haughtily, "You are some kind of sly fox or badger spirit, not my brother. By what principle can someone who has died come back? Did you, sly spirit, knowing how much I long for my brother, come here wanting to confuse me?"
>
> Ki'ichirō said, "You know not that there are principles that operate outside of common sense. After death there is birth. And then after birth again there is death. Birth and death, birth and death revolve endlessly, and good actions bear good results, while evil actions bear evil results. There is no escaping this. Is it not terrifying? You do not know this principle. Therefore it is not unreasonable that when you saw me, you thought I was some kind of fox or badger spirit. I was reborn in the heavenly realm and received the five godly senses and a divine body that does whatever I wish. When I want to be somewhere, I go just as my heart wishes. So when I thought of you, I appeared here instantly. If you still think I am a fox or badger, your spear will not touch me. Point your spear at me. We shall have a match."
>
> Hearing this, Deishū, half believing and half doubting, took up his spear. When he faced his opponent and began the match, there was no doubt that it was Ki'ichirō. In the old days, he had never been able to best Ki'ichirō, but now he was at least his equal. Nevertheless, they failed to settle the match that night.
>
> Ki'ichirō said, "I think you are still holding back some of your skill. Well, it's not as if I am not holding back as well. I'll come again tomorrow." So saying, he easily rose past the clouds and ascended to heaven. Deishū yelled and called for him, but there was no reply. Suddenly, the dream was broken.
>
> When he woke up, his body was covered with sweat, and his bed was drenched with it. The next night, Ki'ichirō came and said, "Let tonight be the night we each use our secret techniques and fight to our hearts' content." Deishū agreed, and they both took up their spears, bowed to each other, and crossed spear points once again. It was a ten-point match. Deishū had already won nine points and would certainly have won the remaining one as well, but out of courtesy he let Ki'ichirō win one. At that point Ki'ichirō said happily, "Ah, you have trained and polished your natural talent for the spear to achieve this level! I can no longer keep up with you. Now, for the first time, I can rest easy. Farewell, I shall take my leave of you for the rest of time." So saying,

---

5. [Abe Masahito, ed., *Deishū Ikō* (Tokyo: Kokkōsha, 1903).]

he ascended on roiling mists up into heaven. Deishū, mad with grief at the parting, shouted, "Brother! Brother!" at the top of his lungs and suddenly awoke.

Deishū sat up in bed and wiped the sweat from his body, but, in a daze, he was unable to shake his sense of sorrow. For a while, he was in a stupor. Eventually he wondered if he could meet his brother if he went to Renge Temple (in Komagome). Dawn had not even broken, but he made preparations and rushed out, hurrying toward Renge Temple. When he arrived, the temple gate was not yet open, so he beat on the gate and made them open it. He went immediately to his brother's grave and, like a madman, screamed "Brother!" as loud as he could, but no one answered him.

At this point he thought, "I'll never meet my brother like this. Wouldn't it be best to cut open my stomach and follow him?" He shrugged his shoulders out of his kimono and took up the sword on his belt. Fortunately, just as he was about to do it, people came running and stopped him. Deishū experienced a sudden moment of self-reflection. Apologizing deeply, he hurried back and arrived at his house just as a faint glimmer of dawn was beginning to appear.

He was a slave to his emotions. But is this emotionality not the deep feelings of ancient times? Utilitarians who laugh at this would, in other words, find it amusing that Nanshū threw himself in the water.[6]

In the third month of the third year of Ansei (1856), when the shogunate's school for martial arts was established, he was appointed as an instructor of spear techniques. With his skill in budō and his upright character, he finally became the very model of a shogunal retainer.[7] In the twelfth month of the second year of Bunkyū (1862), when Yoshinobu, then the shogunal guardian, went to Kyoto, Deishū accompanied him, leading a force of samurai to protect him.

In the third month of the next year, the shogun Iemochi went to Kyoto with a force of several hundred rōnin led by Udono Kyūō (1808–1869). The shogunate had gathered rōnin for the first time and put them under the leadership of Matsudaira Kazusanosuke, but they were a rebellious lot and there was no way they were ever going to accept someone so conventional. Eventually, the rōnin rejected Kazusanosuke, and the above-mentioned Udono Kyūō replaced him.

However, even Kyūō did not satisfy them. In the end, the rōnin appealed to the shogun to be placed under Deishū. In the shogun's stead, senior councilor Itakura Iga[8] ordered Deishū to the position.

Deishū had originally been opposed to the shogunate's conscription of rōnin, and now he firmly refused to accept the appointment. However, he was appealed

---

6. [Saigō Nanshū (Saigō Takamori, 1828–1877), in an act of friendship and loyalty, attempted to drown himself alongside his friend Gesshō, whom he had failed to protect from political intrigue.]

7. [That is, a hatamoto, or direct retainer of the shogun, as opposed to a retainer of a daimyo.]

8. [Itakura Katsukiyo (板倉勝静, 1823–1889); "Iga" is a title.]

to with such earnestness that he eventually accepted. He became the *rōnin* manager and instructor. It seems the *rōnin* were extremely pleased to be under his command. It was around this time that Deishū received the junior fifth court rank and was appointed governor of Ise.

However, while on the one hand Deishū was respected by the samurai, on the other hand his uncompromising personality did not sit well with the small-minded people in the shogunate. In the fourth month of the same year (1863), he returned to Edo with some warriors and presented his ideas about the structure of the nation and the management of the *rōnin*, offering many suggestions to the senior counselors, but they stubbornly refused to adopt even one. In the end, he resigned his commission.

Quite contrary to accepting his advice, those foolish petty officials, concerned about his loyalty to the emperor and new ideas, and fearing the military power gathered around him, went as far as to try to bring him down with slander. For a while, they investigated him on allegations of rebellion and tried to pass judgment on him. He narrowly avoided that and ended up under house arrest.

However, when a fire happened to break out in Edo Castle in the eleventh month of the third year of Bunkyū (1863), his good faith was reestablished. Finally, in the twelfth month of the same year, he was released from confinement and reinstated as the caretaker of Ninomaru (Nijō) Castle in Kyoto and instructor of spear techniques.

On the twelfth day of the first month of 1868 (the first year of the Meiji period), Yoshinobu lost the Battle of Fushimi and fled back to Edo. The shogunate roiled with disorder. Some people indignantly lamented the evil that the world had fallen into, while others thought it might be about time to give up on the Tokugawa clan and settle down into civilian lives. There were also some bold individuals who shrewdly sought to take advantage of the confusion, like thieves who show up at the scene of a fire. Basically, no one could come up with a plan. In the first place, no one knew what Yoshinobu's course of action should be. The senior counselors even advised Yoshinobu to commit suicide.

Upon hearing this, Deishū could no longer remain silent. He felt that it was meaningless and quite dangerous for countrymen to fight each other. Furthermore, he was ever mindful of interference from countries with ill intent, who cast their predatory gaze on Japan. The nation was in a state of great peril. If the internal strife was not resolved with all possible haste, all Japanese citizens would fall into a terrible abyss. Moreover, the idea of making Yoshinobu commit seppuku was not only a terrible plan that would not achieve the desired result, but also, as Yoshinobu's retainer, Deishū found it atrocious, irrational, highly treasonous, and blind to the emotional bonds between them. The only good plan was for the shogun to earnestly display his submission to the emperor.

So thinking, Deishū, beside himself with anger, turned his horse toward the main castle. He planned to seek an audience with Yoshinobu and carefully lay out the current situation for him. However, petty government officials refused him and would not receive him no matter how he implored them. For seven days and nights, he stubbornly continued to try to force his way through. He finally realized that he was not going to get his way, but unable to set aside his anger, he gave up and sought an audience with senior counselor Ogasawara Iki[9] and, in a voice mixed with tears, argued for submission to the emperor. In the end, they wept together and swore to uphold the nation. Among the senior counselors, Iki was the one who was genuinely concerned about the state of the country—a true samurai.

Even so, the petty officials were extremely obstinate in stonewalling him, and it seemed that he would not have his wish granted after all. Nevertheless, his unrelenting advocacy of submission won in the end, and thereafter he was finally granted an audience with the shogun. Moreover, during this whole time, Yoshinobu, being who he was, thought it strange that the governor of Ise (Deishū) had not come to see him. The errors of petty men are always like this.

During this time, Kaishū had shuttered himself up in his house. Though the shogun's submission sprung from Deishū's insistence on it, it seems like people have been taught that Kaishū alone made the shogun submit, negotiated with Saigō,[10] and handed over Edo Castle.

In fact, Kaishū himself said the following. This is an account directly from Kaishū in response to Abe's question about the state of Edo Castle when the shogun returned from battle:

Kaishū said, "Well now…it was like when children fight outdoors and one of them gets serious, and the other gets scared and runs into his house in a frenzy; is there any reasoning there? What good could they possibly have done after running away to hide in a hole? It makes me want to vomit. I have no idea what the last shogun was doing when he returned to the castle. Since I had shut myself away at the time I don't know for sure, but *he was probably engaging in some rustic play*.

"That Takahashi guy…he had always been talking about devotion to the emperor, so when the shogun came back to his castle having been branded a traitor to the court, he wasn't happy. So he set out for the castle right away to tell the shogun a thing or two.

"But he wasn't being *stupid* at all. He thought it out pretty well. Everyone in the palace knew what Takahashi wanted to say. They all said that things hadn't yet gotten to the dismal point where they had to bear the humiliation of declaring submission,

9. [Ogasawara Nagamichi (小笠原長行, 1822–1891); "Iki" is a title.]
10. [Saigō Takamori, the leader of the imperial forces at that time]

but Takahashi stubbornly took his case to Ogasawara. Ogasawara was *wise*, so he understood the reasoning and agreed, but his fellow senior counselors were a bunch of idiots and they had a hard time making any progress.

"That's when Ōkubo (Ōkubo Ichi'ō, 1818–1888) came in, as you'd expect from him. He saw that things weren't getting anywhere using ordinary methods, so he told all the details to the shogun, and stated, *"This is when we need Katsu to come in and take charge."* It wasn't the kind of situation where I had the time to sit around shutting myself in and being useless. So, I once again took up my posts as magistrate of the navy and director of military affairs. Then I went straight to the castle and heard everyone arguing loudly. Later, I explained the state of affairs to them in detail, then I argued that, indeed, there was no possible strategy other than submission. Then what Takahashi had been saying got through. So Takahashi and I went together to the shogun and argued that submission was the course of action appropriate to the times. That's when they decided to submit to the power of the emperor."

If, upon the advent of the glorious Meiji Restoration, Kaishū had possessed the character of an ancient man of virtue, he would have taken Deishū's hands and said with tears of gratitude, "The nation exists today because of your efforts."

Having thus struggled their way to a decision to submit to the emperor, there was yet another concern ahead of them. If, after the shogun finally submitted, one of his disloyal subordinates were to steal the title of shogun, all their efforts would be for naught. Therefore, someone with power would have to watch over those who might succeed the shogun. Deishū undertook this task with total devotion, while Kaishū's role was primarily to look after the paperwork in dealings with the court. Insightful people were already worried about the paths these two figures would take from there.

It was decided that Yoshinobu would retire to Mount Tōei on the twelfth day of the second month. Instead of the ceremony that usually accompanied shogunal travel, he left the castle as if he were fleeing in the darkness of night. Deishū, leading elite shock troops, protected the shogun as he retreated through Ueno, while Kaishū stayed in the castle. After that, it seems there were many things that warranted investigation.

It is a well-known fact that when his highness Arisugawa-no-miya led a large force of loyalist troops eastward, Yamaoka Tesshū went alone to Sunpu to meet Saigō. However, people seem to think this was done at Kaishū's instigation, but the reality is quite different.

Originally, Deishū himself was supposed to go on this mission. When Yoshinobu heard that the loyalist troops had entered Sunpu, he was very worried and so summoned Deishū. Yoshinobu ordered him to hurry to Sunpu to tell the court directly that the shogun planned to submit. Deishū, having received the order, set about right away to depart for Sunpu. However, the shogun suddenly called him back, saying, "Ise, Ise, wait. If you leave now, I can't say that my subordinate samurai will not revolt in order to take me back. But aside from you there's no one who will fully carry out my orders, and aside from you there's no one who can subdue my subordinates. Isn't there someone else who could go in your stead?" So saying, he broke into tears. My pen having written this far, I think of the feelings between lord and subject, and I too cannot contain my tears. Those words ring true.

It was a time when the question of submission was not entirely settled. Every day the chief retainer of the Sakai Domain, Matsudaira Gonjūrō, came to the shogun's camp and argued forcefully that Deishū should lead soldiers from the twenty-three domains of Ōu into battle with the emperor's force without delay. He cornered Deishū and said,

> First of all, let's wipe out Ii [Ii Naonori, 1848–1904] and the rest of the ungrateful traitors. Let's get the golden fan standard[11] from Tōshōgū Shrine, and swiftly prepare an expedition. Let's look to Ieyasu as our model.

He argued this vehemently for seven days.

However, Deishū countered that this was contrary to the trend of the time and, fortunately, was able to forestall this line of thought. Even when Enomoto Buyō[12] and his followers deserted, they left inconspicuously at night after promising to carefully consider Deishū's dissuasions. If Deishū had not been there, who can tell how it would have turned out?

So Deishū thought over Yoshinobu's request and recommended Tesshū as emissary in his stead. As for Kaishū, Tesshū did no more than consult with him on his way out. It was Deishū's plan from beginning to end, and Kaishū was not involved at all. In Tesshū's miscellaneous writings as well, there is this:

> Towards the end of the second month, a messenger came to my house and told me to come quickly to the shogun. Accordingly, I went immediately and saw my brother-in-law, the governor of Ise, seated at the shogun's side. The shogun ordered me to go to Sunpu and meet with the head of the loyalist army in order to carry out the plan to submit to the emperor.

Tesshū also expressed how happy he was that, because his brother-in-law, the governor of Ise, picked someone as unworthy as himself, he was able to pay back one ten-thousandth of the debt he owed his country.

One thing I cannot fail to write about is the selfish rewards for distinguished

---

11. [The golden fan was the battle standard of Tokugawa Ieyasu, the first shogun of the Tokugawa shogunate.]

12. [Enomoto Takeaki (1836–1908) was the vice admiral of the shogunal navy. He refused to turn over his warships to the loyalist forces when the shogun submitted to the emperor.]

service given out by the new government. Since long ago, there have been many dubious awards of this kind given. However, around the fourth or fifth year of the Meiji period, there were quite a few that are very strange. First, the court sent out notices to all the heroes of the Restoration telling them to submit records of their accomplishments. Tesshū received one of these notices but did not respond.

Getting no response from Tesshū, the Imperial Household Ministry sent an urgent summons to him. He quickly went to present himself and see what it was about and, of all things, it was an investigation of his accomplishments. The council members could not very well ignore him, so they asked him about his accomplishments, which they already knew perfectly well. It seems Tesshū was irritated and flippantly said that he did not have any accomplishments, but they did not give up. Nonetheless, no matter what he was asked, he insisted: "I forgot," eventually told the officials not to make up such lies, and left.

Immediately afterward, he went to Deishū's retreat (Deishū had cut off all ties with the world since the dissolution of the feudal domains) and told him how he had been summoned to the Imperial Household Ministry, went to see what it was, and of all things, everyone there was going over his record of accomplishments, all but saying he was the greatest hero in the world. They had written everything up just like they themselves had done it, so there was no need for him to say anything. He had just said "he forgot" to everything, and left it at that. He told Deishū that Katsu was there as well, but he had written everything himself, saying "Right? Right?" So Tesshū had just said "Sure."

Ōkubo (Ichiō) said with great indignation,

> Katsu hates you as well, so not even a whiff of what you did appears in the record of meritorious service. They're all a bunch of little goblins, like village heads without houses, or sumo wrestlers without opponents. I thought it was pathetic, so I pretended not to know anything and left.

But Deishū just told him he did not care about that kind of thing, and the two of them shared a good laugh over it.

After that there is one more story related to Yamaoka's award for distinguished service that is famous. It is when Inoue Kaoru drew the short straw and was made a provisional imperial messenger and sent from the Imperial Household Ministry to Yamaoka's house carrying the award.

However, Tesshū firmly refused to accept it. "I do not have any exploits to my name that would warrant the bestowal of an award for distinguished service. Even if I did, there is no way I could be bestowed with something so far removed from the norms of reward and punishment." He pushed it away and stubbornly refused to accept it.

At that time as well, Tesshū told Deishū indignantly,

They went ahead and decided on their own achievements. Even what peerage they should receive, at what rank, whether the award for distinguished service would be first-rate or second-rate; all of it they just did on their own. So they feel apologetic and offered something to me, but I categorically refused it. Besides, they're all people who just received wealth from their parents, or else took it from someone else. With all their bluster about what they had accomplished after much hardship, it felt like they were just giving me charity, so I flatly sent it back. If you had received some appropriate awards, I could have accepted it without embarrassment; but since they were trying to do the exact opposite, that's what I did.

It is laughable when you think of how they gave Tesshū the award after he died. And everyone was made into provisional imperial messengers; they really handled it poorly.

Tesshū was right to be indignant: Why was Deishū neglected the way he was? Surely it is not as if they considered Deishū's wish to retire quietly and thought that troubling him with worldly rewards was not the way to treat a man of such noble character. If that were true, then the people of the new Meiji government would have been an admirable lot. A new star would have been born in the heavens in their honor. In the fourth month of the first year of the Meiji period, Deishū went to Mito to protect Shogun Yoshinobu, who had been placed under house arrest, and on the twelfth month of the same year he followed Yoshinobu in moving to Shizuoka. After the dissolution of the feudal domains and the establishment of the prefectures, he embraced his long-held desire and never went forth into the world again.

Why did Deishū cut himself off so cleanly from the world? He shared his master Yoshinobu's fate until the end. His pure sentiment took no notice of his master's desolate fate. Besides, no matter what he did, he would probably not have been able to make a comeback, and he could not bear to rub elbows with those arrogant, rustic layabouts from Satsuma and Chōshū.[13] Even as he set out, the outcome was obvious. The origin of his sobriquet "Deishū" (a boat made of mud) speaks to this. At first, he called himself Ninsai, meaning "hidden grace," but then he made up the following poem:

狸にはあらぬわが身も土のふね、こぎ出ださぬがかちかちのやま

Tanuki ni wa / Aranu wa ga mi mo / Tsuchi no fune / Kogi idasanu ga / Kachikachi no yama

---

13. [Samurai from the Satsuma and Chōshū Domains had been on the imperial side during the Restoration and occupied prominent positions in the new government.]

Although different from the racoon's, I too am a boat of mud, so I had better not row
out, just be "crackle crackle" (win win) mountain.[14]

Afterward he changed his name to Deishū, which means "boat of mud."

However, it seems the Meiji court did keep him in mind and tried to have him
serve as the administrator of Ibaraki and Fukuoka Prefectures, but that was a mistake from the beginning. Also, it seems they thought to make him an adviser to the
Meiji government, as was done with Date Jitoku Koji (Date Chihiro, 1802–1877),
and expended some effort trying to do so.

Here there is an interesting episode from the *Collected Works of Deishū*. It
takes place around 1883, the sixteenth year of the Meiji era. One day Sekiguchi
Ryūkichi (1836–1889), a pupil of Deishū's who was at the time serving as a leg-
islative adviser to the council of senior statesmen, came to visit Deishū and stayed
the entire day. He was constantly fidgeting, and it was clear he wanted to say something. When Deishū asked him, "What is it?" he finally spoke and beseeched him,

> The truth is that we have long been the recipients of your kindness. You convinced
> the shogun to submit to the emperor. You didn't give in to the appeals of the domains
> but stood your ground and fought from the center, and we avoided the worst. Truly, it
> was a great accomplishment. But the fact that the court hasn't bestowed you with any
> reward is our fault. His majesty was unaware of this oversight; truly we cannot apolo-
> gize enough. It seems that you no longer have any intention of going forth into the
> world, but we aren't content with that. After discussing this with Yamaoka recently,
> I have come to ask you if there isn't any way you would once again enter government
> service.

Deishū laughed. He asked, "If I do as you say and exert myself for the sake of
the nation, could I be recommended as prime minister?" Sekiguchi responded that,
well, no, it would be difficult to do at once, but eventually they would definitely
reach that goal. Deishū chuckled and asked,

> What is difficult about it? Just report what I say to the emperor and it will surely be
> successful. (The stunned Sekiguchi was mystified.) Enomoto and his lot ignored the
> orders of their master, deserted, fought the loyalist forces for a while, lost, surrendered,
> and were hauled away in chains. Yet now they are in positions of prominence. What

---

14. [This poem refers to a folk tale about a rabbit that plays tricks on an evil raccoon (*tanuki*).
First he sets fire to a bundle of kindling the raccoon is carrying on his back. When the raccoon hears
the crackle of the fire, the rabbit tells him he was just saying the name of "crackle crackle" mountain
that they were passing, throwing him off guard until the fire reaches the raccoon's back and burns him.
Later the rabbit tricks him into a boat race. He uses a boat made of wood while giving the raccoon
a boat made of mud. The mud boat dissolves in the middle of the lake, and the raccoon drowns. In
Japanese, "crackle" is a homonym of "win."]

merit was he rewarded for? The difference between myself and them is as large as that between heaven and earth, yet here I am unrewarded, living in seclusion in this rude shack. What mistake was I punished for? If Enomoto was rewarded for resisting the loyalist forces, how regretful that I did not take the several thousand samurai under my command, along with the soldiers of the twenty-three domains of Tōhoku, as the emissary from the Sakai Domain, Matsudaira Gonjūrō, recommended, cross the Hakone mountains, fight the loyalist forces, obtain a great victory, restore the glory of the shogunate, and advance myself. Even if I had lost, I could have surrendered in the Enomoto style, used some clever sleight of hand and come crawling back to court, and become a high counselor; it would have been a piece of cake.

So said Deishū laughingly.

It seems Sekiguchi went home dumbfounded. Deishū was not being particularly boastful. His poem of recollection sounds most appropriate to me:

野に山によしや餓うとも蘆鶴の、群れ居る鶏の中にやは入らむ

No ni Yama ni / Yoshiya uu tomo / Ashitazu no / Mureoru tori no / Naka ni ya hairamu

On the plains and mountains, even if hungry, the crane does not join the chickens that flock

Sekiguchi Ryūkichi, as expected from a student of Deishū, was a person who grasped both beauty and utility. After the Hagi Rebellion, when he was the administrator of Yamaguchi Prefecture, he forgot all ceremony and paid Maebara Issei a visit in prison to console him. The sincere Issei was not the only reason he cried.[15]

Just to drive the point home, I will insert Kaishū's evaluation of Deishū:

What can I say about Deishū? He was a colossal idiot. These days, would any talented person do something that stupid? I heard that when he was young he used to practice spear techniques, but he would practice all day and night for several days, forgetting to eat and sleep, putting his life in danger. Is there anyone that stupid in the world now? That's how he climbed his way up to being the governor of Ise—with only a single spear.

But as a samurai, there was no fault to be found in him. During the Restoration, when I entrusted him with the defense of the shogun, I saw that he lacked subterfuge, so I thought, "Well, in that case," and gave him that mission. Fortunately everything went well. Also, he had taken an oath to retire from the world with his former lord; he made his lord retire and then upheld the oath all on his own. His whole life he was

---

15. [Maebara Issei led a revolt of samurai dissatisfied with the direction of the new government called the Hagi Rebellion. His army was eventually defeated and he was imprisoned and executed.]

content with that oath and poverty, like a pig wallowing in mud; certainly not a person of worldly talent. Isn't that truly foolish? That's why I called him an idiot.

Only passionate individuals like him, who think of people and are concerned about the world, can truly savor nature. Just like many Eastern sages, he lived half his life among people and half his life among nature.

> In the morning I take the dew from the chrysanthemums on my hedge
> Pour it onto my inkstone, and portray my inner heart
> And the pines and bamboo that keep me company
> How could I desire my worldly name?
> Separated from it thus by water and mountains
> I will live out the rest of my life wholesomely in this humble hut
> The birds in the garden do not fly away
> The deer in the fields do not startle at me anymore
> Simple and quiet, not a single disturbance
> Finally true rest
> *   *   *
> Although my humble door never closes
> It is quiet, cut off from worldly affairs
> I submerge my desires and watch the mystery of nature
> Belonging to no party, having no bias
> In the morning I watch the azure waves
> In the evening I look upon Mount Shouyang[16]
> I call out to green mountains, but there is no answer
> Flowing water passes away, never to come back
> Everything returns to its origin
> Words fail to capture this truth

The sadness of the worldly man is that he cannot see nature as more than a thing. Sometimes he is deluded by a kind of artistic intoxication, and it seems he can overcome this limitation; but for most, this is only a momentary happiness. Only a man of high virtue can, with his meritorious inner heart, grasp the significance that the depths of nature hold for human character.

> The wild orchid, born in a narrow valley of fragrant grass
> Prouder than the other red flowers

---

16. [Mount Shouyang is where the Chinese sages Bo Yi and Shu Qi are said to have died in solitude. They starved to death in protest of an unrighteous government.]

Its scent borne on pleasant breezes
It brings comfort to me in my loneliness
Languidly I sit down on top of a jagged cliff
Paying no heed to the slanting rays of the setting sun
The evening winds urge me to turn my walking stick toward home
The birds in the woods send me off with their song
When I turn and look back
There are only white clouds forming

   *   *   *

Nothing happens at my hermitage
At my desk I am always reading books
Or laughing with the ancient sages
Or lamenting that I have not yet attained the Way
When I open the window the moon shines above the mountains
The bell has already rung the third watch[17]
The cold wind that blows into my hood
Rustles through my lonely garden
It always stirs my emotions
When the crickets chirp in the bush
I will relish them all tonight:
The sentiments of heaven and earth that defy reason

Deishū has another set of evocative poems difficult to ignore:

Ko no ma moru	The hazy moon
Tsuki mo kasumite	Leaks out from between the trees
Shiba no to ni	At the door to my thatched hut
Ume ga kakaoru	I can smell the plum blossoms
Haru no yoha kana.	In the middle of this spring night.

   *   *   *

Natsumigawa	Natsumi river
Mada yo o nokosu	At dawn
Akatsuki ni	When the night still lingers
Kishi no ashihara	In reed-choked fields near the shore
Kuina naku nari.	A marsh hen calls.

   *   *   *

Yūzuku hi	In the evening sun
Kagayaku Yama no	The mountain blazes

---

17. [From 11 p.m. to 1 a.m.]

Momiji ba ni	In the turned leaves
Hatenaki aki no	The endless colors of autumn
Iro zo miekeru.	Are suddenly visible.

*   *   *

Satsuma gata	In the bay at Satsuma
Iwa ga ne yusuru	The rough waves that shake
Aranami no	The rocks to their core
Nani o kokoro to	What were they trying to break open
Uchikudake kemu.	With all their might?[18]

These were composed on the occasion of Nanshū's death, but do they not possess a certain inexhaustible grace?

The judgment of *shi* as to whether to go forth or retire is, unquestionably, not based on calculations of profit and loss. Human beings' cunning, calculating intellect is surprisingly shallow when it comes to profit and loss. On the contrary, unsullied emotion will forever give value to the decision to go forth or retire. When looking at him, we surely realize that the *shi*'s adherence to principle means streams of hot tears underneath stern power. He consigned half a life's heroic achievements to be a mere dream and spent more than thirty years contented with poverty and enjoying the Way. In 1903, on the thirteenth of February at six in the afternoon, at his house in Yarai in Ushigome, he passed on unexpectedly. He was sixty-nine.

---

18. [Satsuma Bay is a poetic name that refers to Kagoshima Bay, the place where Saigō Takamori attempted to drown himself out of loyalty to his friend. Since this event occurred in the winter, the four poems reflect the progression of the four seasons.]

9

Faith and the Ultimate Act of Loyalty
On Kusunoki Masashige (楠木正成, 1294?–1336)

The most regrettable of human activities is idling one's life away. Truly, what kind of life is there without deep emotion? To lay down one's life for a friend is a samurai's constant desired state of being. Wanting to die a hero's death is the wish of the common man. *To go to the seas and die soaked in the waves, to go to the mountains and die in the tall grass; wherever I die, I want to be close to the emperor* (Man'yōshū 18). This is the vow of the Japanese people. However, deep feelings are difficult to attain, and life is full of illusions. Dealing with serious and difficult matters in a world easily spent in endless dreaming, one's words and deeds are lost in confusion.

Ah, Nankō [the enshrined spirit of Kusunoki Masashige] who, long ago in the Genkō period (1321–1324), when the whole country was in turmoil and the people were in misery, accepted the imperial edict and feared not the opposing powers as his enemy. He was not rattled by a onetime success or failure. He opposed a strong army of thousands and, in the end, he made possible the emperor's aspirations. What a great achievement of loyalty and valor! The emperor graciously said to him, "You are a loyal defender, humbly and swiftly performing distinguished deeds for a great cause." Without a tinge of pride, he performed his duty. Nankō praised other people's merit, and he served under them with comity and humility. At the end of the Kemmu period, the emperor's power was overturned again. A plot to restore the emperor proved futile, and Nankō faced death calmly, vowing that if he had seven lives to give, he would crush the insurgents. So devoted was he to the imperial cause that he offered up his kinsmen in service to the emperor. Nankō manifested the true, pure spirit of heaven and earth. His heroic spirit and solemnity protected the nation. Feeling Nankō's spirit, fierce gods weep; hearing of Nankō's deeds, even the low-spirited rise up. Ah, Nankō!

1.

Upon hearing the name "Kusunoki Masashige," one unconsciously and reverently braces-up. Deep in one's heart of hearts, one feels compelled to address him with honorifics, as "Nankō." The name leads Japan's subjects to the holiest halls of worship, felt in the depths of their being.

The name "Nankō" moves me with boundless love and respect as well as reverence. One of my remote ancestors, long ago in the Shōhei era (1346–1370), was a soldier who rode in the army with Nankō's eldest son, Masatsura, and who died in action with "Little Nankō" in the battle of Shijō Nawate. I spent the years of my impressionable youth around Shijō Nawate and read voraciously any and all books about Nankō. During spare time from school, I made a pilgrimage to the historic sites of Nankō: from Iimoriyama to Akasaka and Chihaya, visiting the temples of Kanshinji and Kongōji. I drank thirstily from the fount of deep emotion. The geography of the mountains and rivers was impressed upon my memory, and Nankō's legacy was inscribed on my heart and engraved on my bones.

Happily, I did not succumb to learning wanton amusements, and I liked the study of Bushido. I came to immerse my thoughts in the teachings of Confucius and Zen. This was all owing to a knowledge of Nankō's noble character, which to no small degree depended on the study of Confucianists of the Song period and the teachings of Zen. Advancing to higher school, I was inspired by Nankō, even when encountering the trends of socialism and anarchism, just as Nankō's influence inspired even the nameless populace around the mountains of Kongō to determinedly resist the unceasing rebel attacks. Even someone as ignorant as myself is encouraged by Nankō's heroic spirit to devote oneself to the teachings of ancient wisdom, not giving in, not yielding.

As for Nankō, I had been contemplating him since those times within a "sacred silence," as Thomas Carlyle long ago so aptly described in his treatise on hero worship. However, May 25 of this year (1935) was the anniversary of the death of Nankō, who committed suicide with his own sword in Minatogawa six hundred years ago on this day—an occasion commemorated in a nationwide observance. At the behest of these kindred spirits, and moved by their earnest emotion, I decided to author this passage, including my sentiments, as a biography of Nankō. That night at an inn, though ill, I took up my brush to write. Facing the mountains, I suddenly felt that I had returned to the Iimori Mountains of my youth, twenty years before.

2.

Kusanagi Enseki (1817–1868), an eccentric character from Sanshū, composed this poem about Nankō in the last years of the Tokugawa period:

> There is a saint in Japan
> His name is Nankō.
> Born by mistake into the period of warfare
> He was made a sword-wielding hero.

In these lines, one can feel Nankō's spirit approaching.

What is considered religion is a contemporary concept imported from the West, not our ancestor's pure way of thinking. However, borrowing this already widely understood terminology, Nankō's later years were, psychologically, those of a sacred religious state, even while he wielded a sword. The final article on Nankō is recorded in this famous passage from the *Taiheiki*:

> Masashige sat in a high place, faced his brother, Masasue, and said, "In the final hour of one's life is determined whether the next life will be good or bad. While living in the nine worlds, what will you pray?" To which Masasue laughed loudly and answered, "In seven lifetimes I would like to be reborn the same person, and want to destroy the enemies of the emperor." Masashige replied with a sigh of happiness. "Even though I feel deeply sinful and have evil thoughts, I think the same way. Well, then, if I am to be reborn the same man, I will attain my long-cherished ambition," he swore, falling on his sword together with his brother, bending down on the same pillow.

In terms of a story, what historian reciting historical fact could place such significance in a depiction of Nankō's mental state? At the same time, I express deep respect for the creators of the *Taiheiki* for the passage I have just quoted. What a solemn and intense moment of one's fate in life. What a solemn, what an intense moment, indeed!

Day by day, Nankō knew the distant shore of salvation, transcending compassion and enmity, deepening his inner drive for Buddhist nirvana and enlightenment. Coming to this juncture of imminent death, Nankō didn't talk about his own demise. Though Masashige felt deeply sinful and had evil thoughts, one would still wish to kill the enemies of the emperor, even if reborn the same person for seven lifetimes. This is the way I think, too, he thought. Well then, if one is reborn the same person and, by submitting to the reality of persistent malediction and war, fulfills one's long-cherished wish to devote oneself to loyalty and patriotism—this is a human being at his most heroic and sacred. This is "a saint born by mistake into the world of warfare, who was made a sword-wielding hero."

About the time I was finishing higher school, I read *Thus Spoke Zarathustra* by Nietzsche (1844–1900). I was filled with wonder at his idea of "the overman" and eternal recurrence. However, one day while perusing the previously quoted passage from the *Taiheiki*, I unexpectedly came upon Nankō and cried out loudly from deep within my being:

> Nietzsche—it is a misfortune of global proportions that I could not have you know my Nankō and could not have you read the *Taiheiki*. If you could do so, frail and impassioned as you are, so excessively excitable and emotional, perhaps the onset of

insanity would have been quickened. A few centuries before your so-called overman Zarathustra, Kusunoki Masasue and his brother Masashige already actually existed in my Japan. Furthermore, they were not driven insane like Zarathustra, neither were they loquacious; they were a real presence, enveloped in a sacred silence. Your theory of eternal recurrence that caused a sensation among the literati of Europe was recorded magnificently in the *Taiheiki* and has advanced the spirit and flesh of Japan's *bushi* warriors for several hundred years.

Zarathustra, it goes without saying, was the name of a Persian sage of antiquity who was the pretext for Nietzsche's book, which illustrates his thinking and his ideals of the overman. Nietzsche wrote this book with preternatural inspiration and stimulation, and with a poetic rendering. This so-called overman, Zarathustra, treats compassion and empathy as feminine, and considers them despicable vices, since they will be obstructions to the improvement of man. He rejects any form of ingratiation and compromise. Even if the real world of human beings, cursed and warlike, is full of various ugliness and defilement—nay, because it is full of ugliness and defilement—he of the fierce will of a lion and extraordinary character is the Übermensch, decidedly not seeking to become a winged sage nor ascend to paradise, but meant to conquer and purify—all the while being, himself, thoroughly human and of this world. He must be "one who perfects the meaning of earth" and "one who corrects the future and saves the past," that "while being a human who is a part of the muddy lowlands, is the great sea that is never defiled."

He then goes on to explain the eternal recurrence. Completely different from the Gospel of salvation expounded by Christianity, and different from the Six Domains—the six realms of transmigration taught by Buddhism—eternal recurrence is likened to the firm conviction of a terrible Ashura.

Ugliness, defilement, and vileness fill the world—especially the past of human beings. No one who thinks so can endure the endless shame, regret, anger, and curse. Or, if one tries to forget, he is not able to forget. Or they suffer, trying to compensate, or becoming angry demons, they agonize in revenge. The ugliness, defilement, and vileness of the past worsens more and more; they hold sadness and gloom for the future. They destroy the great earth and befoul the great ocean.

Should one cover one's eyes to this, and should one resign oneself and pass it by as an inevitable route that leads to the world of ideals? Turning one's back, should one enter the way of the world of ideals? Nay, such is not the moral resolve of the overman who is devoted to the human world. The overman, Zarathustra, on the contrary, opens his eyes and faces the reality of the past. Amid the whirling world, full of ugliness, defilement, and vileness, in various entanglements—shame, anger, regret, malediction—he fiercely pushes forward. Not fearing or evading the reality of the past, he yearns for this and must transform himself.

All humanity, as it is, does not change in the least but experiences eternal recurrence. Do not think you are finished with resentment, conflict, shame, and the like, and, once finished, do not think that is the end. That is the eternal recurrence. Turning back, alternating, it is obvious as it is forever before your eyes. You cannot help but see it, even when you try not to see it; you cannot escape it, even if you seek to. Well, then, what will you do? What will you do?

It was precisely the overman Zarathustra who boldly welcomed this—not evading it in the least—the one who, confronting the obstacles head-on, had to be a conqueror. If fighting one's sworn enemy, that is very well; changing in death, changing in life, always continuing the struggle, one must deliver a scathing philippic to the sworn enemy. This is actually the teaching of the eternal recurrence.

Nietzsche's psychological state inexorably reached this point, his writing composed triumphantly in his poetic rendering. But unable to abide in this world, unable to find rest, he eventually died insane. Nankō's kinsmen, calm and tranquil, were, in their zealous quest for enlightenment, the embodiment of the thoughts of Nietzsche. *Bushi* warriors of Japan resonate passionately with this idea and, one after another, continue in its wake. Awesome to behold, it is the blood relative of Japan's spirit. If any kind of hegemon in the world were able to capture Japan, he would have to yield immediately before this spirit.

3.

In the first year of Genkō (1331),[1] on the twenty-fifth day of the eighth month, at the hour of the ox—the so-called time when "trees and grass sleep" (between 1 and 3 a.m.)—an unusual line of several people, riding swift horses, silently made its way southward, ever southward, on the thoroughfare from Kyoto to Nara. While resting their horses at Kizu (north of Nara), monks came hurriedly to greet them, and finally they arrived at Tōnan-in, within Tōdai-ji in Nara. The next day, they headed north and arrived at Kondai-ji in Watsuka city, Yamashiro Province. Departing again on the following day, the twenty-seventh, they came this time to the Kasagi-dera. Present there were Emperor Go-Daigo, Fujiwara Fujifusa, and others, with their attendants, all of whom had been driven from the capital; they had fled the Rokuhara forces of the Kamakura shogunate when their secret plan to overthrow the shogunate had been revealed.

In Kyoto, Kazan'in Morokata, who had been impersonating the emperor since the prior evening, donned imperial robes and fled to Mount Hiei. The Rokuhara forces, tricked into believing the "emperor" would flee, attacked Mount Hiei on the twenty-seventh day, just as the real emperor arrived at Kasagi-dera. Monk war-

---

1. 604 years before today.

riors of Mount Hiei became vaguely aware of the ruse and didn't put up much of a fight. Both Imperial Princes Son'un (Morinaga) and Sonchō (Munenaga) escaped to temporary lodging in Kasagi. Thus, Mount Hiei capitulated, without a great struggle, on the twenty-ninth. However, the shogunate forces were dismayed when they learned that the real emperor had escaped.

An imperial edict went out immediately from the emperor's lodgings, calling upon all loyalist samurai to enlist. Through Hino Toshimoto, Hino Suketomo, and other court nobles, a substantial response was generated from loyalist comrades centered in the Kinki area. But because the plot was detected so soon, samurai who had hastened to join in the fray were few in number. They were no more than Ishikawa and Nishikigori from Kawachi, Asuke from Mikawa, and a few others. On that memorable third day of the ninth month, Kusunoki Masashige made his heroic appearance. Responding to the imperial edict, he answered the call of duty to the throne with confidence and trustworthiness.

> The recent high treason committed by the eastern barbarians against the emperor invited a righteous response. The emperor will mete out heaven's punishment to the traitors when their power wanes in time of turmoil. This is just. However, success in founding a new country depends on military tactics and resourcefulness. If we fight based on power alone, even by assembling soldiers from sixty-some provinces, it would be difficult to defeat just the two regions of Musashi and Sagami. If we fight with a strategy, the power of the eastern barbarians will not, of itself, be sufficient to do more than destroy our vanguard. The barbarians are easily deceived and we need not fear them. As for learning the lessons of war, the outcome is not determined by victory or defeat in any single battle. Hearing that I, Masashige, alone survive, know that divine providence will open up before you. (*Taiheiki*)

Nankō's wisdom and intelligence, enabled by natural talent, learning, and scholarship, understood the current reality of the Kamakura shogunate. The actual power of the shogunate had been deteriorating gradually since the Mongol invasion; its misgovernance could not be hidden. The motives for revenge and the old grudges of powerful regional clans—who were not few—had, since the Jōkyū era, continued to fester under the sustained persecution of the Kamakura shogunate. Dissatisfied with the shogunate, the tide of reformists secretly continued to grow and, inevitably accompanying this, the awakening of a spirit of loyalty to the throne—the "divine providence that will finally open upon us." Masashige believed firmly that he alone possessed the moral fiber necessary for the great undertaking of turning the tide. The day after his audience with the emperor, Nankō guided Prince Takanaga, Shijō Takasuke, and others, and returned to Akasaka, boldly raising the flag of righteousness. Not long after, Prince Morinaga also left Kasagi to join them.

Kasagi-dera was a strategic location, surrounded by precipitous cliffs on three sides and commanding a view of the torrents of the Kizu River. However, it was a narrow strip of land, unsuitable for facing a great army over an extended length of time. Nankō—heroically steadfast and confident of success—was resolved to accelerate the rise of a righteous army under heaven to wage a protracted war. Rather than challenge their stronghold at Kasagi Temple, he instead decided to face the great army of the shogunate in his ancestral homeland. There, Nankō had the advantages of steep, mountainous terrain and sympathetic people loyal to him who would help bring affliction upon a disorderly force, fatigued from a long march.

Nankō's genealogy is not very clear, even to this day. Even his father's name is not established, being called Masatō, or Masayasu, or Seigen. In a word, his was a family belonging to the Tachibana clan (descendants of Emperor Bidatsu) that flourished long ago in the vicinity of Iyo, Sanuki, and Kawachi, which at Masashige's time was home to nothing more than a provincial samurai clan possessing thirty to fifty thousand *koku*. Their power, centered in Minamikawachi, swelled to Kii and Izumi. His title was officer of the guard in the statutory office, and he was posted in service to the shogunate, but this was not unusual for a provincial samurai.

The region where Nankō wielded authority, Kasen Kishū, the center of which was Akasaka and Chihaya, had unparalleled natural defenses by virtue of its steep terrain. The name "Kongōzan" (*Vajra* or Adamantine Mountain) was an apt designation that could not be gainsaid. Commanding a view of the open fields of Sekkasen (Settsu, Kawachi, and Izumi), the front had the advantage of inaccessibility. On the other hand, were one to approach from the open fields, one would encounter hilly ground, and moving a great army through woods and over small peaks would be extremely disadvantageous. In the back, two rivers—the Yoshino River and the Kino River in the lower reaches—flowed to the open fields of Yamato and Wakayama, and the adjacent Kii mountain range offered a strategic position. If the advantage of transportation was maintained, the center protected, and Kōya and Anafu fortified, the place held a threefold advantage over any other.

In the meantime, if benevolence and strictness were carried out together, the hearts of the people won over, samurai trained, and plans laid, there could have been no doubt that divine providence would be on their side, especially since the shogunate was already deteriorating. Nankō's report to the emperor was not simply an act of righteous indignation, and it was also more than a meticulous calculation. Rather than judging it a difficult situation with no easy solution, he responded boldly with a plan of courageous force: to return to Akasaka and raise a righteous army. This stunned the Kyoto nobility, who circulated it as a groundless rumor.

At Kasagi, on the sixth or seventh day of the ninth month, the attack of the shogunate army finally began. Before the middle of the month, the army from

Kantō was mobilized and on its way to the capital. Drawn by the news, on the twenty-seventh day Ashikaga Takauji also joined in the attack on Kasagi. The shogunate forces spread fires and attacked furiously. The emperor, probably thinking to move to Nankō's mansion, was able to flee the temple, but unfortunately he lost his way and was seized by the rebel army two or three ri^2 northwest of Kasagi, at a place called Ariōyama, in the neighborhood of Ide. The shogunate forces promptly incarcerated the emperor in the capital, backed the new emperor, Kōgen, and savagely attacked the solitary castle at Akasaka. There, Prince Takanaga, overcome with empathy for the emperor, at last left the castle and, as he made his way towards the capital, was felled at the hand of a retainer of Kanazawa Sadafuyu.

The attack on Akasaka began on the seventeenth or eighteenth day of the tenth month. Several hundred soldiers converged at Nankō's solitary castle, which was on a small patch of level land amid the hills. The shogunate army, organized into four units with tens of thousands of men, marched majestically toward the castle, their feelings described in the *Taiheiki* as, "Oh, the pitiful state of the enemy, were we to hold this castle in one hand to throw, we would be able to throw it!" This was a preliminary test for Masashige. The emperor already having been taken, he had to proceed very carefully. He engaged the enemy forces only lightly, just enough to instill some fear in them. Then, on the twenty-first of the tenth month, he set fire to the castle, making it a pyre of dead bodies to deceive them—and disappeared.

For about a year after that, news of his whereabouts was vague, and it was unknown whether he was dead or alive. The shogunate was in a quandary over how to capture Nankō. During that time, Nankō traversed the mountains of Kasen Kishū around Chihaya and devised a secret plan with Prince Morinaga and others. This was a very surprising thing to do.

Regarding this matter, we must realize, more than anything else, how much Nankō embodied virtue and could thereby so easily win the hearts of the people in the provinces. For a long time, Nankō lent his patronage to the monk-soldiers, suppressing the Yuasa clan, which had persecuted the monks of Mount Kōya. His family temple was Kanshin-ji, an important temple of the Shingon sect, associated with wise and famous monks of the day. He rewarded officers and samurai for meritorious service, using up all of his resources, and he did not shirk in caring for the peasants.

Prince Morinaga, in collusion with Nankō, issued commands and ruled over Yoshino Province, while concentrating on enlisting a righteous army of loyalists. The emperor, secluded in Kyoto and in the third month exiled to Oki, occasionally communicated with the Prince by letter. Without the shogunate's knowledge, Nankō was promoted to the rank of Minister of the Left.

---

2. [Japanese unit of length, about 3,927 meters]

Around the sixth month of the second year of Genkō (1332), a rumor spread that Prince Morinaga was hiding in the capital, greatly unsettling the populace. Toward the end of the month, one Takehara Nyūdō (a lay monk), commanding his whole clan and monks living in the Kumano area, invaded the shogunate's territory of Ise, destroying its military governor, its armed forces, burning down administration buildings, conquering near and far, and then finally withdrawing in the direction of Kumano.

Come autumn, a widespread rumor was that Nankō had appeared in the steep castle of Chihaya. Other reports spread that the monk-soldiers of Mount Hiei (where Prince Morinaga was a head monk) were fomenting action against the Rokuhara. The shogunate, at the beginning of the twelfth month, having run out of patience, issued a subjugation order against Kusunoki Masashige and the Prince of the Great Pagoda (Prince Morinaga). Bitō Danzaemon-no-jo proceeded to the capital as the advance guard, where he was met by Hōjō Tokimasu, Nakatoki, and others from the Rokuhara, and thereupon an army of the Kinki region was mobilized.

At this point, Nankō made a surprise attack on Yuasa Magoroku (known as the lay monk Jōbutsu), who had occupied Akasaka Castle, and forced him to capitulate. At the beginning of the third year, Nankō ambushed the shogunate general of Kishū, Inoue, Yamanoi and others, and all their kinsmen, at Kainoshō in Minami Kawachi; he demolished them and made a sweeping conquest, like a thunderclap in a hurricane, of Kawachi Izumi. The Prince of the Great Pagoda eventually set up headquarters in Yoshino and gained the support of monk soldiers from the temples of Kōya Kumano, Kogawa, Matsuo, and Kunu, thereby greatly increasing the military might of the imperial force.

The Rokuhara army attempted to subjugate Nankō's army and took under its control Tennōji, the main artery of northern Kasen. Nankō made Shijō Takasada general of his army and, commencing on the nineteenth of the first month, launched one furious attack after another, from morning until deep into the night, vanquishing the enemy. On the twenty-second, he rested his troops and made a triumphant return to his stronghold in Tōjō and Chihaya. The valiant general of Kantō, Utsunomiya Kintsuna, galloped toward Tennōji the next day, but it was too late. The scouting party dispatched to Akasaka had already, to the last man, been rounded up by Nankō's army.

Alarmed by the grave situation, the Kamakura shogunate, toward the end of the first month, assembled fifty thousand elite soldiers in the capital and divided the army into three forces: Osaragi Takanao, Nikaidō Dō'un, Kudō Takakage, and others went to Yoshino from the Yamato Basin; Nagoya Genshin entered Kishū from Izumi; and Aso Harutoki, Nagasaki Takasane, and others started the attack on Chihaya. Rewards were advertised for capturing the Prince of the Great Pagoda and Nankō: To the one who took the prince would be given a manor in Madé of Ōmi Province. Even unemployed resident monks of all temples, even if they belonged to a band of vile profligate rebels, would be rewarded for their success. To the one who took Nankō, whatever his status may be, would be given the Funai manor in Tanba Province.

The Imperial Court issued this decree across Kyushu on the seventh day of the second month:

> The Buddhist monk Takatoki and his kinsmen, rebels all, for excessive deprecation of the power of the Imperial Court, have been found exceedingly outrageous; therefore, they are to be subjugated. Hidetoki, Moroyori, and their drones are to be tracked down and killed.[3]

Dated the twenty-first day of the second month, this order was posted throughout the San'in and San'yō regions (southwestern Honshu Island):

> Whereas the eastern barbarians, descendants of Hōjō To'otōmi Zenshi Tokimasa, governor of Izu, who since the Jōkyū era held the four seas in the palm of their hand, have disparaged the Imperial Court. Especially in recent years, Takatoki Sagami, the lay monk, and his kinsmen not only have deprecated the Imperial Court through military strategy, but also demoted the current Mikado (emperor), living in exile on the island of Inshū. The emperor's heart is anguished, the country is thrown into confusion, reaching the point wherein retainers are supplanting their lords. Therefore, it being extremely outrageous, and for attempting a conquest, in order to restore the emperor, military forces are hereby enlisted from within the fifteen provinces of the Seikaidō. All the emperor's virtue shall return, commanding the hosts to march into battle, regardless of time and date. By imperial command of the Prince of the Great Pagoda.

Would not the sympathy of military men of the provinces be moved by this? Aso Korenao and Korezumi and their kinsmen went so far as Tomonotsu in Bingo in order to join in the attack on Kongōzan. But, coming across this announcement, they resolved to return to allegiance. They retraced their steps to their province to raise a righteous army. The rousing of spirits by Doi and Tokunō in Iyo was also a result of this influence.

By the twentieth day of the second month, tens of thousands of the shogunate army had flooded the Kawachi highway, rushing toward their target, Chihaya. Kusunoki's army first drew them to Upper Akasaka Castle (Akasaka during the

---

3. Translated from the Sino-Japanese text.

Genkō era was Lower Akasaka). Hirano Shōgen and Kusunoki Masasue fought fiercely at the outer walls of the main castle, inflicting great damage on the shogunate army, but eventually, their energy exhausted, they were forced to capitulate. Masasue fled to Chihaya. The Yoshino headquarters also fell under the attack of Nikaidō's army, and the emperor was driven to Kōya.

In this way, the Chihaya Castle literally became the solitary castle and the target of all the armies in the land. From this time through the fifth month, indomitable and indefatigable, Nankō fought tooth and nail and was mysteriously transformed—a marvelous sight for the whole world to see. It is not unreasonable that Nankō would become like a god of military strategy for posterity.

Still today, hidden in the steep terrain of Chihaya village, is the idea that "if one man protects the gate, ten thousand men cannot enter." Chihaya Castle was on the side of Kongō Mountain, surrounded by cliffs and deep ravines. Directly in front lay Chihaya Valley and Furotani Valley to the rear, with valleys on either side: Myōken on the left and Kita (or Kongō) on the right. Two rivers entwined the castle, the Kitatani River and the Myōken River, which flowed together as the Chihaya River in front of the castle. There was no lack of water in the castle. Rising from Chihaya Valley, Akataki Mountain formed a barrier, mountain after mountain creating a natural defense, holding sway over the main roads of Yamato and Kii. Kitayama, also called Tekimiyama (View-of-the-Enemy Mountain), towered above the rear of the castle and from there, one could see the whole expanse of rivers and fields.

Nikaidō, Nagoya, Osaragi, and others were the valorous generals of Kantō, commanding tens of thousands of brave soldiers who came to savagely attack the indomitable castle. However, they could only ineffectually surround the castle, owing to its natural defenses and its holy general. Observing the situation during this time, a righteous army from all the provinces finally mobilized. Gaining the assistance of the soldier-monks of Akashiyama Temple, Akamatsu Norimura left Banshū and conspired to steal away the emperor, who had recently been sequestered in Kyoto. Ryōchū Hōin joined the fray, advancing toward Mount Maya from Hyōgo and, on the twelfth day of the third month, beat back the rebel army at Segawa. Doi, Tokunō, and others, along with the righteous army from Iyo, destroyed Hōjō Tokinao, military governor of Nagato. Hailing each other as the righteous army of Gei and Bi Provinces, it seemed they might attack the sea routes of the capital.

Before that time, at the end of the intercalary second month, Emperor Go-Daigo easily escaped to temporary accommodations, was greeted by Nawa Nagatoshi, and established imperial quarters at Ōyama Temple on Mount Senjō in Hōki. An imperial decree calling for the defense of the emperor was relayed throughout the land. Responding, Kikuchi Taketoki gathered his courage into a righteous force and attacked the military governor of Hakata, Hōjō Hidetoki. Because of Shōni Ōtomo's betrayal, Taketoki bravely died an honorable death, but his whole clan rose, one by one, to action. In addition, the Takama brothers, noble compatriots of Yamato, answered the imperial call. Suddenly, threatening Rokuhara from Yamashiro, they retaliated against the army, fiercely attacking Kōfuku Temple in Nara, the backup support to the Osaragi army. This took place around the twenty-third of the third month. In addition, before long, the soldier-monks of Mount Hiei also seemed as if they might attack Rokuhara.

The shogunate gradually grew restive and impatient, and lost its morale. The strong castle on Mount Kongō stood starkly as of old. Barely managing to contain all the men of the righteous army, the shogunate could not now, even for a day, lightly disregard the solitary castle of Chihaya. It was a grave matter and must be brought down as quickly as possible. On the twenty-seventh day of the third month, Takatoki dispatched the highly reputed Ashikaga Takauji, Nagoya Takaie, and others. This indeed would become Takatoki's fatal blow.

Valorous Takauji then saw clearly the imminent collapse of the shogunate and firmly resolved to usurp military authority from the Hōjō clan. Departing for the front with Nagoya and other men, he dispatched a secret emissary to the imperial lodging on Mount Senjō, pressing for a return to allegiance. Upon receiving the imperial decree at Ōmi Kagami that the emperor had accepted his allegiance, Takauji, without disclosing his changed loyalties, calmly entered the capital toward the end of the fourth month. In opposition to this, the serious Nagoya Takaie, while on his way down to San'yōdō to face the attack on Mount Senjō, died in battle at Koganawate, fighting fiercely the righteous armies of Akamatsu and Chigusa that had advanced to Yahata Yamazaki.

Takauji, who was supposed to have been on his way to Mount Senjō down the same San'yō highway, was for a time at Nishioka. However, he retreated to Sasamura in Tanba, whence this missive was written and dedicated, at Hachiman Shrine, on the twenty-ninth day:

> Hachiman Great Bodhisattva is the shrine deity of my family, the protector of the imperial household. Takauji, a descendent of this deity, is the successor of the clan. Is there anyone superior to him in archery and horsemanship? Through this, enemies of generations of the Imperial Throne have been destroyed. Rebels of the ages are killed. The sage masters of the Genkō era, in order to worship the deities, in order to give advantage to the people, in order to save the country, call forth a righteous army to be enlisted during the time of this Imperial Mandate. For that reason, I occupy the houses of Tanshū Sasamura and plant a white banner at the foot of the willow. Beneath another tree here is a shrine. Inquiring of the village people, I was told it is an altar to the Great Bodhisattva. It is an omen of the fulfillment of the righteous army;

a miraculous sign of swift military commanders. Tears of gratitude flow in secret. There rises respect and trust. If this request is fulfilled immediately and our family flourishes once again, shrines and altars will be solemnized and paddies and fields will be donated. We hereby petition the *kami* and buddhas toward these ends.[4]

With the issuance of this command, banners of the righteous army were first unfurled. Receipt of the imperial order was widely announced, armies enlisted, and it induced men to join the army in surrounding Chihaya Castle.

On the seventh day of the fifth month, Takauji's army, all at once, began to charge Rokuhara, now in a state of confusion. From every direction, Chigusa and Akamatsu's righteous armies rushed onward from Yamazaki, Yahata, and Uji. Hōjō Tokimasu attempted to race to Ōmi, but on the way he was felled in the area of Ōsakayama by the flying arrow of a rogue samurai. On the morning of the ninth, Nakatoki, trapped with no place to advance or retreat, took his own life at the base of Banba Pass. On this news, the army surrounding Chihaya suddenly collapsed and was slaughtered by Kusunoki's fiercely pursuing army. The generals retreated bitterly to Kōfukuji, but eventually most of them were killed.

Before this occurred, in the third month after the imperial message was presented from the palace, Nitta Yoshisada escaped from the armies sent to surround and attack Chihaya and returned to Jōshū. Nitta raised loyalist armies in front of Jōshū Ubushina Myōjin on the day following Takauji's attack of the eighth. Pushing forward on the Kamakura highway from Musashi, they entered Kamakura, causing a melee. On the evening of the twenty-first day, Takatoki, his generals, and more than 870 men were able to put an end to the honor of Kamakura samurai; he died a heroic death. Hidetoki, military governor of Kyushu, subsequently killed himself. Tokinao, military governor of Nagato, surrendered.

One hundred forty years of hegemony, since the time of Yoritomo, was destroyed—as fittingly stated in the words of a poet, "reduced to smoke and dust." The sudden collapse of the shogunate all over the country gave pause to consider how extreme was its nadir—its utter and complete fall from power.

Kitabatake Chikafusa (1293–1354) also exults in his *Jinnō Shōtōki* (Chronicles of the authentic lineages of the divine emperors),

> Without consciously having planned it, in the same moon all the provinces of Kyushu and over faraway Dewa of Mutsu,[5] the provinces became quiet. For such unity to occur at one time, over a distance of six or seven thousand *ri*, simply as a result of fortune's chance, is indeed a wondrous thing.

---

4. Translated from the Sino-Japanese text.
5. [Northern Japan]

News of the fall of Kamakura on the second day of the sixth month spread quickly and reached the ears of the emperor from Nishinomiya in Hyōgo, on the way to his return to Kyoto. Kusunoki came from Chihaya to state his desire to escort him and could at last gaze upon the imperial countenance. Can a human being experience deeper emotion than this? Is there any such scene of honor and deep emotion in the literature of any other country? In the *Taiheiki* is recorded,

> While the emperor was in procession, on the second day of the sixth month, Kusu-noki Tamon Hyōe Masashige and more than seven thousand soldiers were given audi-ence with him. How extraordinarily valiant they looked! His supreme highness rolled the screens up high, beckoned Masashige to approach, and said, "The speedy restora-tion of imperial rights was achieved because of the loyal battle you fought." Respect-fully, Masashige modestly replied that it was not his achievement: "Were it not for my lord's virtue, the virtue of His Supreme Highness Emperor Jimmu, how could a minor official, with the smallest of plans, charge against a strong enemy and surround him?" From the day that His Highness left Hyōgo, Masashige had ridden at the head of seven thousand men, leading the way, uniting the might of the five provinces. Along the eighteen *ri* of the emperor's procession the armies marched. Men of the righteous army, with their halberds, shields, and battleaxes, marched on both the left and right sides of the road. Following the emperor's litter were all the loyal ministers, then came the six armies protecting them, the five-colored clouds (heaven) tranquil and happy.

4.

The imperial reign became known as the Kemmu era (1334). It was essential that Kemmu be the era of reestablishing the rule of Emperor Jimmu. The power of armies and horses and finances, used privately and self-indulgently, must be controlled by the state, and every key official must be completely devoted to administering the imperial command.

If, at this point, Ashikaga Takauji and his brothers, and Nitta Yoshisada and others had joined forces with the Prince of the Great Pagoda and his supporters, and had the character and discernment to carry out the abolition of domains and the establishment of prefectures, forming a new government under an emperor— something like the Satsuma-Chōshū alliance that enabled the Meiji Restoration— how much brighter, one wonders, would the history of Japan have been? Unfortu-nately, the reality of the Kemmu era was defined by the establishment of govern-ment by a stagnated warrior class. Nothing could be more regretful.

Historians argue about the failure of the Kemmu Restoration, enumerating many reasons: the allocation of army and cavalry among the clans, losing the hearts of samurai by mishandling rewards for meritorious service, the arrogance of the court administration early on, and falling to profligacy. Law and order lapsed into chaos, causing despair among righteous samurai. These were, at any rate, superficial problems. On deep reflection, one realizes that the underlying problem was a human contest of shallow avarice.

Lord Fujifusa despaired of the governance of the Kemmu Restoration and took the tonsure, as it is recorded in a biography contained in *Dai Nihon-shi* (The great history of Japan),

> When peace came to the country, Gon Dainagon Fujiwara Saneyo received an imperial order to accomplish the restoration of entitlements. Military officers and men competed for rewards. Tens of thousands of people assembled, most of them feigning military service. Saneyo could not judge the cases. After a month passed, only twenty or so people had been selected to receive rewards.
>
> Almost all of the commanders and samurai who deserved entitlements were forgotten, resulting in anger and dissatisfaction. Those who had not already received notice of appointments returned to their villages without waiting for another report, secretly lamenting the injustice of the times. Those sympathizers angered by the misfortune of the unrewarded were perhaps several thousand in number.

If one earnestly ponders the reason for the restoration's failure, the answer soon comes to mind, does it not? The greatest sources of evil that led to such confusion and disorder were the personal interests of favored retainers and spiteful envy.

The one who received the favor of his supreme highness on every occasion, who aspired to incomparable careerism, always seeking to extend his influence, a man of unbridled ambition, was, of course, Ashikaga Takauji. Granted the title *chinjufu-shōgun*, he reached the courtly grade of the third rank, was *shugo*[6] of three provinces (Musashi, Sagami, and Shimo), held the ministerial position of *sangi* (councilor), and also received a personal honorific name from the emperor.

It was often argued that Nankō, by comparison, although first in meritorious deeds, failed to get his just reward. At the time he was *kokushu* (governor) of three provinces, Settsu, Kawachi, and Izumi, but his rank was merely lower fifth rank— Saemon Shōjō—nothing more.

However, in these times, many boasted of their family name and argued their lineage. Nankō was nothing more than a local samurai from Kawachi. Even though he fought valiantly in battle for the emperor, from the perspective of these scheming braggarts, he himself had not attacked Kyoto or Kamakura. Nor had he killed a military governor. People holding important posts in the new administration, in both the Office of Litigation and the Office of Records, criticized Nankō for

---

6. Governor of Kamakura and Muromachi shogunate.

having only protected a solitary castle. Nankō's reward, perhaps by some accounts, would have been excessively favorable treatment. Or perhaps these were more or less the feelings toward him even by Lord Chikafusa, intimations that are not unheard of in the *Shōtōki*.

In any case, Nankō was not interested in the conferral of honors. In the midst of a loyal battle, even if he petitioned the *kami* and buddhas, there could be no requesting prosperity for himself and his family, as Takauji did with his other generals. It is said that in Kikuchi Taketomo's *mōshijō* (entreaty) to the throne vis-à-vis reward for service during the time of the Genkō, Nankō addressed the emperor:

> Even if it is said that there were many of the most faithful during the time of Genkō who deserved to be granted awards, they are still alive. The one person who, through imperial order, gave his life, was Kikuchi Taketomo—the most faithful, the most committed.

How beautiful are Nankō's emotions, as reflected by his humble response to the emperor during his audience at Nishinomiya. It was Nankō who was devoted to the spirit of *matsuri* (governing), the most honored principle of the Japanese *Volk*. And through Nankō, the neo-Confucianism (Sōgaku) of the Song dynasty, with which he was familiar, manifested its most solemn transformation.

The *Raiki* (*Book of Rites*) says, "When serving the lord, dedicate yourself and do what you sincerely believe." As it says in the *Kuyōden* (*Gongyang zhuan*),

> Do not concern the throne with your private matters; if you serve the lord, do not reject loyal work because of your private matters. Do not consider your private matters when you work for the lord.

"A subject will serve not only with all his might, but also with faith and truth, all to protect his lord," as it says in the *Saden* (*Zuo zhuan*). All these words speak of Nankō.

The following words, believed to have been spoken by Nankō, have in later years moved many distinguished compatriots, including Wakabayashi Kyōsai (1679–1732, Edo era scholar of Confucianism): "If even for a moment you have stirred bitterness in the emperor's heart, recite the name of God Amaterasu." Such words of admonishment are worthy of Nankō, especially considering the times he lived in.

Nankō's character, consequently, influenced and inspired people. Previously I have expounded on how Nankō captured the hearts of the people when he disappeared and then reappeared during the year after retreating from Lower Akasaka. Another thing that must not be forgotten is the fact that he frequently turned his

bitter enemies into followers, precipitating a change of heart, increasing his kinsmen, and causing them to devote themselves to the emperor. Even a man such
as Yuasa Magoroku, a lay monk, in spite of his long-held malice toward Nankō,
surrendered to Nankō and, experiencing a change of heart, devoted himself to the
emperor. The Noda clan, manorial lords of Kawachi Noda, had been defeated by
Nankō but subsequently distinguished themselves as loyalists, laboring diligently,
even after Nankō's death, until Masanori's generation. The Tange clan in Kawachi
was another conversion.

This thought and character were desired by the nobility and military generals alike, including the Takauji brothers. Nay, cultivating these thoughts, this faith
and resolve was, after all, essential to governing the country. The Kemmu Restoration itself was made possible through the nobility, including the emperor, Chikafusa, Fujifusa, Suketomo, Toshimoto, other nobles, and Nankō, who aspired to
thoughts and character as described above. This, I think, must not be forgotten.

5.

An eruption of flagging morale and unfairness among the samurai
houses eventually threatened the new government of the imperial court, which
from the beginning was not strong. In taking advantage of this situation, the
steadily growing influence of Takauji and his brother inside and outside the court
was threatened by two people they could not risk ignoring: Morinaga, the Prince
of the Great Pagoda (a compatriot with deep ties to Nankō, of course), and Nitta
Yoshisada. However, the pedigree and reputation of Yoshisada, modest and honest, was far and away beneath Takauji's. The real source of Takauji's fear was the
talent, wisdom, and the majesty of character that belonged to the Prince of the
Great Pagoda.

Before Takauji became the next Yoritomo, Prince Morinaga believed that he
had to deal with him quickly. The radical opposition hatched a rumor that the
prince, as military commander, would besiege Takauji's mansion (*Baishō-ron*). On
the twenty-second day of the tenth month, when the prince visited the palace, he
was held in custody while at the imperial court, then banished to Kamakura.

There were various unfounded rumors circulating about the prince: One was
that he planned treason against the emperor; the genesis of this was in aspersions
cast by Takauji through the consort Ano Yasuko (the *Taiheiki* version). Another
rumor sought to blame the prince for what was, in truth, the emperor's secret plan
to make Takauji retire (the *Baishō-ron* version). These were only two of the many
rumors in the air. At that time, Nankō seems to have been in retreat from the capital to make a punitive attack on the remaining Hōjō clan in Kishū. What emotion
must have filled his heart upon hearing these things!

A still more unusual occurrence took place on the twenty-second day of the sixth month. Saionji Dainagon Kinmune, long bound to the Hōjō clan, conspired in secret with Hōjō Takatoki's heir, Tokiyuki, his younger brother Tokioki, and others to kidnap the emperor on his maple-viewing excursion to Kitayama. However, the plan to snatch the emperor was exposed. Nankō, who was in the capital, appeared to have arrested the conspirators.

Come the seventh month, Tokiyuki gained the support of the Suwa clan of Shinano and attacked into Musashi. In a battle at Fuchū, he crushed the army of Kamakura's Tadayoshi. This was known as the Nakasendai Rebellion. Tadayoshi departed for the front at Idezawa of Bushū and met defeat. Tadayoshi then made Fuchibe Yoshihiro, sworn enemy of the Prince of the Great Pagoda, commit the heinous act of murdering the prince and fled to Mikawa.

On the twenty-fifth day of the seventh month, Tokiyuki occupied Kamakura, sending a shockwave throughout the *bushi* warriors of the eastern provinces. At this point, Takauji ordered a campaign to subjugate Tokiyuki and sought the title *sei'i taishogun* for himself. Without waiting for an imperial order, he commanded his army eastward on the second day of the eighth month. He met Ashikaga Tadayoshi at Yahagi in Sanshū Province and continued to advance, while destroying the Hōjō army. On the eighteenth day of the eighth month, Kamakura was reclaimed.

The government sent an imperial message to Takauji to reward him for his service and invited him to return to Kyoto, the capital, so as to receive the distribution of rewards. However, Tadayoshi was opposed to this, arguing against the coexistence of the aristocracy and the military; he exposed Yoshisada's plot to try to persuade Takauji. Though more generous, sympathetic, and grateful than his brother Tadayoshi, Takauji, however, ultimately resolved to reject the imperial message, and, making Tadayoshi and Kōno-Moronao his teeth and claws, he reestablished the shogunate in place of the Hōjō clan.

Takauji publicly conducted a distribution of rewards for the men who served faithfully under him. On the second day of the twelfth month, he sent his brother a missive to punish Nitta Yoshisada and enlisted an army to carry out the order. The government was astonished when it first became aware of Takauji's disobedience, and Prince Takanaga was made general of the imperial army and Nitta Yoshisada was sent marching down the Tokaidō. However, the army of the court was defeated at Takenoshita Hakone, beaten back, and counterattacked by the rebel army. At the end of the twelfth month, Kō no Moronao of the advance army and others had already spearheaded a ferocious attack on Ōmi, and Kyoto once again had become a sea of halberds and shields.

Feeling the infringement and violation of these circumstances, the government issued an order to raise troops, and Nankō's army put a stranglehold on Uji. Nawa Nagatoshi and his army headed toward Seta. In the direction of Yamazaki, they dispatched Wakiya Yoshisuke to prepare for the Akamatsu's rebel army from Saigoku. Yoshisada would position himself at Ōwatashi.

On the first day of the new year, the battle started from Setaguchi. However, the imperial army was initially defeated on the tenth by an attack from the direction of Yamazakiguchi. His supreme highness retreated quickly to arranged quarters at Higashisakamoto, Yoshisada withdrew from Ōwatashi, and the strong forces of Kusunoki and Nawa finally retreated on the eleventh, following the emperor's entourage.

The rebel army invaded Kyoto, setting fire to the Imperial Palace. They continued to advance, attempting to attack the provisory accommodations of the emperor. Just in the nick of time, the Kitabatake clan, father and son, came to help, directing a great army from Ōu, the northern provinces, which served Prince Yoshinaga. The spirit of the loyalist army was roused to a fever pitch. The opposing armies fought to the death until the thirtieth day of the first month, continuing the exchange a number of times in battles on the streets of the city. Pressing harder and harder upon the rebel army, Takauji was eventually stampeded down the road to Tanba. In pursuit after pursuit, the loyalist army chased him to Nishinomiya and then to Segawa. On the twelfth day of the second month, Takauji and his brother managed to escape to Kyushu by a sea route.

As soon as Kikuchi Taketoshi (third son of Taketoki) of Higo Province [Kumamoto Prefecture] heard that Takauji was coming, he swiftly led his army to the north. Overpowering the rebel general Shōni Sadatsune at Dazaifu, he then advanced to Tatarahama of Chikuzen Hakata on the second day of the third month, where they attacked Takauji and fought a furious battle.

Even the great Takauji was, on this occasion, resigned to his end, attempting several times to fall on his own sword. But perhaps fate intervened, as a north wind stirred up the dust and sand and tormented the loyalist army. The situation changed, and the loyalist forces fell in a bitter struggle. Taketoshi, most regrettably, had to gather all his men and retreat. The very pleased Takauji, then commanding from Dazaifu, instantly recovered his strength, and swiftly departed Dazaifu on the third day of the fourth month. He would once again recapture the capital, advancing eastward, by land and by sea, like a whirlwind.

While the disarray of the new Kemmu government had yet to be settled in the capital, in the second month Takauji had been forced to retreat to Kyushu. However, the imperial forces had no time to adequately prepare a decisive counterattack on Takauji. Nitta Yoshisada departed for Chūgoku at the beginning of the third month to punish the rebels, but he was obstructed at the Akamatsu Castle in Banshū, and in the middle of the fifth month, beaten down by Takauji's forces, had to retreat to Hyōgo. An emissary was urgently dispatched to Kyoto to relay a message to the emperor that countermeasures against Takauji were needed. Visibly shaken, the imperial court immediately convened a meeting of court officials and decided that, no matter what, they must quickly send to Nankō for reinforcement. Against a second attack from the great army of Takauji, which burned with a spirit of revenge, a clash with Nankō and the fatigued, smaller forces of the loyalist army would most certainly fail to give victory to Nankō, at least if conducted by conventional warfare. Nankō expressed his humble opinion that an expedient plan would be to draw the enemy to the capital, whisk the emperor away to Mount Hiei, and to attack from two sides: Nitta from the foot of the mountains and Nankō from Kawachi. But the court officials could not agree because they felt escaping from the capital would be frightening and disgraceful. On the other hand, Takauji had made this his headquarters before, and when he had descended on the capital commanding a great army of valiant soldiers of Kantō, he was crushed. Takauji had survived the great battle at Chikuzen Hakata. Now the imperial army would attack his counterattack. The popular view was that a loyalist victory was a foregone conclusion. By Bōmon Saishō Kiyohara's decision, an order was issued for a swift departure to the front in any case as Yoshisada's reinforcement.

In the *Taiheiki* it is recorded, "There were no objections to the decision," and that Nankō, without making a commotion, made his final resolve and departed. The *Baishō-ron* gives a somewhat sanguine view: "Consequently, Masashige's life, were he to go on living, would be in vain. He was the very first to say one should lay down one's life for the cause." Well aware of the true state of affairs of the court ceremonies, discerning the direction in which the current circumstances were moving, already sure of the outcome, he held in his heart a realization that the average human being cannot grasp. However, this was a case of giving up one's life, like a quiet flame, to follow an imperial order as the most earnest, the holiest of Japanese Bushido acts; in other words, *matsuri*, from the verb *matsurau*: to obey something holy.

Nankō then told his heir Masatsura (eleven or thirteen at the time, or twenty by some accounts) exactly what he should do after Nankō's death and made his solemn farewell at Sakurai station. Exactly three years before, on the thirteenth day of the third month of the third year of Genkō (1333), Nankō, overflowing with emotion, gave high praise to Kikuchi Taketoki, known as the lay monk Jakua, who raised an army in response to the imperial order. Kikuchi, amid a bloody war with Hakata's military governor, had left an admonishment to his heir Takeshige at Sodegaura: "Return to your homeland and raise loyalty to the throne, dispel the emperor's enemies, and put the emperor's heart at rest. Avenge me after my death." Cutting his flesh-and-blood, parent-and-child relation, he was able to depart, scolding his beloved son for wanting to die together in battle, that this was a matter of duty to the emperor (*Murakami Sōdōshi Junchū Kikuchi-shi Daichi Zenshi*). This evidence of unswerving loyalty in the whole country, like two halves of a token united, will live in posterity with great depth of feeling and weeping.

There was no time to dispatch a messenger to Hyōgo and to have a heated discussion with Yoshisada. The rebel army came, crossing land and sea, causing heaven and earth to tremble. Nankō made all of Yumeno, from Egeyama Mountain, northeast of the Minatogawa, his stronghold. From early morning on the twenty-fifth day of the fifth month of the first year of Engen (1336) began the great, bloody battle of Minatogawa. Nankō and his brother fought unreservedly, with their minds set on taking down Takauji and his brother. While delivering a crushing defeat to Tadayoshi, the Yoshisada army made a tactical error and retreated. Regrettably, Nankō's army was completely surrounded. For six long hours, he put up a hard fight, but, his sword broken, his strength exhausted, they withdrew to the north of Minatogawa. Finally, the brothers met their heroic end. (The spot where they fell on their swords is not clear. Lieutenant General Hayashi Yasakichi argued that Nankō had stormed into the rebel army on purpose so as to facilitate Yoshisada's retreat. Masashige's age at the time of his death can be estimated by comparison to Masatsura's.) Deeply moved, Takeyoshi, younger brother in the campaign, dispatched by Kikuchi Takashige, followed Nankō by taking his own life. Twilight was about to fall on Minatogawa.

Nankō's spirit lived on and was exemplified by Masatsura and solemnly carried on through Masanori; an entire clan gave their utmost for the emperor. Nankō's dignity and majesty in holding to his convictions and his military planning were held in awe and respect by all samurai in the country for many years to come. Nankō, in reality, is a model for samurai of great integrity and a guide for Japan (in Bōnan Jakurin's assessment). His spirit will live with heaven and earth in eternity (*Maki Izumi Kashōroku*) and will protect and preserve our national polity.

10

Bushido as Viewed by the Japanese *Volk*
On Gandhism, Mohism, and Bushido

1. Gandhi and *Satyagraha*

The name, Gandhi, became the focus of discourse for a time in Japan, accompanying the rise of the Indian independence movement, and frequent newspaper and magazine articles were written about the movement, his thought, and his character, all becoming a topic of conversation.

Responding to the spirit of *ahimsa* (the principle of nonviolence toward all living things) and practical activism, the pillars of his *satyagraha* (a policy of passive political resistance), people sang hymns of praise and raised their eyes in admiration, as if to say, "At last!" Now he is called Mahatma (Great Soul) in his native land of India and by his followers throughout the world. I, too, am one who is deeply moved by his thought and action.

When people speak of Gandhi, they promptly recall his principle of nonresistance (the literal interpretation, "nonresistance," should not be strictly adhered to). Gandhi remembers his inspiration from learning a Gujarati poem at school when he was a child: "When someone gives you a cup of water and you recompense for the cup of water, there is no virtue of any kind in this. Real virtue is recompensing good for evil." After that, he always strived to realize this teaching in his life.

His reading of the New Testament also made a great impression on him. In particular, passages from the Sermon on the Mount gave him immeasurable joy:

> Ye have heard that it hath been said, "An eye for an eye, and a tooth for a tooth"; but I say unto you, that ye resist not evil: but whosoever shall smite thee on thy right cheek, turn to him the other also. (Matthew 5:39)
>
> But I say unto you, love your enemies, bless them that curse you, do good to them that hate you, and pray for them that despitefully use you and persecute you, that ye may be the children of your Father who is in Heaven. (Matthew 5:44–45)

Half his lifetime was spent in strenuous efforts to personally embody this feeling of religious ecstasy and deep emotion. But the real world, since time immemorial, is a bleak desert. Pursuing a course through this desert, one exhausts the religious ecstasy and deep feelings of one's youth. His heart, however, incessantly filled to overflowing, like a bubbling spring.

Bravely and calmly, Gandhi walked the great road of faith and belief, leaving behind worldly possessions. Bolstered by his personal convictions and practicing the abstinence of an ascetic, he embraced resolution while enduring all manner of afflictions. With a heart full of compassion, he stood before the oppressed, in South Africa and in his native India, like the Goddess of Mercy who hears the prayers of the hopeful and comes to help them.

Many times, he was thrust into the sadness and gloom of prison, like an animal. Sometimes he was attacked by villains and left moaning and groaning in the mud. But he kept silent and endured through it all. The agonies that he endured were one and the same with the persecution of the oppressed he loved. Their afflictions were his afflictions; as long as there was one of the oppressed to be saved, how could he seek his own comfort? He was like a bodhisattva, come to serve humankind.

For the sake of the oppressed, he suffered all manner of persecutions; for the sake of England, he never tired of offering great sacrifice. According to his statement made before the court of Ahmedabad on March 18 of this year (1922), his public life began in 1898 in South Africa in troubled weather. His first contact with British authority in that country was not of a happy character. He discovered that as a man and an Indian he had no rights. More correctly, he discovered that he had no rights as a man because he was an Indian. However, he was not exactly overcome by humiliation. On the contrary, he gave the government his voluntary hearty cooperation, criticizing it freely where he felt it was faulty but never wishing its destruction.

Accordingly, in 1899, when the Second Boer War threatened British rule, he voluntarily recruited his countrymen to serve, bringing together a courageous detachment to serve field hospitals, and, at times, join in the hard fighting. During the Zulu War of 1906, he enlisted a corps of stretcher-bearers, and gave his all through till the end. Again in 1914 as well, when war broke out between England and Germany, he assembled Indians living in London and organized men for military field hospitals. In 1917, the English recruited soldiers from among Indians, and Gandhi, then being of a sickly constitution, helped with the recruitment campaign in Kheda. In other words, he sought transformation of the malevolent government of the British Empire by offering benevolence toward the resentment of the oppressed in his native country of India.

Those efforts were in vain, however, because the infamous Rowlatt Act (1919) expressly stated, "This law was drafted to revoke all freedoms of the people of India in order to suppress any uprising." Then-Brigadier General Dyer, acting selfishly and arbitrarily, massacred Indians in Amritsar—an act unjust and unforgivable before God and man. In the audacious gesture of the British peace treaty, they betrayed 70 million Muslims in India. To hope for at least some justice from the British government, a nation of whites, was, in this regard, completely hopeless. In the end, they were demons. They were Asura—fighting demons. We must detest evil. Any kind of accommodation or compromising with evil must be rejected.

Thereupon, Gandhi had to fiercely proclaim his noncooperation movement over the principles of nonviolence. This was a proclamation of severing relations with England. This meant a complete rejection of all forms of cooperation and submission to the laws of the British government—paying taxes, purchasing British goods, schooling and education, and garnering of decorations and bonuses. His strategy of *swadeshi* was to survive on native Indian manufacture, not British goods, and thereby achieve *swaraj*: to stand independent from England as Indians.

If this is not India's moral self-consciousness and progress of human character, what is it? This is a solemn reality that warrants serious reflection; Gandhi's policy of nonviolence and the noncooperation movement, pursued by his followers—the people of India—attracted worldwide attention. For what reason is this a solemn reality that merits serious reflection—especially one that attracted worldwide notice? Contemporary generations will have to ponder this carefully.

I think this reality—the movement of Gandhi and his followers in India— this alone affirms the moral progress of the entire human race. We can acknowledge that mankind is actually making steady progress toward an ideal country of the human race, what is now called utopia, our human ideals.

The realization of *ahimsa*, requiting malice with virtue, the principle of nonviolence, until now was limited to the life of an ascetic found deep in the forest, or simply nothing more than an ideal for obtaining one's hopes as an individual—nay, a daydream perhaps for ordinary people. Look! In this case, is there not proof that *ahimsa* is far from a daydream? Or, put another way, is this not proof that the limits of the spiritual lives of humans continue to expand higher and wider? If this great joy is not embraced, socialism and democracy—nay, all of religion and morality— will suddenly lose their light.

Gandhi was an extremely gifted child, not unlike the great men who were his predecessors. He was indeed worthy of the name Mahatma. I sing his praises from my innermost being, and one must pray that he will inspire a deeper moral sense for the future and not end up, in the words spoken to Hakuin (Zen monk, 1686–1769), "as an empty inconsequential *arhat* but one who will reach a state of true enlightenment." Even if he were to become a "scabrous animal," he would not boast of today's accomplishments.

2. The Principle of Nonviolence: An Inquiry into *Ahimsa*

Conversely, here is a problem that we must consider afresh. This is not only a problem for Gandhi or the people of India, but a serious problem directly before all of us. How are we to take Gandhi's principle of nonviolence? That is what we must consider. I feel disconcerted: Have people not misunderstood the spirit of *ahimsa*, Gandhi's principle of nonviolence? Is it not foolhardy to take it too lightly? Unfortunately, it seems Gandhi himself worried about this. It requires grave reflection.

To people today, Gandhi has been communicated by the principle of non-resistance. This "nonresistance" as a translational equivalent is an exceedingly ambiguous, inferior term. The word "resistance" today certainly does not carry its original meaning of fighting with brute strength. Rather it is used in a vague way to mean "to oppose" without yielding. In which case, the principle of nonresistance is interpreted simply and shallowly, and thought of as merely to *yield oneself without resistance, even if it is unreasonable and unjust.*

This interpretation is tinged with a faint hue that is sympathetic to the thinking of modern people. First is today's conservative, pacifist thought. Painful suffering of wars of all kinds stems from the conflict of two powers. With one-sided power only, if there is no opposing power, then war will not occur. There will be absolute peace, and life will always love peace. The principle of nonresistance is rational as a means of realizing peace.

Second is the kind of thinking of evil naturalism and carnal affirmation of decadent principles. The satisfaction of desire is the most fundamental of human tendencies. However, indulging in desires makes for the unavoidable breakdown of necessary life, and trying to tighten the reins on uncontrollable desires and passions is a normal requirement for human nature. Thenceforth, moral anguish deepens and deepens. Modern people, however, with their corrupted will and emotion, and their flaccid human character, are exceedingly weak in enduring this anguish. For them, a higher order of conscious living is too cold. A higher-order consciousness is first manifested with the structure of denying a low-order consciousness. That is, one must of oneself take up arms against one's beloved low-order consciousness.

The manifestation of the teaching of the principle of nonresistance toward this is, for them, like the proverbial blind turtle searching for a floating log. They can merely indulge in peaceful indolence. They can escape moral anguish.

This kind of nonresistance, however, must be called a "slave mentality," an expression spat out by the firebrand, Friedrich Nietzsche; it is a lazy and cowardly way of thinking by those who prefer the comfort of nonconfrontation. Because of this nonconfrontational thinking and slave mentality, we spread the disease of the impoverished thought of self-consolation, of worldly desires, of *tariki* (other power) salvation (not in the Original Vow), and, unable to handle disorder in domestic affairs, we disgracefully become satisfied with unsupportable diplomacy.

At the very least, one who desires to stand under the sun and dance to life's rhythms must listen again to the solemn and dignified voice. Gandhi certainly was no supporter of nonconfrontation and slavish nonresistance. On the contrary, did he not undertake a great resistance? To cite one example, if his movement of non-cooperation was not a thorough resistance to English rule, what was it? He refused to pay taxes, rejected English education, and would not submit to English law. Moreover, he boycotted the machines of factories that had been built at great pains as "the cursed civilization of the present day." In actuality, is this not a committed resistance? This is what he said about nonresistance: "I am not talking about sub-mitting docilely to the will of the devil. I mean resisting and challenging the will of the tyrant with all the human spirit."

How could the admirable Mahatma (Great Soul) so marvelously change it so easily to its exact opposite spirit of nonconfrontation and servitude: "submitting docilely to the will of the devil" and "submitting wincingly to the will of the tyrant, shedding the human spirit"?

At this point, we must personally understand in depth the spirit of *ahimsa*, the principle of nonviolence:

> When a certain man called himself nonviolent, Gandhi reasoned, "What manner of man must he be?" He ought not hate the man that hurts him. He doesn't wish ill of him but prays for his happiness. He certainly doesn't curse him. He doesn't cause him any physical harm either. This person will submit to diverse misfortunes at the hands of the treacherous one. Thus, nonviolence is completely without causing harm. Perfect nonviolence is to harbor not the slightest ill will toward any living thing. Therefore, in addition to humans, he does not exclude even birds, animals, fish, and insects from this. Certainly, they were not created to be sacrificed to human brutality. If we could sympathize with the heart of the Creator, we would have more consideration toward the significance of all creation. Nonviolence is having good will toward all living things for their positive significance. This is the pure love that can be read about in sacred Hindu texts, in the Bible, and in the Koran.

This goodwill toward all life—or compassion, in other words—is the essence of *ahimsa*. *Ahimsa* without this essence is not true *ahimsa*. That would be nothing more than the practice of not taking life. From time to time in this merely empty shell, diverse evil parasites appear.

True *ahimsa*, the spirit of nonviolence, is a fully charged, living force. It must be "a great and magnanimous spirit that permeates heaven and earth," as the saying goes. As something that antagonizes us, a mutual reciprocity does not exist. There is also the old proverb, "The compassionate man has no enemies." Gandhi too said,

I wish for people to be cautious about the fundamental nature of *ahimsa*. I don't say, "Your enemy is who you think is your enemy," but rather, "Your enemy is who you arbitrarily think is your enemy." That is why, for those who follow the doctrine of *ahimsa*, there is no room for an enemy to enter.

Precisely for this reason, one will be able to submit to all manner of pain and persecution. Moreover, there is the significance of perseverance. Strictly speaking, it is not that perseverance as such is an imperfect condition but more of a "perfect condition."

The calamity of nonconfrontational thought and a slavish spirit make this the most imperfect condition. It turns a great, strong spirit into a small, feeble spirit. That is because truth and the unreasonable ultimately manifest themselves in similar figures. This is especially so because in today's mechanical, material age, humans constantly tend toward an unstable, floating existence in which deep contemplation of the self is difficult to achieve.

3. Two Heresies

The next problem arises from a misunderstanding of the concept of nonresistance as described above. Must humans, as a matter of course, pass through some kind of process in order to attain the spirit of nonviolence, true *ahimsa*? Clearly, the answer is noncooperation—and rejection. But noncooperation with what? Rejection of what? Needless to say, not cooperating with evil and rejecting the unreasonable.

Gandhi also said,

Rejection has the same meaning as approval. Rejecting the unreasonable is of the same importance as approving the truth. All religions teach that two conflicting powers operate above us, and that human endeavor is linked to the eternal sequence of rejection and approval. Noncooperation with evil has the same responsibility toward the true and the good.

However, herein lies concealed the trap of a paradox into which it is easy for ordinary people to fall. Rejecting *evil* and hating the *evildoer* is a mixture of acceding to violence against the evildoer. Strictly speaking, one cannot say that because one rejects evil, one can hate the evildoer. More correctly, because one rejects evil, one must say one loves the evildoer. As Christ teaches to love your enemy, or a man of integrity says that he hates the sin but not the sinner, we must seriously contemplate this principle.

The evildoer, whatever he is, is not the same as *the evil itself*. There is no absolute evil in the world. The most evil of persons is not an evil thing but a human being. He is someone who can be saved. The more earnest our heart's desire to expel evil from human beings, the more eager it becomes to eliminate that *deep-rooted evil* from the individual. You will feel more pity for a person who is trapped in such enduring evil. Buddha and Christ—indeed, all great religious teachers—were noble people who had such hearts, brimming with compassion.

Since one loves the evildoer, how can one do harm to his life? The taking of life is the gravest of evils. It crushes every form of hope in the world and goes against one's natural will. "The pursuit of truth does not permit violence on one's opponent. Rather, one should draw the sinner away from his erroneous ways through patience and empathy."

Gandhi hated the unjust rule of the English, but he didn't hate England. Even as Brigadier General Dyer, the perpetrator of the Amritsar Massacre, lay moaning on his sickbed, Gandhi said he would comfort him.

This is a vital trait indispensable to the human spirit. In Bushido, the enemy's character was most highly respected.

Once, violence as a form of revenge met with approval. Revenge is a rule of the human world and was, for a time, obligatory. Gandhi said, "In our ignorance and arrogance, we take up violence to resist violence, which leads to the development of indignation. This was considered practicing the human ideal." However, an "eye for an eye and a tooth for a tooth" is truly despicable. For human beings, to whatever extent they may strive, cannot attain moral improvement. And violence, again and again, can be approved as retribution for evil. It goes without saying that this is a low and vulgar way of thinking.

Formerly, in the world of criminal law, the principle of retribution was carried out with the understanding that punishment for a crime was meted out as retribution. But today, punishment has come to be understood as nothing more than a method aimed at protecting society. This concept of retribution (*Vergeltungsgedanke*), however, is deemed to be an instinctive part of human nature and persistently guides humans toward violence. This is what Gandhi always feared. In actuality, the people of India repeatedly gave in to retribution.

Through this, one can comprehend how difficult it must be to internalize this so-called principle of nonviolence, the spirit of *ahimsa*. Were humans not nonconfrontational and slavish in attitude, they would fall into a thought process that is vengeful, retributive, and violent, not knowing where it might lead.

4. Nonconfrontational Thought and Relative Retaliatory Thought

Seen from one side, the ideal is like encountering mountain after mountain. Once one has reached the summit of a mountain, yet another high peak rises up to meet one's eyes. Human life, after all, is eternal progression, and satisfaction swells within one's own efforts. "Adequate effort means what is adequate to succeed," as Gandhi has said.

This notion of effort is important. A feeling of focused concentration is important. A great and magnanimous spirit that is cultivated by grasping the straight and direct is important. What is meant by "straight and direct"? The straight and direct must be *not deluding oneself*. This must entail making judgments straight and true and following one's convictions concerning good and evil, right and wrong, and seeing beauty as beauty, and ugliness as ugliness, just as they really are. Clarity and expansiveness of the spirit—this is the straight and direct. This is the dynamic force that pushes human beings toward the ideal.

The driving force of the straight and direct is also called valor. One of the most respected of Confucius' disciples, Zengzi (505–436 BC), explains great courage:

> If, on looking within, one finds oneself to be in the wrong, then even though one's adversary is only a common fellow, coarsely clad, one is bound to tremble with fear. But if one finds oneself in the right, one goes forward even against men in the thousands. (*Mencius* 2A.2)

As the foundation for the moral life of human beings, as the basis of a moral spirit for all people, valor is the most significant element, I think, and it must be held in high honor. Before we can consider *ahimsa*, the principle of nonviolence, I think rather it is necessary to distinguish it from the aforementioned principle of nonconfrontational slavish nonresistance and the retributive violent way of thinking.

Now, let us take a look at a group of young people, all students in the same class. Among them, one young man is proud of his physical strength, always looking to pick a fight with people, relying on violence, and is a bully. The remaining students, on the other hand, fall into these five categories: (1) afraid of violence, he meekly accepts the situation; (2) he considers the student mean and violent but lets sleeping dogs lie and does nothing; (3) he despises the tyranny of the student and schemes for a chance to show his toughness; (4) he does not despise the student but he despises his actions; at the right instant, he will strike back at the bully, first to make a show to the others and second to chastise the offender as if it were divine punishment that delivered the blow; and (5) the last one is the man of virtue of the middle way, or one who operates in the style of Gandhi.

Under the circumstances, it is necessary to make a comparison between 1 and 3, and also between 2 and 4. Of the two, which do people choose, 1 or 3? For 1, there is no focus or vital force whatsoever in his life or in his character. Some have only atrophy and stagnation. Contrariwise, 3 still has flexibility. He strives vigorously to advocate life. Of the two, I would choose 3. However, of course, 3 is a vile creature.

What then do we make of 2 and 4? As for 2, he holds a bright recognition of morality. His behavior, however, is thoroughly selfish and conservative. He is *one who sees principles but does not embody them.* This certainly must be called one who knows what is right and does nothing (not recognizing the necessity of a morality that considers both wrongs of commission and wrongs of omission).

Or, under these circumstances, perhaps 2 is one who says, "I pray for his sake." As a minimum, the teaching of *ahimsa*, the principle of nonviolence, can become a fine excuse for him. Nevertheless, this is in fact an act of self-deception. Through this, he is able to build a two-layer aspect of wrongs.

Finally, 4 is a mental attitude that is, I think, closest to the path of the Way. He is also, of course, cognizant of the bright truth, and his life focus, if struck, would ring clear as a bell. His life has momentum and thrust. Is he not worthy to speak of the spirit of *ahimsa*, the spirit of nonviolence? I would like to refer to this as "relative retaliatory thought."

Relative retaliatory thought distinguishes clearly between the person and the wrong. That the evil and the evildoer are not the same thing is discernible. That the evildoer is also a fellow human being worthy of commiseration is also well-known. But he esteems human character. To lapse into evil, to commit a crime, does not exempt persecuting someone, however vile his character. Moreover, he feels a victim's resentment. And in this world, there is a feeling that no peace would exist were there no recompensing good with good, and recompensing evil with evil. In other words, his flailing of his arms at the evildoer certainly is not because he despises him. But rather this is heaven's retribution.

Observing them, it is necessary to distinguish between the violence of 3 and the violence of 4. The violence of 3 is because of hatred toward the person, because of sudden rage. If this is called "provoking violence with violence," 4 is not actually violence but must be called punishment from heaven—should it not?

From ancient times, a person of absolute purity within the so-called chivalrous or humanitarian was namely this relative retaliatory advocate. More than anything, a person must first be true to himself and to life. He must be a person of dignity and gravity. A correct judgment of good and evil based on actual conduct and a pure sensibility are needed. Recognizing evil for evil, a strict judgment that despises evil, with straightforward sensibility, in that way it is possible to love good and do good. Loving the good is recognizing evil for evil and despising evil. One should do good and at the same time cast off evil. Moreover, love of truth must mean becoming one with the object. Loving the good is, in the end, casting off evil.

In this regard, the psychological power of such people must be considered an admonition that penetrates the scathing needle of truth toward the moral conscience of human beings, whose consciousness would otherwise be dull and paralyzed.

One school of thought, that of Mozi of China, truly possesses a psychological foundation that is relevant here.

5. Mozi's Thought and Society's Two Great Evils

In colloquial speech there is the saying, "Strike it, and it will ring." Mozi (墨子, Mo Di 墨翟, ca. 470–ca. 391 BC, of the Warring States period), I think, was certainly this kind of person. The phrase, "Strike it, and it will ring," refers to a person of character who has deep and powerful emotions toward the truth. At the same time, we can assume that this person does not just feel deeply, but that his emotions extend directly to his actions (to his character), making him straight and direct.

Let truth be a mallet and a person, a bell. Once a person is struck with the truth, the person would set the open air to roiling and ringing, an attribute lacking in modern men.[1] Mozi was certainly a person of this order. And he was, as Sakamoto Ryōma commented on Nanshū (Saigō Takamori), a person who, when struck quietly, rings quietly, and when struck loudly, rings loudly. Although he was a philosopher of the late Zhou dynasty, shoulder to shoulder with Confucius who is rather contemplative and poetical, Mozi was, compared to Confucius, a remarkably pragmatic person of an academic disposition.

A careful observer of the chaos of his times, Mozi discovered two sad, fundamental evils in society. One of these was that human beings lived reciprocally, solely on their base and selfish impulses, like beasts. The other was that impartial, moral principles were mistakenly limited only to the personal sphere and not applied to the actions of statesmen or authorities. Because these two great evils were allowed to run wild, society became even more disordered and could not be managed.

Between parent and child, master and servant, between all people, each one thinks narrow-mindedly only of oneself, not considering the other in the least, and conflict arises each to each. Without exception, the disorder was engendered from *lack of mutual love*. As mentioned before, mutual love is reciprocal, becoming one. Therefore, in order to secure peace in society, there is no other way than to expand "love," a love that is an inherent virtue. If, for example, one country views another's internal affairs as if they were occurring in their own nation, and the two regard each other from this common perspective, then certainly things would go amicably.

At the same time, the prerequisite for social peace is the consistency of moral law, from the individual to the state. Not departing from that moral law under any circumstances is, in turn, the key to ongoing social harmony. If a person steals property or assets, naturally, he will be punished under the laws of the country. The same is true of one who kills or causes harm. Yet when it comes to the occasion of "invading another country," everyone affirms and praises this, without any suspicion. Is this not a brazen contradiction?

If a man looks at a dark-colored object and calls it black, then looks at a pitch-

---

1. [Yasuoka also mentioned this "moral simplicity" as a foundation of Eastern character.]

black object and calls it white, he would be laughed at. If we consider seizing a person's property a great crime, so then must invading another country be an even greater crime. To accept one while condemning the other is a contradiction beyond belief.

In actuality, authorities in all countries, on the one hand, control the crimes of their subjects through national law and, on the other hand, bolster their own egoistical inhumane aspirations internationally, using invasion to do so. If the situation is left to run its course, in the end the expansion of love—the universalization and absolutization of morality—cannot be conclusively realized. These two great evils should not be tolerated or ignored—not even for a day. What must those faithful to the truth do to make this come to pass?

This is what Mozi thought. We have two schemes. One of them is the enlightened person who preaches the good news of love to the masses through his speech and behavior. The other is the actively involved enlightened person who creates unity through love, brings cooperation, opposes the party of unreason, and allows no room to wreak violence. When need be, the violent ones are assailed and punishment is meted out against them.

For this to transpire, each individual must personally realize a deep sense of humanity and, at the same time, must be brimming with a fervent force (of life and of human character). A master of budō may well first espouse the crime of violence. Powerless individuals, trying to admonish aggressive ruffians for the cruelty of brute strength, do nothing more than aimlessly provoke violent incidents or earn their antipathy and scorn. Conversely, it is understood that those who are deep in their mastery of kendo, or great priests who have tempered the inviolable authority of human character, can bend these ruffians to their will and make them change their violent ways.

Mozi had arrived at deep truth. He taught and learned fervently, preaching the gospel of love on the one hand, while thoroughly studying military strategy and weapons and giving military training to his disciples. He faced the invasion of wicked lords by helping the invaded country and thereby attempted to overcome (and not give in to) bestial treachery with the sword of justice. Truly, he was a noble man to be held in high esteem.

6. Mozi's Moral Character

Before expounding on Mozi's fervent social movement, I first must address his pure exhilaration and fidelity to truth.

All ideologies and movements are inevitably accompanied by an underside of extreme danger. That is because amid the struggle and championing of the ideology of a movement, kindred souls at some point lose their original spirit, their truth and love, and blindly run wild with their comrades, aimless, like a flock of sheep.

Or, losing the vestiges of early emotions, they entertain selfish motives beneath a vocabulary of empty, beautiful names. Some of the people test the waters of an ideological movement, embracing selfish motives from the start. I think philosophers such as Yang Zhu (440–360? BC) would abhor such thinking.

On this account, Mozi was a person to be loved and respected. Reading the existing works of Mozi, we feel keenly in our hearts his deep emotion toward truth, evident in his anecdotes, and can sense an unshakeable, pure integrity. His thought and principles, crying love and advocating peace in an age at the height of egoism and imperialism, were seen to be futile in practicality, as can easily be imagined.

Once, a friend of Mozi's said to him,

> We live in times of moral degeneration. However much meaning and value morals may have, it doesn't matter since they are not observed. So whatever hardship you experience in going around explaining moral principles, it cannot possibly have an effect. Maybe you should just give up altogether, don't you think?

Adjusting his collar, Mozi replied,

> Let's say there are ten men. Among them are nine idlers and only one man who tills the fields. The one man cannot afford to idle his time away. Well, if the masses of society are now in such a degenerate state, then you should, of course, urge me to insist on a moral life, encouraging me more and more. But, to the contrary, you suggest "giving up"?

If the world is taken up and everyone is sullied, I too, in its wake, am enjoined in their midst, soiled by the dirt, attempting to ride the wave. If the masses become intoxicated, I too want to eat and drink. Mozi's passion could not possibly accept this accommodation and apathy toward society. He was, of course, an individual with the grateful heart of a bodhisattva that shares the illnesses of the people. Serving a social movement with a passionate body solely from a pure moral motivation, he strove never to lose clear moral self-consciousness under any circumstance.

The following story should move people to a deeper understanding.

> Mozi once recommended someone for government service in the state of Wei. The person served in the position but before long came back. Suspicious, Mozi asked him the reason for his return. The man replied proudly,

The duke of Wei is a perfidious ruler who speaks with a forked tongue. He promised me 2,000 *ryō* for service, but finally after having served for a while I received only 1,000 *ryō*. I have no desire to serve such an untrustworthy ruler.

Mozi asked him in return, "Well then, what if you were paid in excess of the promised amount of 2,000 *ryō*? Would you still resign and return home?"

"No, of course not," the man declared in amazement. At once, Mozi stated solemnly, "You returned not because the duke failed to keep his promise, but because the wages were insufficient."

People like the man in this story misrepresent their own selfishness while deceiving others and are apt to use the pretext of high repute. How much antisocial, antinational behavior is conducted under the banner of socialism and nationalism? How much crime is committed profligately under the good name of religion and the arts? Enough to make a person shudder. How many people, when facing a gang, could actually choose to be Mozi?

Mozi sent his disciple Shōshaku (Sheng Zhuo) to Qi to serve Kō Shi Gyū (Xiang Zi Niu). His intention was to bring the great invader under the influence of his disciple's virtue. However, Shōshaku received a fine stipend from Kō Shi Gyū and didn't do anything other than sit vacantly as an idle spectator. Shōshaku followed his master in several invasion campaigns.

Mozi sent another one of his disciples, Kō Sonshi (Gao Sunzi), to make Shōshaku resign from his position. Being responsible for promoting morality while sitting by idly is like trying to lead a horse by the nose with a whip—thus, there was no avenue by which Kō Shi Gyū's conscience could emerge. This is something the likes of Shōshaku ought to have known. Mozi deplored that fact that Shōshaku enjoyed emoluments and rested on his laurels.

Kō Sekishi (Gao Shizi), conversely, was an excellent disciple. The lord of Wei invited him to court and paid him handsomely. He rose to the rank of state minister. Each time Kō Sekishi visited the palace, he spoke heatedly, advocating a moral government, but he never saw his counsel implemented. In spite of his high rank and handsome stipend, he quit his post and left Wei.

When he met his teacher Mozi, Kō Sekishi complained, speaking earnestly of the injustice:

> The lord of Wei treated me very lavishly, but in the end he had no intention of conducting a moral government. That is why I came back, giving up everything he gave me. I'm afraid he might think me a madman.

Mozi replied happily,

> If you left in accordance with the Way, I don't care a whit whether or not you were a madman. Zhou Gong, the duke of Zhou, weary of the suspicion and criticism from Guan, the king's son, abandoned all rank and lived a penitent. People then said he was mad, but today all revere him as a saint. What is more, practicing righteousness means

not being afraid of the will of society. If one believes oneself to be in accordance with the Way, then one thinks nothing of censure and praise.

The master's words struck his convictions like a thunderbolt.

> No, that certainly is not a worry. I left in accordance with the Way. And I have complied with your words: "When there is no Way in the world, a man of virtue will not stay for high remuneration." Were I to live off the rank and entitlements from service to the lord of Wei, who does not practice the Way, I would be a good-for-nothing.

Impressed by his beloved disciple's daring disposition and his pure spirit, Mozi joyfully summoned his first respected disciple Kin Kotsuri (Qinzi), telling him in amazement, "Listen, I have heard often of people who oppose righteousness and pursue profit, but Gao Shizi is the first time I have seen someone oppose profit and choose righteousness."

These men lived lives of deep emotion and inspiration. Modern intellectual education has a general tendency to weaken this invaluable moral inspiration. Observe how multitudinous are the morally incompetent among the educated classes of today. They are generally able to distinguish between good and bad, right and wrong, but are too mediocre to do anything about it. For this reason, the man of virtue loves the rustic, simple person.

7. Mozi's Movement

Mozi and all his disciples burned with a pure moral enthusiasm. They earnestly promoted the spirit of universal love for all people and sought to destroy the prevalence of violence by humans. They rallied comrades of strong will to realize a moral government and to eliminate immoral tyrannical rule, giving their all to campaigning for peace and negotiating between states. Mozi always watched for a tiny spark of a moral spirit, even in the heart of an immoral invader, and he sought earnestly to nurture that spark.

If the invader had mentioned words tinged with even the slightest morality, Mozi would close in and make him self-aware of his moral responsibility. When he just wouldn't listen, Mozi would intimidate the invader, instilling fear in his heart. He exhibited an unreserved antagonism, as if to say, "I have the sword of truth and justice against whatever you may attempt to do."

One of the most famous stories involves Kōyu Ban (Gongshu Ban), the renowned military strategist at the time the states of Chu and Song were at war with each other. As the commander of Chu, Gongshu Ban was about to invade Song using the latest scaling ladders he had developed. Mozi dispatched Kin Kotsu

Ri (Qin Hua Li) and other disciples as one military unit to Song, prompting the Song army to prepare for battle against the Chu army. Mozi himself visited the Chu army and negotiated personally and repeatedly with Gongshu Ban and the king of Chu. Mozi at last convinced Gongshu Ban to abandon his stratagems and thereby completely defused the war.

The following episode is recorded in Mozi's *Gongshu Collection* (墨子公輸篇) and, by its conclusion, resonates with his prestige and influence. Gongshu Ban, who realized he had no chance of success at all in engaging with Mozi, said nonchalantly, his face quivering with a flash of bloodthirstiness:

> Indeed, I have exhausted all means. Yet I still have one way to avoid your interference. But that needn't be said.
>
> Mozi: No, I know exactly what you mean. However, I too will not presume to say.
>
> King of Chu: What can't you say?
>
> Mozi: Nothing but this. The final measure of Master Gongshu's intentions was to try to kill me. If I were just eliminated, the invasion of Song would be a simple matter. We see now that that didn't come to pass. Even if I were to collapse on this spot, my disciple Qin Hua Li and others have already carried out my plans and have fortified the Song castle; so they are on the alert and prepared against a Chu army invasion. So you see, even if I were to be annihilated, that is no certainty that events would go well.

This, however, certainly was not his true meaning. His true meaning was strictly this: the realization of a moral government, without resorting to violence, and in maintaining peace based on love for humanity.

He lamented that a smaller, weaker country that was focused solely on military preparations against a larger country ultimately invites only self-destruction. Consequently, he insisted that small countries establish themselves through righteousness, putting internal affairs in order, and sustaining education. In facing the authorities of a large country, he advocated preaching the calamities and cruelties of war and using this power to become true builders and keepers of peace.

He then wandered about from Lu, Qi, Wei, Song, and Chu, present-day Shandong, Henan, Shanxi, and Hunan, oblivious to life and death for the sake of truth and the masses.

Through him, I am able to know the actual joy that is led by ideals and taste the true power of love and its preciousness. Ideals are not fantasy. Ideals are not an abstract concept. They must be a force that can directly move reality. Our individual history is, in other words, uninterrupted ideals and aspirations. When considered deeply, ideals are limitless self-realization. Thus, a person can occupy for the first time, as a man of character, a position among all creation that is the final absolute.

To speak of humanity and explain ideals lightly, with a brush or with the tongue, is, after all, meaningless. To console oneself with the likes of "weak as a god" while being violated like a woman for the sake of the devil and trying to mask one's outward appearance is the most unseemly of all. Gandhi and Gandhism surely ought not to be explained in a confused, disorderly fashion. One must at least know and savor fully the thought and action of someone who came before, such as Mozi.

In this regard, I rather feel that the desideratum, in any case, is a new national self-consciousness of Japan's forgotten Bushido.

8. The Japanese *Volksgeist* Symbolized in the Three Sacred Treasures

Wang Yangming deplored human ignorance, saying, "People throw away what they already have in unlimited abundance to take a bowl in hand and emulate a mendicant monk who goes from door to door begging." Truly, what is easy for one to lose is not life, it is not assets, but actually the self. As a result of losing the self, we experience the beginning of all manner of anxiety, impatience, and groping for solutions. Today, too, is a time when we have fallen to the depths of such bewilderment. Having discussed Gandhism and Mohism, I too, not surprisingly, had to inquire into my own spirit. We have grasped the significance of Gandhism and Mohism. However, instead of depending on those teachings, having cultivated the noble Japanese *Volksgeist*, what joy for us to be able to recognize the nourishment of our souls from our native land.

In olden times, when the monk Saigyō Hōshi went to visit the Great Shrine of Ise, overcome by his emotions, he cried tears of piety, and composed this poem:

Although I know not
What is enshrined, here,
My tears fall
With an awesome
Feeling of respect.[2]

Remembering Saigyō, I once again traced the origin of the founding of Japan, thinking back to the three sacred treasures that are a symbol of imperial succession in our nation, and I felt an irrepressible, deep, and sublime feeling that is not in Gandhism or Mohism, but that is permitted only to Japanese.

This is the myth of the founding of our country as it has been passed on by word of mouth from our ancestors. Izanagi and Izanami, the male and female gods that are the two pillars, made solid the land of Ōyashima (Japan). Amaterasu, the eldest child, reigned over Takamagahara, the great plain of heaven. Her

---

2. [Translation by Dr. Yoshiko Dykstra]

brother, Susanoo, descended to Izumo and obtained the treasured sword to subjugate the land. This sword, the Murakumo no Tsurugi, he presented to Amaterasu. Later, Amaterasu told Ninigi, her grandson, to reign over the land of Toyoashiharamizuho-no-kuni, and presented him with the mirror (Yata no Kagami), the jewel (Yasakani no Magatama), and the sword (Murakumo no Tsurugi), commanding him to make prosperous the imperial lineage together with heaven and earth. Such is the origin of the Three Sacred Treasures, given to the emperor and transmitted by him.

Appropriately enough, Amaterasu is the spiritual origin of national life that symbolizes, most nobly, a creative evolution in which the realization of self occurs through ideals. When Amaterasu said, upon the descent of her heavenly grandson Ninigi, to make prosperous the imperial lineage to the end of heaven and earth, was she not making a declaration of the infinitude of our nation's creative evolution? And the mirror, jewel, and sword that she granted him are the three virtues of an ideal creative activity that is clear and infinite—as represented by their three fundamental functions.

The mirror, in other words, is wisdom that springs from sincerity. The jewel is a resplendent benevolence—making all creation a harmonious whole (benevolence), and while so doing, manifesting all things clearly and distinctly (wisdom). The action of the one and the many dissolving into oneness, freed from obstacles, is verily the existence of Japan's land of the emperor. Valor (virtue of the sword) acts to free us from obstacles. Valor is nothing other than making contradiction uniform. That the Murakumo no Tsurugi was presented to Susanoo, who used it to subjugate Izumo, is naturally a marvelous thing, is it not? (Many Shinto treatises have affirmed the notion that the Three Sacred Treasures exemplify the three primary virtues: valor, wisdom, and benevolence; some examples are found in Yoshikawa Koretari, Miyake Kanran, Amemori Hōshū, and Kumazawa Banzan, among others.)

Thus, the Three Sacred Treasures as a symbol of imperial succession well represent the mission of the spiritual life of the Japanese *Volk*. These are the three great virtues of the Japanese *Volk*: benevolence that envelops all creation; wisdom, arising from selflessness, that illuminates the inside and outside; and, accompanying these, valor that constantly elevates. Above all, the Murakumo no Tsurugi (also known as Kusanagi) with the passage of time became the Japanese sword and led to the development of a vibrant Japanese Bushido, producing men of valor who held high the earnest aspirations and ideals of our people.

The reverential acceptance of the Three Sacred Treasures is the *satyagraha* of the Japanese *Volk*.

People nowadays, who do not comprehend the value of symbols, demonstrate a shallow cultivation of intuition and insight. Deceived by abstract concepts, they are too distant from the fount of life and cannot feel with their hearts what these symbols convey. Toward those who scoff at the Three Sacred Treasures as an old superstitious custom, I feel only sorrow for their imprudence. Yet how numerous are those who speak of the Great Shrines of Atsuta or Ise without knowing the meaning of the Three Sacred Treasures.

9. The Essence of Bushido

Calling a Japanese male who holds the Sword and embraces the Mirror and the Jewel a "*bushi*" is actually very appropriate. The origin of the *shi* (士) of *bushi* (武士) has various meanings. In ancient times, it was used to refer to a judge. Its meaning can be seen in the phrase from the *Shujing*: "The emperor said, 'Kōyō (Gaotao), you must become a *shi*, judge'" is one example. In the Zhou dynasty, *shi*, or scholars, belonged to the four classes, just below *taifu*, the great men. After that, it seems everyone in government service who received an official salary was called a "*shi*."

In the *Saden* (*Zuo Zhuan*) and other sources, men who commanded troops on the battlefield were called "*shi*." It is thought that such usage derives from military men who served below commissioned officers, commanding soldiers, thus referred to as "*kashi*" (*ka* means *lower*) or noncommissioned officers.

Eventually, the term came to mean warrior or samurai in general and also referred more broadly to a man. The term "*shi*" also has a deeper level of significance: in other words, "one who carries out duty," one who is the subject of moral behavior. Zengzi, one of the most respected men of virtue among the disciples of Confucius, made this priceless statement:

> *Shi* must be compassionate and strong-willed. His duty is heavy and the road is long. Making benevolence his personal duty, is it not heavy? Even unto death the burden must be borne; is the road not long?

Mencius also argued, "Only '*shi*' can have a mind of virtue, even though he lacks fortune." Put another way, *shi* can never be a slave to any material possession, is not driven by worldly passions and desires, and is nothing less than a man of character, truly free and autonomous.

Shi has also been explained in the *Book of Han* as one who has social standing and is learned. Learned means, as mentioned before, making life's foundation clear. There is also the etymological interpretation that the character for '*shi*' (士), written with 'ten' (十) and 'one' (一) signifies that "counting begins with one and ends with ten; to support ten and unify into one makes *shi*."

Even a life that does not overcome complex carnal desire springs from the function of one's heart, as do spiritual activities. *Shi* is nothing other than one who establishes a moral character without delusion, who examines life thoroughly. Expressed another way, one who embraces the mirror and the jewel is a *shi*.

Then, what of the meaning of "*bu*" in Bushido? The character "*bu*" (武) is made up of *hoko* (戈) (weapons) and *todomeru* (止), to stop; to stop weapons. Tsurugi, the sword, is definitely not an instrument for taking life. It is the power to perfect the virtue of the mirror and the jewel. The virtue of Tsurugi is rather in not killing, or *ahimsa*. A one-character translation of ahimsa would be "*bu*." Thus, *bu* must forsake the intent to kill and be in sympathy with advancing life. It must be "to follow directly the will of heaven." The virtue of this *bu* is called *buyū*, valor. If understanding the will of heaven is in *shi* (士), then *bu* and *shi* should coincide from the beginning; the virtue of *bu* is the virtue of *shi*.

Matsudaira Nobutsuna (1596–1662), also known by the illustrious sobriquet Chie Izu, or Izu the wise, told an anecdote to Kumazawa Banzan about Yagyū Tajima (1571–1646)—that when he crossed swords with him, he was struck by the light glinting so brightly from Yagyū's eyes that he could not look upon him. After a while, Banzan said, "He would have been even greater had he made the light shine within." Yagyū is said to have progressed one step toward the ultimate through his studies with the Zen Buddhist, Takuan Sōhō.

Takahashi Deishū, a behind-the-scenes elder statesmen at the end of the Tokugawa shogunate who went by the name Yari (spear) Ise-no-Kami, excelled at spearmanship and mastered the secrets of the martial art to the extent that the holy priest Unshō Risshi shrank before him. Receiving moral teaching from the Buddhist monk Rinzui Oshō of Dentsū-in Temple, he achieved great power.

It was the sword that was beneficial to Japanese males as the most effective power to banish the clouds of delusion, in order to forge a noble and free moral character, and to fulfill a benevolent life. What a wonderful designation "*bushi*" must have been to these great men and heroic warriors.

Our study, I think, is the enhancement of ideals through everything that is true, good, and beautiful, in all their aspects.

The venerable Miwa Shissai, scholar of Wang Yangming teachings, when asked what is the way to learning, answered, "Have the heart and mind (心, *shin*) of *shi* (士): (*shishin*)." The inquirer then asked what is the meaning of *shi* (志), to which Miwa replied, "*Ikidōri*" (憤), moral indignation. The movement of the seasons, quietly, without interruption, is the *ikidōri* of heaven. Living nature, endlessly springing forth, is the *ikidōri* of earth. Humanity and justice, faithfulness and devotion, at times not unsympathetically, is the *ikidōri* of humans. This notion of *ikidōri* is not a sentiment of self-interest. It is to hate evil; to hate evil, and to exclude evil. Loving the good, becoming one with good, and hating evil and excluding evil are, together, the inseparable functions of *shishin*.

In "Seppo's Grain of Rice" in the *Hekiganroku* (*The Blue Cliff Record*), it is said,

One who finds new teachings—and a great man, by all means, who can kill without the blink of an eye—he has the potential to awaken a sense of Buddha in someone where they stand.

What is called the realm of nonviolence—people with *shishin* or *shikon* (士魂, samurai spirit) are the ones who are qualified to speak about it. Without understanding Bushido, I do not think one can appreciate what nonviolence is. And to return to the beginning of this chapter, I think kendo must be examined with this background in mind.

11

Learning the Way and Moral Indignation
On Ōshio Chūsai

Letter to Satō Issai:

Respected Master Satō,

I am originally a petty official from a distant place. Following the command of a superior official, I was engaged in all issues regarding litigation and punishment and received wages for doing this and thus lived my life. Not seeking anything else in particular, I would have been fine with this. However, while I began learning the Way by myself, embracing high ideals, I was restless and thought: Why can't I, without finding acceptance in the world, without being loved, exist without following misbegotten plans? Even if someone who understands me can empathize with my intentions, someone who does not understand me sees my misbegotten plans as a crime. And rightfully so.

Up to now, I have experienced three transformations in my thinking. At age fifteen, I read my family's pedigree and discovered that we are the same lineage that served the Imagawa clan. After the destruction of the Imagawa clan, my ancestor was an attendant to Lord Ieyasu and was given a bow of honor for his meritorious deeds in capturing the enemy commander in the battle of Odawara. He also received land in the village of Tsukamoto in Izu. Because of his advanced age, he did not join the campaign in the battle of Osaka. He protected the Kashiwazaki fortress in Echigo, and after peace prevailed he finally became attached to the Bishū Domain. Generation after generation of heirs continued the family name, and the youngest child became an official of Osaka. This person was my father.

I was thrilled to learn my pedigree. And I felt deep shame for being in the company of ineffective petty officials. From that time onward, I wanted to somehow show the will of my predecessors; driven by nothing but the idea of great accomplishment and moral fiber, I succumbed to days of melancholy.

Unfortunately, my parents died when I was seven years old. So, at my early age, I simply had to follow in succeeding my grandfather in his profession. Consequently, the type of people I came in contact with every day were criminals in red kimono or the petty officials who handled them, and I heard nothing but their tales and laments of making a living and making money. Doing nothing but reciting the rules and regulations, I made not the slightest advance in realizing my previous ideals and passed my twentieth year while dawdling my time away.

However, officials and their like are not particularly given to study, so even if one were to commit a peccadillo, there were no friends to remonstrate against it; they thought nothing of deceiving authority themselves, taking advantage of others, or of profligacy. They were led into various evil practices. But no person is without a moral consciousness. Were one to examine oneself in secret, one would see innumerable actions and achievements that defy logic. After all, there is but a hair's breadth of difference between myself and the criminals in red kimono sentenced to a whipping or a caning at one's feet.

All the same, there is no human who feels not a sense of shame for his own lowliness and baseness. In this case, if one is to press a judgment against their crimes, however vile, and to stabilize the insecurity in society, then naturally the diseases of the inner self must be healed too. Just how does one go about healing these diseases? This is what I thought: following Confucianism, reading the texts and meditating on them, one can make healing possible. Thereupon, I took up the study of Confucianism. For this reason, my intentions of self-aggrandizement changed completely.

At that time, however, I was not yet truly conscious. It seems I had mistakenly assumed that simply through acquiring knowledge I could improve my faults and develop a correct moral character. Consequently, human beings are not exempted from going from clever to superficial. I, too, over time, was made to follow the so-called Confucian education of just reading the classic texts and commenting on the words and phrases, merely altering poems and passages. As a result, my studies, of course, also fit the conventional model—deluding the desire for sincere interiority, merely manipulating words and becoming unashamed of it, keeping up appearances, to the extent that it was thought that the sickness became even worse than before.

With the original intention to live a life of moral character that truly brings freedom, reflecting earnestly on one's self, how is it possible not to regret being so far removed from those intentions now? Thereupon, I abandoned everything and retreated to study on my own. I studied hard, suffering almost indescribably. Yes, I had to depend on providential help, and I was suddenly able to obtain an imported edition of *Shin Gin Go* (呻吟語, *Shi Zheng Lu*) by Master Ro Shingo (呂 新吾, Lu Kun, 1536–1618). In this book, Master Ro recorded words that cannot be counterfeited, recorded from the sickness of a painful heart, much like my own painful suffering. Getting my hands on this book, I read it passionately, relishing every word.

It is precisely in this serious anguish—is it not?—where the true path lies. Fascinated, I felt that I had touched the light of self-awareness. The feeling was like a sharp needle piercing my chest and releasing pent-up pressure. I had not yet reached the point of having completely correct feelings, but I was at least able to go beyond the hair's breadth of difference between myself and the crime and criminals in their red uniforms.

From then, I ascertained that Ro Shingo's thoughts came from Wang Yangming, and that three scholars of Wang Yangming studies in Japan were Nakae Tōju, Kumazawa Banzan, and then Miwa Shissai. Thereafter, it became extinct in the Kansai region, and no one lectured on the subject. So, I secretly sought out records of *The Great Learning* and Wang Yangming's *Denshūroku* (伝習録) that reprinted Miwa's version. Furthermore, I accumulated means for fulfilling something of an inner life and persuaded other people about this, forgetting the idle introspection of the past, and made a complete about-face from the tendency to run about mechanically.

Accordingly, my purpose, in a word, was in pure freedom of will, and I realized that the means to achieve this was in expanding the inevitable inner desire that was pure and earnest. After that, I never considered the before and after, only what came in front of me; simply going forward energetically, I merely did the day's work of an official, thoroughly, attentive to accomplishment. To that extent, secretly repaying my debt of gratitude to my Lord, my debt of gratitude to my parents, repaying the teachings of the ancient sages' virtue, I went as far as to believe that I need yield to no man.

However, running counter to my expectations, I earned a false reputation in the provinces, and I thought deeply about it. In spite of not yet becoming such a human being, trying to enhance a false reputation was called a taboo of heaven. At this point, I resolutely retired from my position and returned to a quiet life of rest. I was not afraid of suffering the calamities needlessly caused by others. I was then thirty-eight years of age.

Now, at forty-one, I live a quiet, secluded life, cultivating my heart and mind, and I make an effort, though small, toward enhancing moral character. Unfortunately, however, I have no good friends or teachers. With the oncoming age of fifty or sixty, there is no guarantee I can maintain my present concentration. I worry about this night and day. What must I do from now on to be able to wander in the realm of self-renunciation, to make my present will stronger and stronger? You too, Master, are someone who has experienced Wang Yangming's intuitive, innate-knowing school of learning. Therefore, were I to study under you, Master, who has a grasp of the Way, then you would certainly have a disciple in me just as Confucius had in one of his disciples, Ru Bei. Would you accept me as a student of yours? With this in mind, to inform you of my intentions, and to ask to learn from you, I have written this letter first of all.[1]

This letter, attached to a copy of *Senshindō sakki*—a record at times brimming with pious thought, the words of a wise man that pierced his soul as if from a light on high for half his life—was sent to the old Confucian, Satō Issai. In the letter, he opened his heart to Satō Issai, a man he had not yet met, without including the slightest look back on his own half-spent life.

Well-heeled worldlings, too given over to gold, adoring power—having *raga* (desire), lewdness, being wily, abject—who try to measure a person's worth through judgment of this earth alone, would do well to quietly and carefully read this letter. Coarse, soulless men as well, who try to fabricate a false worldview, manipulating one-sided, cold logic while scheming solely to usurp authority and the distribution of wealth, offending the eye with obstinate, spiteful gaze and dominating arm—wholeheartedly hateful—these men would do well to try to read this letter and to reflect deeply on themselves.

He definitely was not a person who crept about the face of the earth like a sly fox or a vile swine. He was a person seeking the Way, always pursuing lofty ideals, deepening his earnest introspection. To use the words of German foreign minister Walther Rathenau (1867–1922), he was always "illuminated by the light of spirit emanating from the kingdom of the absolute, fulfilling his role brightly on the stage of phenomenon." Broadening the way that seeks a life path, he was truly a protagonist in a tragedy who, in the end, fell to misbegotten plans, unaccepted by the world and unloved by people.

---

1. Translated from *Satō Issai's Writings*

Dear reader, please forget the confusing conventional titles applied to him—ringleader of insurgents, revolutionary, direct behaviorist, and so forth—and peruse this letter without preconceived notions.

According to what was reliably heard by Chūsai's senior disciple, Utsugi Kyōho, Chūsai, from his youth, was extremely short-tempered and violent. And because he couldn't help bullying other children in his group, his grandmother was worried and took him every day to Sumiyoshi Myōjin shrine, praying that his temperament might be cured. One day, a used-book vendor came to his grandmother's house selling his wares. Taking up a volume from among the other books, she saw that it was *The Great Learning*. She quickly bought it because she was an avid reader. Later, finding the book, Chūsai wondered what it was about and asked his grandmother to teach him. While being badgered by him, she taught him phrase by phrase, and the young Chūsai began to study in earnest. After that, his recklessness somehow or other also subsided (*Okada Kōan kikigakisho*).

That story is convincing when we look at Chūsai's later years. Having learned how to read, he quickly began to show extraordinary genius. In the third year of Bunka (1806), reaching the age of fourteen, he succeeded his grandfather, Masanojō, apprenticing as an officer of the law and serving at the guardhouse of the magistrate of Higashimachi, Osaka. As he also explained in his letter to Issai, he had to take the employment because his father, Heihachirō, had died when Chūsai was young.

For a person like him, with the temperament of an ox, having to endure such abuse as working for the police and being thrown together with petty officials lacking backbone—at a time, moreover, when his youthful ambition was engaged—brought him unbearable unhappiness. Then, by chance, searching his family's genealogy and other documents, he learned the fact that his predecessors were part of the Imagawa line, who served the house of Tokugawa and were presented with territory in Izu for their meritorious service. This greatly stimulated his sense of heroism and made his present social position all the more disagreeable.

The irresistible force of this unfairness he dissolved with single-hearted training and discipline in the martial arts. With this strength, he excelled at Nakajima-style artillery and mastered the Saburi-style of spearmanship. It is said that at the age of eighteen or nineteen, he dispatched a band of thirty or more pirates who were rampaging in Osaka.

Had Chūsai been born during the chaotic world of Sengoku, the Warring States period, perhaps he would have rolled up his sleeves, spat on his hands, and achieved great accomplishments, as well as wealth and rank. Or perhaps with the use of his sword, he could have cut his way through the entire region of Settsu, Kawachi, and Izumi. In actuality, that he was exceedingly good at strategic ruling is recorded with wonder in many commentaries (e.g., Shimamoto Nakamichi's *Seiten Hekireki*, Sakamoto Teisai's *Kōsai Hiki*, and Ishizaki Tōkoku's *Biography of Ōshio Heihachirō*).

However, in a world of peace replete with rules, the social standing of a petty official in feudal times would do nothing but despoil the spirit of even a hero. A true hero could turn his head away from things of this world and become an immortal sage. Wielding the power to catch a tiger and slay a dragon, a martial artist can also enter the way of philosophy. As the loved and respected sage Cheng Hao (1032–1085) observed, in jest, of the mysterious philosopher Shao Yong (1011–1077), "a great villain of troubled times." However, this ought not to be seen as a frivolous jest all the same. Therein lies a profound meaning, I should think.

Chūsai, an extraordinary genius, from the tender age of twenty was able to turn his pride and yearning for so-called great reputation and accomplishments toward familiarizing himself with learning and scholarship. It is said that from this time, he traveled to study in Tokyo and became a disciple of the Hayashi family. For the development of moral character and the pulse of life, no matter what obstacles are confronted, power must be expended in some direction.

While serving as a petty officer at the rank of *yoriki*, Chūsai's young pure heart, burning like a flame, vividly reflected the unsavory world around him. In his environment there was nothing to give value to deep emotions. Every time they came together, the petty officials thought of nothing but ways to conduct themselves as shrewdly as possible in the world, set intently on counting money or calculating the price of rice.

Before these men, the red-kimonoed criminals who were suspected of committing their own crimes and vices shuddered in terror, remorse, and excuse. Those who judged, who ought to have been merciful, were instead the arrogant officials. How were they actually qualified to judge? What indeed is the actual difference in worth between the judge and the judged? How could they even be given a fair trial?

Having nothing to look forward to, he frequently fell into deep contemplative thoughts. Whenever in this state, he felt an unspeakable anxiety and shuddered. He had to take up studying. He had to seek the truth. He had to create an educated man of character. This was, in other words, a keenly felt desire that was pressing upon him. Accordingly, driven by a deep inner desire, he knocked earnestly at the gate of Confucian learning.

Even amid these thoughts, he carried out his professional duties, always and relentlessly wielding the shield of justice, unlike his colleagues, unafraid in the least to stand up for his convictions or to face favoritism. He could not evade the territorial dispute that had remained unresolved for a long time during the Bunka years between the Kishū Domain—which was founded by relatives of the Tokugawa shoguns—and the Kishiwada Domain. Chūsai was assigned to the case and, within less than a month, ruled imposingly that the Kishū Domain was illegal, with Kishiwada Domain winning the lawsuit. So it has been told.

Once one has become self-aware, for him, life is an abyss that always lures the traveler with deep sighs of grief. Awakened to the meaninglessness and worthlessness of his life as an official, he thoughtfully considered the importance of education and again knocked intently at the gate of Confucian learning. This time, he was bewildered about the significance of learning, about so-called education. So-called Confucianists, at that time, either simply taught young people the commentary and reading, without comprehending old books such as the *Analects* or *Mengzi*, or made students learn formal literary works with assigned topics. So, if there was no listening to students' serious complaints from their innermost thoughts, neither was contemplation or criticism carried out. In other words, their education was meaningless and mechanical. In this regard, today's education in schools is in an even worse state of this bad habit. For Chūsai, brimming with life's creative energy that made him leap with joy, he once again became an unhappy man, given to melancholy because the urgent plea of his innermost desires fell on deaf ears. This was in the twenty-fourth year of his young life, radiating vitality like the verdure of spring.

The bud of his life was about to burst open. Now he needed only wait for a warm rain for the flower to blossom. Finally, "by the hand of providence," he unexpectedly acquired an imported volume of *Shin Gin Go* (*Shi Zheng Lu*). *Shin Gin Go* is a valuable book in which the author, Lu Kun of the Ming dynasty, compares his personal deep thinking about life to the moaning (*shin gin*) of a sick person. How hungrily Chūsai must have read it, his heart pounding in his chest. This speaks to the infinite meanings included in the few words of his letter.

This was the driving force at the beginning of his query into the study of Wang Yangming's intuitive/innate knowing, his fierce life force at last discovered in this his future path. His famous school, Senshindō (Senshindō gakudō, Academy of the Cavern of the Cleansed Mind) was also established at this time. His dignified appearance—pale complexion, long, narrow almond-shaped eyes, a bracing, slim stature of five-and-a-half-feet in height—became, for a long time, the idealized image of young people's enthusiasm.

In the first year of Bunsei, when he was twenty-six, he took by common-law marriage a wife named Yū. A foster daughter of the village headman, extremely level-headed, educated, though not a beauty, she helped Chūsai immensely and, it is said, managed family finances.

The following year, Kondō Jūzō was appointed chief archer of the magistrate of Osaka. Jūzō was a man of great discernment, and the two of them formed a close connection. The year after that, Takai Yamashiro-no-Kami, who headed Yamashiro Province, assumed a position in the Magistrate's Office in Higashimachi. Already past the age of sixty, he was a person of acute powers of judgment, a man of virtue, full of consideration and prudence. From the start, Chūsai's character was recognized, and he was selected to occupy a special chair as investigator, despite his humble status.

Chūsai's life, both interior and exterior, finally came into focus. Already, through attaining a deep understanding of Wang Yangming learning, he had convictions in his attitude toward life and of the self. As he had written in his letter to Issai, his inevitable innermost desire, which was pure and earnest, was aiming to perfect a moral character that was free to follow the ultimate life. Not in the least ought he to strive for conventional, traditional heteronomy. Whatever one is driven by depends on the solemn voice in one's heart. Consequently, things like authority and favoritism, becoming some kind of motive that determines behavior of the self, even for the self that is an official, are impossible. One can only accomplish one's natural responsibilities, including responsibilities pertaining to one's work.

Perhaps in the same way that obstinate *kleśā*, or worldly desires, are sermonized against, he fought bravely against the oppression of unjust power and favoritism. The stubborn and violent personality he was born with added fuel to the fire. A master observing this temperament might think the volatility could be harmful. Deploring this, a man of virtue would fear that it could go in the wrong direction. A coarse man wandering about like a fox or a pig, in the worst foulness, lacking a purpose in life, an idler—what honor would he have in the first place, standing before Chūsai?

In the spring of his thirty-second year, the seventh year of Bunsei (1824), Rai Sanyō first paid a visit to Chūsai, accompanied by Shinozaki Shōchiku (1781–1851). One was a hot-blooded man of tender sensibilities, the other a man of revolutionary temperament, a sincere and direct firebrand. They became friends and kindred spirits. At that time, Chūsai's Senshindō was gradually becoming successful, his heart and mind more and more inclined toward the enterprise of education to instruct young lives. He had a chronic lung affliction and suffered from a vexatious public office involving influence and favoritism that took a heavy toll on his physical well-being. He frequently divulged his intent to resign to Takai Yamashiro-no-Kami, who valued Chūsai highly as a man of talent, consoled him, and convinced him not to quit.

As time went on, he was entrusted with resolving various social problems. One among them, in the tenth year of Bunsei (1827), was the extermination of heretical believers. In any age, when the human heart deteriorates, inevitably, ascetics of a dubious nature appear. During the Bunka years, there was an ascetic called Mizuno Gunki, a man from Kyushu. He was the kind of character that fit the part—certainly not an ordinary person. He was well-informed, from beginning to end, in Buddhism and the study of divination. He was discerning in Chinese and Japanese history as well, and in personal physical appearance looked like a general. But because he was never honest in his disposition, he failed many times, and he was a vagabond between the capital and Kyushu. He became a Christian and learned hypnosis and other things, becoming capable of performing various miracles. Gradually, believers were converted, but holding secret ambitions, he constantly hatched a number of schemes. At the end of the seventh year of Bunsei, he died, empty-handed, unable to accomplish his intentions.

Incidentally, there was a woman named Toyoda Mitsugi who was his disciple. She was originally a *yūjo*, a prostitute, from the newly developed area in Kyoto's Nijō. Later, she became the wife of a certain yin-yang diviner. But, soon abandoned by her husband, she moved from place to place, became a disciple of Gunki's, and learned diverse secret arts. A place of prayer called Toyokunijin was erected in Yasaka, Kyoto, which became popular and attracted the foolish citizenry.

Her subordinates included women of dubious character, Harimaya Kinu and Kyōya Sano. Other people continued to gather around her: doctors, priests returned to secular life, and *rōnin*—masterless samurai warriors. From Kyoto and Osaka to the Banshū region, the secret religion started to expand. Because of this, numerous crimes were committed, and rumors of improprieties were rampant. But in the Magistrate's Office of Kyoto, no firm action was taken against them. It was said that the office could not interfere because many nobles and bureaucrats were privately involved.

Someone of extraordinary courage and resourcefulness was called for in order to resolve this problem. Takai Yamashiro-no-Kami put Chūsai in charge to make the arrests. Chūsai spent several months searching around Kyoto and determinedly apprehended more than sixty prominent people who were implicated. But since the case belonged to the category of religious beliefs, it actually took three years until they gained the Tokugawa shogunate council's approval. As a result of Chūsai's efforts, not a trace of their secret religion remained.

The following year, on the twenty-ninth day of the eleventh month of the eleventh year of Bunsei (1828), Chūsai celebrated, at his Senshindō, the three-hundredth anniversary of Wang Yangming's death. Three hundred years before, on the same day of the same month, the sage Wang Yangming, on his return from his last military expedition, never again rose from his sick bed and entered his eternal rest in Nan'an. Tanomura Chikuden, an eminent artist at the end of the Edo period, received purification and drew an image of Wang Yangming for Chūsai.

During that time, there was a cunning man called Yuge Shin'uemon, from the western division of the *yoriki* police, who tried hard to gain favor with the magistrate at the time, Naitō Hayatonoshō, and who, using the authority of his office as investigator, repeatedly committed crimes. Under his supervision were birds of a feather: Seigorō, Yasubei, Kangorō, Kichigorō, and other ruffians, who were administrators of police work at the four main precincts at that time: Tenma, Dōtonbori, Tennōji, and Tobita, respectively. With the master of the Shinmachi brothel as their right-hand man, this cohort conspired to make the law-abiding citizens suffer, while their own profits grew and grew. Although there were some among the officials who could see this outrageous behavior, and there were quiet rumblings about stricter enforcement of rules against such officials, what could they do? Yuge Shin'uemon was Naitō Hayatonoshō's favorite, and Seigorō, Yasubei, Kangorō, and Kichigorō were each chief of their respective precincts. There was no one telling higher authority to take notice and act against them.

The role of arraignment again had to wait for Chūsai. The government officials—the so-called capable and intelligent ones—did not do anything. Officials like this have no sincerity and consequently no moral valor and no consistent fundamental policy. Yamashiro-no-Kami's feelings toward the ailing Chūsai, not wanting Chūsai to leave his side, can also be sensed from this incident.

The handling of this difficult situation fell upon Chūsai, who burned with righteous indignation and reacted with rage toward it. This time he would put his hand into the den of iniquity of the viper that was uncoiling in the Magistrate's Office. The scoundrels that were sprawling across town would be executed. The more one pulled in the tendrils of crime, the stranger the areas they seemed to reach. When Chūsai wielded a wide-bladed knife at these crimes in his official position, he, of course, had to be resigned to the fact that his own life could be cut down in an untimely fashion.

In the spring of the twelfth year of Bunsei (1829), in the third month, Chūsai's beloved wife, Yū, shaved her head and was taken away into her father's estate. The people who knew them were deeply moved by the couple's resolve and preparation.

Chūsai's prosecution astounded them like a thunderclap in a hurricane. At once, the four precinct chiefs were sentenced to crucifixion; Yuge's sentence was *seppuku*, ritual suicide. Many years of crime were cleaned up in one sweep. The townspeople were grateful to Chūsai, as if he was the sun shining over them.

In times to follow, famine occurred in the countryside and peasant riots grew more frequent. During times of peace, the degeneration of the wealthy class of government officials worsened, and the people's fatigue and uneasiness darkened Chūsai's heart day by day.

It was the first year of Tenpō. In early spring, Chūsai also carried out the elimination of corrupt priests. The degeneration of priests in those days was remarkable; not a few of them gave rein to subversive customs concealed under the shadow of religion. He had a directive controlling customs issued beforehand, then strictly surveyed temples with priests and had every last depraved priest arrested.

As an investigator, Chūsai constantly achieved great results, as demonstrated above, and he received special treatment from Takai Yamashiro-no-Kami. His reputation as a scholar, a personality, and a famous official rang throughout the Kansai region. And at the same time, it must have deepened the envy and resentment of petty officials toward him. But this would pose no particular problem for Chūsai, who always had a direct, strong, and fierce character.

But a person of sincerity would feel a deep emptiness of self beneath the reputation. Though Chūsai had a strong personality, he was, however, weak as a god in front of the Way. What is more, he had chronic lung disease. At this time, he was only thirty-eight and still in his prime; but because of his health, he devoutly hoped to retire. Unexpectedly, in the seventh month of that year, Takai Yamashiro-no-Kami, growing infirm with old age, submitted his letter of resignation to the shogunate, at which time Chūsai pressed ardently for Yamashiro-no-Kami to accept his resignation and finally got his own wish to have his body return to feeling free as a bird in the sky. This struck terror in the hearts of the people of the world, who knew nothing about Chūsai's personal motivations.

As Chūsai said in a poem,

> Last night in the still house I first dreamed in quiet
> This morning, my mind like a hermit's
> Who knows my true friends are yet not a few
> How white the blossoms of autumn chrysanthemums

From then on, he devoted himself to the project of education, as a scholar polishing in earnest the spirit of revered memory, as a man of noble character now out of office. In the spring of the fourth year of Tenpō (1833), his *Senshindō sakki* (Cleansing the mind), a renowned work, was published at the request of his students.

Having been out of office, his easily excitable heart could not long remain calm. Society was already in collapse. It could not be stabilized unless some kind of world reformation came. Scandalous incidents frequently broke out in various places. It was a world that would "sadden a man of benevolence." Fortunately, a famous magistrate, Yabe Suruga-no-Kami Sadakane, had a change of post from Sakai to Osaka. While in Sakai, he soon heard of Chūsai's reputation. When he came to Osaka, he first put his child, Tsurumatsu, in Senshindō to study, treated Chūsai as a guest, and appointed him political advisor.

After Yamashiro-no-Kami, Chūsai gained the warm friendship of Yabe Suruga-no-Kami and was truly happy, an emollient to his volatile emotions. While divulging his burning love of country to Suruga-no-Kami only, he felt some degree of consolation. Or, while having a meal with Suruga-no-Kami and becoming indignant over the situation, he ate an entire fish, a gurnard, chomping it down from the head to the tail, while Suruga-no-Kami's attempts at consolation fell on deaf ears (*Tōko zuihitsu*).

From the end of the Bunsei period, poor harvests continued and violent storms also attacked the crops, making rice prices in the Kanto and other regions soar: 250 *mon* for one *shō*. As a consequence, the price of all goods shot up and showed no indication of coming down. Terrible cries of hunger were heard throughout the land.

At this point, Suruga-no-Kami offered the shogunate his recommendation to loosen the dunning of rice shipped to Edo. He also asked the daimyo of the western part of Japan to increase the quantity of rice shipped to Osaka, while strictly controlling its price. These measures brought relief to the poor and, because of this, the Osaka region was able to maintain comparative calm. He also gave careful consideration to economic policy that would stabilize the present situation.

During this time, riots broke out frequently in Harima and Mino. From the second month of the seventh year, a long spell of rain continued, with gentle rain falling every day, and around May and June a cold snap hit. In July, violent storms swept across the whole nation. Rice plants could not be cultivated; wheat, millet, and other grains could not grow to harvest. All travel in the nation was stopped because of this, and the coming and going of passengers was cut off. Rice paddies and fields were destroyed, and the price of rice jumped to 300 *mon*; corpses could be seen everywhere along the roadside; people lay where they died.

Just when Yabe Suruga-no-Kami, the famous magistrate, had himself secured the safety of the region, he was called back to the executive Magistrate's Office in Edo. After that, a foolish politician by the name of Atobe Yamashiro-no-Kami was assigned to the Higashimachi Magistrate's Office. This might or might not be seen as fate. Now, the world had become such a place that it seemed no one but Ōshio Chūsai, he without any official title, grieved for the people. Moreover, at that time, the borders of Japan were under threat from foreign countries.

With trouble stirring both at home and abroad, Chūsai felt deep regret for the deterioration of the spirit of the people. To inspire the samurai ethos, in the autumn of the seventh year of Tenpō he invited Fujishige Magosaburō, who was then master of Nakajima-style artillery, and his son Ryōzaemon to Osaka. Chūsai, starting with his son Kakunosuke, made the students study cannonry and planned practice exercises on the beach of Sakai for the following spring. However, life being difficult to gauge, his plans turned into irrevocable insurrection with the launching of an assault on the miscreant government and the wealthy.

In autumn, in the eleventh month, threatened by a rice shortage due to continued poor harvests, the Osaka Magistrate's Office, lacking measures or policies, issued severe edicts on reductions in shipping. As a result, the most devastating effects were suffered by people of the Kyoto region, who up to then had looked to Osaka for their rice. They sensed that supply routes would be shut off suddenly and, to make matters worse, the price of rice was boosted even higher by sly accursed merchants.

The people of Fushimi, Kyoto, staggering like hungry ghosts, crept into Osaka to buy a bag or two of rice. But the merciless evil officials of the Atobe faction apprehended every single one of the pitiful, poor people. It is said that up to 56,000 of the Kyoto population of 300,000 people died of starvation (*Sen'andō* posthumous manuscript, vol. 1).

The extremely foolish Atobe, deceiving the people of Kyoto and Osaka to the point of death, as described above, also obeyed orders from the shogunate and, working in the shadows, forwarded rice from Osaka to Edo. Chūsai, while not of the masses, flew into a rage with his entire being. He at once confronted the Magistrate's Office and pressed them to open government warehouses. However, the Magistrate's Office offered no satisfactory solutions. Finally, after being pressed again several times, the magistrate conveyed the message that because of necessary preparations for next spring's inauguration ceremony of shogun Ieyoshi, the successor, to take place concurrently with the retirement of Ienari, the eleventh shogun, relief and aid would be impossible. To such a thoughtless response from the authorities, Chūsai could only give a deep sigh.

At the beginning of the new year (1837), to make matters worse, an epidemic spread far and wide. Because of deaths from starvation and illness, corpses had to be dealt with everywhere on a daily basis, creating more problems. Exhausting his civility to government offices, Chūsai tried to work with wealthy merchants not connected with the government to increase the shipping of rice to Osaka by limiting loans from the merchants to daimyo. The daimyo and the wealthy, however, did not see this as in their interest. Therefore, they took no notice of the problem. Trying various ways to come up with some solution, he applied for a relief loan of 120,000 *ryō* from Kōnoike and other wealthy people, using his own stipend and his disciples' stipends as collateral.

This time, even the wealthy were moved by Chūsai's sincerity and character, and advanced to the point of approving his request without objection. But an understanding of what is important is the foresight of the wealthy. In the end, they inquired into getting official approval of the issue. How strange! And what was Atobe's directive? That Heihachirō's [another name of Chūsai] action of self-aggrandizement and not understanding his social position were an impropriety in the extreme; anyone lending Chūsai money without orders from the Magistrate's Office would be severely punished! Thereupon, the wealthy, lacking backbone and trembling in fear, bluntly refused Chūsai's request, the response to which he had been waiting for in anticipation and expectation.

Heihachirō's fervor was brought to a boil. He threw a book and shouted, "Scoundrels! Have you such contempt for me? Very well, I will do everything possible for the poor, even if I must sacrifice myself!"

These men of unjust politics and corrupt commerce, what authority have they? These men must be eliminated immediately and the life of the people saved. The correct and solemn man of virtue made a complete change of face and became a leader of direct action. On the eighth day of the new year, his group of loyal and faithful men numbered more than thirty.

The warehouse full of books soon became useless. He sold every book in his library and raised 650 *ryō* in funds, which he distributed as munificent relief to thirty-three villages over a three-day period, on the sixth, seventh, and eighth day of the second month. The people, pleasantly surprised, gathered like clouds. The asinine, cowardly Atobe Jōshū did not succeed in trying to stop it.

During this time, Chūsai gave detailed instructions to his family and left them in the care of relatives in Kawachi. On the night of the fifteenth of the second month, his cohorts gathered for the first time at Senshindō and talked over their stratagem. On the appointed day, the nineteenth of the second month, the Festival of Confucius, they decided to launch an assault on the occasion of Atobe Jōshū's inspection tour of the city, when he would guide Horii Iga-no-Kami, newly appointed as the western magistrate.

From that night on, their manifesto was circulated around the neighboring villages:

> The poverty of the masses for a long time has lost the blessing of heaven. When a petty person governs a nation and disasters occur, wise men of old sternly cautioned the ruler and officials of posterity. Lord Ieyasu, too, had said that saving people in distress was the basis of a benevolent government. For more than 250 years, officials involved in important politics have lived luxuriously in times of peace, bribes were made publicly, even trivial people who had some connections with the powerful were promoted rapidly to important posts, working their intellects only to devise ways to fatten their own purses. By ordering excessive burdens on peasants in the domain, the whole world suffered. In spite of there being no one who does not resent such governments, all those officials, from Edo to the countryside, yielded today's results. His Highness the Emperor, since the start of the Ashikaga shogunate, has had the same social standing as a retired emperor. Consequently, there was no avenue by which the people could make accusations against the government. Perhaps heaven knows this and has unleashed earthquakes and fires year after year and various natural calamities, causing crop failure.
>
> These all were acts of divine punishment. Still, the people above paid no attention, the gang of evil petty officials conducted politics as usual, only making the people below suffer, involved only in means to collect rice and money. The hardship of the small-scale farmers made people like us, observing from the shadows, sorrowful. Having no authority nor virtue of high position, we had little choice but to watch helplessly. However, at the worst possible time, the price of rice rose astronomically, and the officials of the Osaka Magistrate's Office forgot any semblance of benevolence, conducting politics for their own convenience. They shipped rice to Edo but not to the emperor's residence in Kyoto. They arrested someone who came to buy no more than a bag or two of rice. It was an outrageous situation; every place should have been treated equally under the Tokugawa administration. What made a distinction was the

absolute lack of benevolence from the magistrates; self-indulgent public notices were sent out repeatedly, cautioning self-importantly of living in idleness in Osaka, as mentioned before, because they were insignificant people to the point of being exceedingly shameless and insolent.

The rich of Osaka, among the "three capitals" Kyoto, Edo, and Osaka, for years made money by giving loans to daimyo and by stealing amounts of rice stipends. They lived in unprecedented affluence and felt no fear watching the recent divine punishment of natural calamities, nor did they make an attempt to save the beggars and impoverished dying of hunger. They ate fine foods, visited the houses of their mistresses, drank expensive sake like water in pleasure houses with the daimyo's retainers, and indulged in their usual amusements with actors and geisha during these times of want. What was the meaning of all this behavior? Wielding the power they clung onto, these officials could not save the people but only played at speculating on the Dōjima exchange on a daily basis—not deeds that are suited to the Way. Their deeds have no forgiveness under heaven.

Confined to this house, we cannot remain silent much longer and not be seen. Unavoidably, I have sacrificed my family for the sake of the country and now have called on sympathizers, first to exterminate the officials who are making the people suffer and then to exterminate the rich, who have grown in arrogance. Those scoundrels should distribute both the rice and money in storehouses. Those of you who do not possess paddies and fields in Settsu, Kawachi, Izumi, and Harima, or even if you do, those who cannot support mothers, fathers, wives, and children, hearing that riots could happen in Osaka at any time, should come running, regardless of the distance. Our purpose is to build again a society of ideals, based on the way of governing of Emperor Jimmu. (*Yasuoka's note*: Abridged translation of the Manifesto)

In the dead of the night, an unusual presence rushed into the official residence of Atobe Jōshū. A Chūsai sympathizer, Hirayama Sukejirō, turned traitor and leaked a report of Chūsai's plot. Dumbfounded, Jōshū had known of no plans taking action against him, and the western magistrate, having just been appointed, of course had no way of knowing. Amid the confusion, one day elapsed. On the night of the eighteenth, Yoshimi Kurōemon, another turncoat, dispatched the same news to the new western magistrate, and no time was lost in relaying the message to the eastern magistrate, Atobe. Night gave way to dawn. Jōshū didn't have anything to do except to spread disorder throughout the Magistrate's Office.

That night, two of Chūsai's loyal compatriots were on duty at the Magistrate's Office. Learning that their plot had been discovered, they turned tail and tried to run off. One of them fell down in the sudden scuffle, and one barely escaped to flee to Senshindō and report the crisis. Girding themselves for the next day's insurrection, sympathizers had gathered at Senshindō for an all-night rally and were in the midst of indignant lamentation over the evils of the times when an urgent report arrived. The big moment had finally come. All present were ready for making a roar before the rebellion—but instead grew quiet.

After a short time, as if holding something back, Chūsai, standing next to Ōi Shōichirō, a man in his prime, commanded him, "Go and kill Kyōho!"

Responding to his voice, as if struck by lightning, Ōi stood up. Tears shone in Chūsai's eyes.

On the evening of the seventeenth day, among the people on a boat to Aji-kawa, came an imposing young samurai of goodly proportions. Accompanying him was a person who appeared to be a student, and after a while they entered the gate of Senshindō. The usually solemn academy was, on this day, brimming with a feeling of unrest. His thoughtful eyes looked about in all directions, half suspiciously, half nostalgically, as if unable to suppress his emotions, and he seated himself quietly in the provided place. Before long, food and drink was presented before him, and Master Chūsai entered hurriedly but smiling. From his greeting it was known that he was Chūsai's leading disciple, Utsugi Kyōho, recently traveling to study in Kyushu.

A man of composure and dignity, courage and resourcefulness, Kyōho, to the boldly fearless Chūsai, was always Chūsai's only reliable man and his joy. Chūsai, holding back the serious matter before him, perhaps too soon to exchange cups of sake in celebration of Kyōho's return to Osaka, looked at his beloved Kyōho and spoke his mind frankly about the recent occurrence, pressing him about complicity in the plot. Kyōho listened silently from beginning to end and, adjusting his collar, replied to his teacher:

> There are any number of reasons for your actions, but what you are going to do is requite violence with violence. Your actions are too rash. As a result, it will cause disruption and end in a disaster—nothing more.

In a tearful voice he remonstrated with his teacher. The mute Chūsai was about to send him home without further ado. But seeing this, the hot-blooded, fervent followers, full of anger, urged Chūsai to punish him first.

Realizing that nothing could be done, and having already reached this point, Kyōho secretly set his resolve and retired quietly to the new classroom within Senshindō.

> To have a finite body and to be able to sacrifice one's self to the infinite Way, in that there is no resentment. Even if I were to die here now, ending my physical body, the truth that was in me shall live. I wish only when I die to prevent, at all cost, any calamity befalling my brothers.

On the eighteenth day, he put down these thoughts in a short letter, deliberately writing his childhood name but no recipient's name, and had it delivered to his older brother, Shimofusa, in his home village of Ōmi, a follower who had been accompanying him for some years.

At the dawn of the nineteenth day, Ōi Shōichirō took up a spear in anger and visited Kyōho in the new classroom. Kyōho had just left the privy and quietly stepped out on the veranda when Ōi shouted, "On Master's orders!" and his spear gleamed like a flash of lightning at Kyōho's chest. "Wait," Kyōho commanded gently, and finished washing his hands, then seated himself upright on the floor of the corridor to receive what awaited him. The one giving the orders, holding back tears, was the master, the one about to meet his death, in silence, the beloved disciple.

On the morning of the nineteenth, they started firing on Kenkoku-ji, the temple that honors Tokugawa Ieyasu, and proceeded to Tenma-machi, then on to Senba. This place is still famous today as a place of residences of the wealthy. The artillery of the righteous army started a conflagration that burned all of north Tenma. A mob that hoped for this gathered, and they immediately helped the momentum of the righteous army. Never had such a catastrophe occurred since the Siege of Osaka. The houses of the rich were burned, beginning with Kōnoike's—Mitsui's, Iwakiya's, Shimaya's, Masuya's—all plundered and reduced to ashes, not a one remaining. Atobe's forces cut down a part of Tenjin-bashi and, keeping guard of the castle, had the air of onlookers. Finally, the soldiers of the castle marched out and began close combat with the righteous army. Atobe Jōshū and Horii Iga continued firing and suffered an ugly defeat. However, the mob and the righteous army pitched with fear when two or three of the leaders fell, and by night the revolt dissipated. Chūsai and his son went into hiding somewhere.

A month had passed since the turmoil. On the twenty-sixth day of the third month, someone reported that Chūsai, father and son, were sequestered at Miyoshiya Gorōbei's house in Osaka's Utsubo-chō. Gorōbei was promptly taken into custody. By the dawn of the twenty-seventh, dozens of guards surrounded the Miyoshiya house. With the roaring of artillery, black smoke billowed from inside the house. When the smoke had faded, the cowardly guards stepped in and found two blackened corpses. On the twenty-ninth day, Chūsai's family were all arrested and sent to Osaka. People tearfully lined the roadside to say farewell.

In this way, Chūsai's forty-five years of life came to an end. From the beginning, his heroic deeds did not escape the criticism of the ordinary people or master samurai. However, now "there was neither right nor wrong." To the masses of society, he has given contemplation and warm inspiration for eternity. In the words of Dante, "O spirit of indignation, will the mother that embraces us ever be happy?"

12

The Essence of Governance
On Saigō Nanshū's Political Thought

When human beings are caged for a long time by worldly affairs, they yearn for a fresh mountain view of fountains and rocks. When so-called culture makes human beings resort to blandishments and fawning smiles, they recall the pleasantness of natural mountains and words of simplicity. These things complement our true feelings as human beings. At this late hour, even without lending an ear to the discussions of civilization's critics, modern life is too much winning by deceit and run by the spurious and the counterfeit, leaving almost nothing to be truly relished and worth saving. Surely no one can think that a hypocritical, deceitful life, as we live today, is absolutely a culture of truth. True culture must be pure, unadulterated nature and an improvement. As for today, I think we desire more honest and simple action, and genuinely want to listen to the words of the earth.

Can the thought, speech, and conduct of political scientists, sociologists, and other thinkers in general really cause direct, new moral feelings in the citizenry? And can the election campaigning and speeches that representatives of each party conduct in continuous rivalry really inform the people of what politics is? The intellectual and political life of the nation, presented through scholars who never tire of playing with concepts, and politicians who, in Zhuangzi's words, "are governed by lowly, popular learning and [are] misled by popular thinking" (*Zhuangzi, Outer Chapters*), seems distant from us today.

Studying the political thought of Saigō Nanshū, the great, trustworthy leader of early Meiji, who appeared at just the right time and who is still considered a great leader today, perhaps one can feel in the heart and mind its pleasant and vigorous power, as if coming in contact with a true man who has mastered the Way. Through him, we can transcend the despicable acts of politicians and scholars that today confront us, and can learn the means and efforts that will open peace to the ages.

Nanshū said in his last injunction, conveying his view of civilization,

Civilization is a word of praise for being able to universally follow the Way. Civilization is not in the empty show of beautiful appearances in solemn courtly dress.

Listening to what people say, one cannot understand in the least what is civilized and what is uncivilized. Of late, I was able to discuss this with a certain person. We argued that "the West is uncivilized," and "No, it's civilized. Why do you insist upon saying uncivilized?" So I said, "Actually, if it is civilization we're talking about, it must be a civilization guided by earnest persuasion, based on kindness toward uncivilized countries, without which it will lead to inhuman atrocities toward the uncivilized, unenlightened country." My saying "self-interest is uncivilized" made him shut his mouth, and his speechlessness produced laughter. (*Nanshūō Ikun* 11)

Putting aside for a moment the heated debate on the differences between culture and civilization, true civilization is not making social life convenient, adorning it with mechanical, structural successes. Indeed, as stated by Nanshū, the underlying principle of civilization must be "practicing the Way universally." What do we mean by "the Way"? It is the work of heaven and earth's developing formation. Humans, too, live in the Way. Through the Way of heaven and earth we have parents and we know our own life, learn to love people, and come to respect heaven. Put in other words, it is development away from individualistic life toward supraindividualistic life, from physical life toward a spiritual life that envelops it.

The national life of human beings, having developed from primitive times, has already made significant progress toward realizing the Way. In this national life, the people don't simply stop at economic self-interest, and the more they strive toward a higher life of great worth, the more it can be called civilization.

Therefore, to say that a nation is civilized means, at minimum, that it has a stature beyond mere existence as a sovereign country. In other words, it is more than simply a rich country with a strong army. Furthermore, a civilization must possess the characteristic of continuing to live under lofty-minded ideals, not engaging in self-interested invasion of other countries. Civilized nations, most fundamentally, must have demonstrated the quintessential qualities of the Way, having striven for self-improvement and self-realization, shining the light on other countries, and facilitating the evolution of heaven and earth.

When civilization today is viewed through the lens of the above ideals, it is something remarkably uncivilized indeed, just as Nanshū proclaimed it to be.

Yoshida Shōin records in his *Shōkasonjuku Ki*, "To begin with, as people, what we should most respect is 'the obligations between a lord and vassal.' As an individual state, the principle that we must consider most is 'Ka-i no ben.'"

"Ka-i no ben" is, namely, the difference between civilization, Ka (literally, "China"), and barbarism—nothing else. One might venture to say that the word "China" (Ka) should not be monopolized by the country of that name. For example, in the preface to his *Actual Facts about the Central Realm* (*Chūchō Jijitsu*), Yamaga Sokō strongly advocates the name "Chu (center)-ka" for Japan.

Consequently, those who are the civilized nations have not the least shame about the matter of a temporary peace. Obviously, because a temporary peace means a life of attachment—without idealism—it is merely an attempt at existence. As Nanshū explains,

> A nation should follow a righteous path and its people should be willing to die in its defense. Lacking this resolve, proper relations with foreign countries cannot be achieved, resulting in submission to their will, mainly for harmony, and cowering at their might. This invites contempt, destroys amicable relations all the more, and ultimately results in capitulation to their system. (*Nanshūō Ikun* 17)

Viewed from the worldly-mindedness of the fundamental desire to live, dying for one's country is unthinkable and would be characterized as an argument of youthful ardor. Of course, in any case, to die in vain is a wretched thing; but surviving full of shame is also not a true life. There are cases of enduring one's shame to live and also cases of giving up one's life to live in eternity.

However, considering that unless one is resigned to living in the eternal now—ready to die at any moment—one cannot achieve true forbearance. In the life of the nation as well, one must realize how great is the significance of resigning oneself to the notion of being able to die for the country.[1]

Not a few are those who believe that declaring a willingness to die for the sake of the nation is a remarkably dangerous and reckless act of its citizenry; this is one line of thought. However, the desire for life is a basic human sentiment—the strongest instinct. Even at the level of national affairs, it is easy to fall into a peace-at-any-price way of thinking, so this concern for reckless danger is negligible, it must be said. Instead, today, the worldly-mindedness that desires temporary peace is too strong. For that reason, the national life runs toward servility and "invites the contempt" of others, all the more destroying amicable relations, somehow accepting "*capitulation to their system.*" In view of diplomacy toward Russia and policies toward England and America, is not this something keenly felt?

Old Nanshū inveighed against these dangers:

> When a country is insulted or disgraced, including the collapse of a country, the fundamental duty of government is to tread the path of justice and adhere to principles. Delving heatedly into daily matters of economy and finance may give the illusion of being heroes and great men. However, when it comes to the matter of potential bloodshed with other nations, they only plan for temporary peace, for the close at hand,

---

1. The true eternal exists in the now. To love the eternal now is to embody the ultimate value. Without this resolve, it would be impossible to cope with a life of abiding shame.

abandoning principles and forgetting the word "conflict." If they fail the fundamental duty of government, calling themselves a commercial law department, it is all the more not government.

Does one not feel consumed by the heated, severe words of the great teacher? We now live in a world in which pacifism, nonresistance, culturalism, and other doctrines are in vogue. For example, being subjected to explanations by distinguished names of various stripes in newspapers, magazines, and courses, one might think: What kind of world is this, deluged with sages, wise men, and men of virtue? However, when we see such people face real-world situations, one wants to murmur, as did Chinzei Hachirō (also known as Minamoto no Tametomo, 1139–1170), "What can a cultured person actually do? It is sufficient that I am an ignorant countryman of eastern Qi."

Since human beings developed scholarship in general, especially since the diffusion nowadays of modern philosophy, science, literature, and the arts, our lives have unconsciously tended toward hollowness. Playing tricks of logic and rousing the peripheral nerves are scholars whose work it is to build concepts. Under the influence of literati who create a world of illusion, everyone tends to lose sight of steadfast devotion to improvement and problem-solving and run wild in their doctrines and movements, busy with petty things, turning falsehoods into truth.

However, when we stand on the earth under the bright sunshine, our lot in life is indeed fraught with difficulties. We must conquer evil through the principles (理 *li*, fundamental principle of neo-Confucianism) of our life, both internally and externally. The fight against evil in all its aspects is the duty of human beings. By evading this, there is no possibility of living a life of truth. However, many pitiful people, when the forces of evil are strong, yield to this, or submit to it completely. They have not yet reached the point of clear self-consciousness of good and evil. In chaos, they are swept up in the current of these forces.

More despicable are people of cowardice and cunning. Even knowing evil, when seeing its strength, as with letting the sleeping dog lie, they assume an evasive attitude that doesn't confront or interfere. They are what is called the band without courage, who, seeing justice and honor, perform it not. Each of them, in the light of the true principles of life, is a character that should be rejected. However, men sometimes embellish their servile character in order to deceive their conscience under the pretext of pacifism, nonresistance, and other doctrines.

Consequently, deceiving their conscience was not their intention from the beginning. These doctrines cannot be spoken of without traveling the difficult path. When spoken of, they lapse into academic, abstract, impractical theories. For one who can become clear of heart, reading the *gathas* (poetic verse of Buddhism) by teachers of the correct path is without doubt a good feeling, but it is completely different from the realm of true enlightenment attained through discipline and training. Nevertheless, in our religious heart and mind, we feel a sense of satisfaction even lacking such disciplined efforts. Mistakenly understanding this as the true realm of enlightenment, were one to lead people to religion with knowledge written down from the scriptures, this would be an egregious *ultra vires*. The existence today of not a few of these delusions in pacifists and non-resisters cannot, in any way, be denied.

A self-styled humanitarian who requites violence with violence is more earnest, *in his inner life*, than someone who drifts about in a false life in such a way. They do considerable harm externally and in their utilitarianism, but they have a rather more vigorous energy. They have the intense will to challenge an enemy. It is this life force that is the basis of growth, and if this life force is lost, a mental and emotional life is all for naught.

Violent, retributive thought, however, certainly must be called infantile. A life of truth does not fall to violence and is found in becoming a virtuous person.

In other words, separating the person from the sin, sublimating in deep benevolence, hating the sin but not the sinner. Save that person from crime however possible, having the resolve to maintain the public welfare of other people. Decry violence, even with a show of strength if necessary, in the case of having one's will ignored. This is called *bu* (武).

As the character shows, *bu* is created from *hoko* (戈, weapon) and *todomu* (止, to stop)—thus, "to stop weapons," meaning natural effort that should realize peace—a life that is truly free. Put another way, an earnest (*shinken*, "real sword") life, is then *bu*, a righteous force. Understanding *bu* this way, one can begin to teach skillfully, with leniency and flexibility, and feel awakened to the significance of true pacifism and nonresistance—the religious psychological state that does not lead one off the true path.

Looking at reality directly, in a capricious life that cannot be lived in earnest, can we hope and pray for true human peace and happiness? Somehow leave behind the idiocy of an eye for an eye and a tooth for a tooth, and transcend an obstinate notion of retribution and a feeling of malevolence. Even so, individually, a religious psychological state has been opened all the same through the spirit of many great men. However, in the life of nations that have developed of late, the still-weak ones are forced to take a slavish or escapist attitude, while the strong ones use violence. Presently, a true *shōbu* (respect for *a righteous force*) state is rarely seen, except in Japan.

Japan is the only *shōbu* state, and the people of Japan are a *shōbu* people. Said differently, *shōbu* means having a powerful will (a great and magnanimous spirit) and striving toward an earnest life. In one dimension, *shōbu* constitutes the *moral principles* that win over the self. In another dimension, it becomes the *politics* that govern a society of laxity. Politics are equivalent to moral principles, the workings of the rule of heaven over human beings—nothing other than the function of the universe in operation, cultivating all creation.

People in the West long ago believed that politics were carried out by God's representatives. After that, as intellect grew, politics was interpreted to be a human contract. In recent times, as humans prospered, they considered politics as their own great household, and they completely lost the feeling of piousness, reflecting only that their own prosperity was the invisible favor of heaven, and that it was God's blessing. In short, politics amounts to nothing more than the nation making its way through the world, in the same way as so-called moralists use "morals" as a way to make a living. This, I think, is the direct source of the evil in politics that is today so despised.

Consequently, in order for politics to become true politics, it too must have a recovery of normative self-consciousness. Statesmen and citizens alike, unless they do not become self-assured-but-unawakened toward their own lives, must cultivate a sense of respect for heaven.

Nanshū wrote in his last injunction,

> Inasmuch as governing the nation as established by the court is to follow the laws of heaven, it must not, to any degree, involve selfishness. Indeed, making one's heart impartial, treading the true path, choosing wise people, electing people who can perform their duties ably and can administer government—this is the will of heaven. Therefore, once the qualifications are confirmed that he is wise and can perform his duties well, one must be willing to yield one's own position immediately. Worst of all is to reward someone, however earnestly he may serve the state, who has been given a position he cannot fulfill competently. I was asked to reply to this question: "Government bureaucracy selects the appropriate person, grants the position, and rewards the person with a stipend for meritorious service, instructing him to use it wisely. Accordingly, in the classics, a prudent counselor of the Yin period said in a letter of appointment: 'to give a high position to a person of high virtue and much remuneration when much meritorious service is given.' Does this mean that a bureaucratic position is to be arranged based on personal virtue and capability, and that remuneration is to be based on meritorious service?" Happily, I replied, "That is precisely the case." (*Nanshūō Ikun* 1)

A person of virtue is assigned to government service, and merit is rewarded with remuneration—this, I think, is a fortuitous circumstance for human beings. Since all virtue is the essential workings inside human beings to accomplish the will of heaven, and since enriching the life of the people is the original duty of government service, naturally a person of virtue must be appointed. Meritorious service generally depends on talent, and talent may be said to be originally one aspect of virtue. However, virtue is usually something overall and unified, and talent, on the other hand, should be understood as various abilities to help in specific aspects of life.

As Shiba Kō (Sima Guang, 1019–1086) argues in the beginning of *Shijitsu-gan* (*Zizhi Tongjian*, Comprehensive mirror to aid in government), one can both "accomplish good with talent" and also "accomplish bad with talent." Accomplishing good with talent is, in a word, the power of virtue; accomplishing bad with talent is a weak virtue. Sima Guang names the one whose virtue is greater than one's talent is called by the general term *kunshi* (君子, person of virtue); one whose talent exceeds one's virtue, he summarily calls a *shōjin* (小人, a petty person).

Though useful, it is easy for a petty person to do wrong. Consequently, the petty person, even with talent, always tends to be detested by the person of virtue. In the *Tōkaki* and in other places, Hō Seigaku (Fang Xiaoru, 1357–1402) wrote the most scathing rejection of the petty person. Sima Guang also argued that if the wise, the saintly, and the person of virtue, taken together, cannot reject the petty person, it is better to take a foolish one. Fang Xiaoru also showed his loathing of the petty person: "Disorder can happen in the world when the wise and the talented run amok."

Kumazawa Banzan characterized the person of virtue and the petty person in the following ways:

The Person of Virtue
- The benevolent person's heart that does not waver is like a great mountain. Because he is without desires, he is still and at peace.
- The benevolent person makes his heart the great vacuity; heaven and earth, all creation, mountains, rivers, and seas all become one in him. Spring, summer, winter, autumn, light and darkness, day and night, rain and dew, frost and snow are his discipline. Right and wrong are the yin yang of life; life and death are the way of day and night. Like what you will, dislike what you will; his mind is calm with righteousness.
- The wise person's heart is not torpid, but like flowing water. It flows from holes and low roads, finally reaching the four seas. He moves the will, does not like cleverness, he responds to all things that must be. His conduct is natural, without intentions.
- The wise person looks at things as things. He does not desire what is similar to him. Therefore, he befriends a wide range of people without discrimination and does not compare. The petty person looks at things as himself. He desires what is similar to himself. Therefore, he compares and tends to befriend those who are congenial to him.

- A virtuous person's will looks inward, discreet in that he knows himself, and does not seek to be known by others and mingles with the gods of heaven and earth. His character is like the gentle wind on a fine day and the moon shining in the sky cleared by the rain.

- When the heart is emptied, there is nothing to possess. Therefore, he likes to inquire. He loves the excellent and shows mercy on the inferior. He does not covet riches or despise the poor and lowly. Wealth and rank become a function of people; they are only above because of their roles. The poor and lowly take life as it comes; they are only below by circumstance. For wealth and rank, if there is no service, disorder will follow. For the poor and lowly, if there is not acceptance of their circumstances, they are destroyed. When one acquires wealth and rank, carry out wealth and rank; when one becomes poor and lowly, carry out poor and lowly. Enjoying all destinies, one simply carries on without undue angst.

- To maintain one's will, one should choose Bo Yi (伯夷), a man of integrity, as a teacher. Wave your robe from the highest mount and let your feet be as if washed in the flow of 10,000 *ri*. Accepting the people, one should learn Liu Xia Hui (柳下惠), who is broad minded and tolerant. One should become like the endless sky, letting birds fly freely, and like the boundless sea, allowing the fish to jump.

- Even if other people think it is all right, he does not do what gods look upon with disfavor. Even if others think it bad, he does what gods find just. He does not kill a servant for a minor crime to gain a county or a prefecture; why would he follow a rebellion or link arms with injustice?

The Petty Person
- When the heart falls into self-interest, there is ignorance. How frenetic it is going in and out of worldly affairs!

- When one's heart and thoughts are turned outward, one is careful to build a front for others to see, or their heads are empty, or they think only of themselves.

- He prefers obedience and hates disobedience, loves life and hates death; only his requests are many. Obedience becomes the seeds of enjoying wealth and rank. Disobedience belongs to the category of the afflictions of the poor, lowly, and troubled.

- Loving, he desires one to have life; hating, he desires one to have death—all know nothing of life.

- When the reputation is deep, sincerity is shallow; when greed is deep, he knows nothing of morality.

- He is envious of those of more wealth and rank than himself. He despises those poorer and lowlier than himself, or he slights them. If there are people smarter or more talented than him, he does not profit from them. He befriends those who follow him. Ashamed to ask questions, he lives his entire life in ignorance.

+ Even if true morality is not realized in something, if it garners the praise of others, he will do it. If true morality is realized but is criticized by others, he will cease it. One who seeks a reputation in the eyes of others is driven by self-interest. A person of fame and fortune is called a petty person; following the desire for form, he knows not the Way.

+ Hearing praise of oneself, even if it is overstated, he is proud and joyful; hearing criticism of oneself, he is surprised when that is what he actually did and angry if he didn't do it. He wears peccadilloes as decoration and does wrongs, but he knows no reform. People all know a person's character, know the bad side of a person's nature, and recite these things. However, he himself thinks he is good at hiding, thinking no one knows. Focused solely on his own desires, he barricades himself against remonstration and cannot accept it.

+ Looking at other's mistakes, he thinks he has wisdom. He cannot help but boast.

+ Differing from the Way, he seeks praise; turning his back on morality, he seeks profit. A disreputable samurai uses flattery as a means to gain an opportunity; the masses seek to deceive others to make a profit. Against this immorality, riches and precious things are like floating clouds. Even if this finally extends to the destruction of their posterity, there is no understanding of its consequences.

+ The petty person thinks only about himself but knows not other people. If there is profit for him, there is no consideration for others' losses. In the near future, his body is destroyed; in the distant future, the whole family is destroyed. These are the ones who are proud and think they are clever. There is nothing more foolish than this. When the masses censure, one should not censure, and when the masses get angry, one should not get angry. Once anger and greed have been cast aside, the heart will finally rest.

Thus light is shone on the character of both the person of virtue and the petty person who has no place to hide.

Nevertheless, the petty person and his cleverness must not be indiscriminately eliminated as a matter of course. The argument of the above-mentioned person of virtue is nothing other than attempting to remonstrate against the everyday conduct of human life. The petty person's use of cleverness to complete his life, and its utility, is, on the other hand, an important problem of life. On this point, however, in the classics, what the prudent counselor of the Yin period said in a letter of appointment still teaches deep precaution.

Nanshū also teaches on this matter:

> Overstating the differences between a person of virtue and a petty person when employing people can lead to disaster. That is because, since the beginning of time, seven or eight out of ten people in the world are petty people; so it is important to consider the feelings of the petty person, take their strong points, assign them to a small role, and develop their gifts and talents. As Master Tōko [Fujita Tōko, 1806–1855] stated, when a petty person has abilities and a role to play, he must be assigned a position. Having said that, as for granting him an important position or installing him in a high office, he certainly must not be given a top position, for fear of his overturning the country. (*Nanshūō Ikun* 6)

As a modern way of thinking, the person of virtue/petty person debate may be meaningless. That is to say, for these kinds of people, a person receives environmental control. Accordingly, they believe the human mind cannot be changed without first changing the surrounding systems. However, there is no separating oneself from one's undertakings. In the words of Nanshū,

> However much one argues systems and methods, without arranging appropriate resources for appropriate places, results will be difficult to achieve. Since it is possible to carry out plans only if one first has the people to do it, people are the greatest treasure. It is essential to try to make oneself such a valued person. (*Nanshūō Ikun* 20)

We might consider the ironic words of the German biologist Ernst Haeckel. If we, as human beings, degenerate into social vertebrate animals, it would be fine to carry on a material life under the laws of nature. But surely, in behaving as human beings, we must make clear our moral virtues. The world we can discover in our moral virtues must be a world of true human beings, and this world must be what is called civilization. In order to create this world, it is impermissible for us to be self-indulgent, unlike the animal world. Without exception, we must have victory over the self. This should be clear already from our discussion on *bu*.

However, even here there is subtle news about human life. Self-discipline is an important teaching for human beings, but merely having victory over self is not sufficient. The ultimate moral truth, through Christian abstinence, the Brahmanism of India, or the Daoism of China, absolutely cannot be observed. Religious precepts must be generated from great ideals of the inner self. Self-discipline is something that must be coupled with a magnanimous disposition; otherwise, it will end in triviality and indiscretion. Nanshū said, "In overcoming the self, victory does not come in dealing with each and every thing at a time. Have the disposition all the time, and then overcome." Or, as he also proclaimed, "One who aspires to learning cannot do so without expanding the scope."

This is also true of the state: The morals of the citizens cannot be boosted without great ideals on the part of the state. Without boosting the morals of the citizenry, results cannot be achieved, even with the encouragement of diligent efforts and economizing expenditures. "Arouse the hearts of citizens" and "cultivate national manpower" become fictive phrases.

In the first half of the Meiji period, for example, whatever blunders may have occurred, we drummed up courage, and development galloped ahead because of a burning national desire to produce great achievements on the international stage. Then, having taken advantage of a number of unexpected opportunities and having jumped to a first-class status as a nation, we have lost the target to be pursued. Our exertions are mostly reactionary and continue to become flaccid and degenerate, do they not? Once ideals are established that should be pursued passionately and with a clear self-consciousness, then a national life is established and focus is maintained.

Nanshū said,

> Without one system of national polity, organizing wise men for all official positions and returning political power to one course of policy, there can be no orderly system. For example, appointing capable people and opening discussion and taking in public opinion without a course of action to decide what to adopt or what to reject adds confusion. Those who feel that orders issued yesterday will change suddenly today feel that way because there is no one place of supervision, and administrative policies are not definite. (*Nanshūō Ikun* 2)

Europe is not alone in having what is called *Seelenlosigkeit*—a loss of spirit. Is not Japan, rather by its own hand, in a seriously "abstracted state of mind"? To once again borrow the words of Nanshū,

> If we are to widely adopt the systems of various foreign countries in order to progress toward civilization and enlightenment, we must first understand our country's national polity, make morals correct, and then gradually consider those countries' strong points and incorporate them. If not so, when we learn from foreign countries in a disorderly fashion, Japan's national polity will decline, and morals will decay, creating circumstances difficult to remedy and, ultimately, putting the nation in danger, under the control of foreign countries. (*Nanshūō Ikun* 8)

The master naturally precedes the whole country and is sorrowful; following the whole country, he is joyful. Nanshū, with his inherently clear vision, born of sincerity, quickly observed the direction of the tide of the country concerning the new Meiji government and must have felt a profound grief. To be sure, we who are born in the present day, reading this now, must feel deep emotion. Nanshū further cautioned,

> The development of human wisdom is the development of feelings of patriotism, loyalty, and filial piety. When one's path is clear, devoted to country and working for family, every kind of business will advance. Those who pursue the development of the telegraph, the laying of railroads, and the creation of steam-driven machines startle us. They, however, pay no heed to the question of why there can be no progress without telegraph and railroads. They indiscriminately envy the prosperity of foreign countries, arguing the advantages and disadvantages. They look up to foreign countries in things from buildings to entertainment, expanding the trend for extravagance. If they waste resources, they exhaust the nation's strength and turn the human spirit to the frivolous. In the end, is this nothing other than Japan's downfall? (*Nanshūō Ikun* 10)

Concerning the "Political Thought" of Nanshū, as cited in the chapter title, I think his thought is actually quite simple. His words are easy to understand. His simplicity and straightforwardness, brimming with vigor, are actually the true Way. It is the form of the most loving mother, nourishing thought and learning. This contrasts with the discussion about thought today, which is like a wandering child adrift in the rough waves of the world, separated from its parents and its warm home. To contemplate Saigō's simple and understandable political thought is of inexhaustible significance, is it not?

13 The Spirit of Kendo

The sword—part of the Imperial Regalia of Japan together with the mirror and the jewel, solemn symbols of the spirit of the Japanese *Volk*—has been described earlier in this book. However, it is kendo—the way of the sword—that has most vividly cultivated the virtue of the sword. For this reason, kendo is seen as the main point of the art of war.

The idea that the sword originally was a weapon for aggressively attacking another or for passively protecting oneself is infantile. Undoubtedly, that is the only meaning it had in primitive times; but the sword, as such, became synonymous with *the way of the samurai* and therein developed a profound spiritual meaning. Certainly this is one instance, I think, that illustrates a *Volksgeist* or spirit of the peoples of the East.

Seen from one perspective, the nature of a *Volk* as it is in European nations is a case where there has been no room to develop a deeply spiritual, introspective life because threats to their security have, regrettably, forced frequent movement of people. To make even a single part of their actual life easier, they tended toward materialism and utility. The magnificent landscape of the material civilization of the West today is certainly a product of this tendency.

Conversely, in China and Japan, the *Volk* has not experienced a great disturbance in recorded history. Notwithstanding the barbarians that surrounded China, the people were racially of the same ancestry, with no great inequality among them. Compared to peoples of the West, they had a remarkable self-awareness and meditative quality because they led a relatively calm existence, experiencing a life in close union with nature. For the people of the East to lament that there is no philosophy as in the West is laughable and reckless (if, by "philosophy," we mean a finely-argued logical structure of ideas expressed in writing, that is, of course, something different). Our predecessors always carried the whole of human life and experienced life completely, purifying it, everywhere creating a state of religious respect for the spirit of the dead. If asked, "What are the special characteristics of the peoples of the East?" I would reply enthusiastically and resolutely: *"their earnestness and seriousness (shinkenmi) and their infinite pursuit of a noble moral character."*

The "*ken*" (sword) in *shinkenmi* (真 剣味), which I have used here instinctively, may require some explanation. For the Japanese, especially because they are endowed with kendo, *shinkenmi* (taste of the true sword)—the way of the sword—is a nebulous concept.

Shinkenmi, needless to say, is one's frame of mind when wielding a bare sword and facing an enemy. I, too, have learned the *kata* (forms) of swordsmanship, taking up the naked sword all day, from the time I was sixteen or seventeen, for a period of two or three years. From that experience, I certainly do not act in the mutual give-and-take of life now. Even in the case of merely practicing the *kata* of swordsmanship, when opponents exchange the clash of sword points and stare each other down, suddenly one's body tenses and breathing seizes involuntarily.

Various polluting thoughts of hatred and delusion (*kleśā*) come tagging along ceaselessly, like the shadow of a demon, no matter how one tries to ward them off. And, when they arrive, I, full of tension, first suddenly subduing the shadow, can return to myself. Every day, as one possessed, I pursued this realm. It was as if my youthful body truly could not bear the fatigue and irritation that accompany flaccidity and delusion. Many times I must have flung aside my novels, pounded my desk, and sped off to the dojo (training hall). And when, standing in the dojo, I held a drawn sword in my hand, I felt the current of my life vividly.

Again I would take up the sword and face off. My opponent brandishes his sword in the *jōdan* posture, holding it over his head, and slices downward toward my head. I step back, parrying with a clash of swords. As I parry, I advance one step and strike my opponent's face. Stepping back quickly, we both return to the *seigan* position, swords pointed at the eye. This is one regular *kata*. Even in a standard form, a single slip results in "the true sword"—one mistake is serious. When one thinks that one's head is about to be split open like a ripe pomegranate—no, even if one hasn't thought so—subconsciously, your heart starts racing. When you first start practicing, the spirit lags behind no matter what; one's body will not move. Only the sword shakes back and forth. But the spirit is extremely tense. At this point, in other words, the inner unity of reciprocal moral character has not become heightened. In the limbo of half-heartedness, one stands petrified.

The naked sword, flashing before one's eyes, pressures a man, pushing him forward on the way to *moksha*—emancipation from worldly attachment. At some point, as repetitions accumulate, if you are one to build up a substantial amount of training with the bamboo sword, the three elements of kendo—*ki, ken,* and *tai*: heart-and-mind, sword, and body (mind-spirit-power)—become one naturally. The actions of the three elements actually become the sole person and the sole action. It is then that the pure unity of flawless moral character first becomes clearly visible.

In philosophical terms, this is precisely the state of pure experience. The state of pure experience means no intellectual conflict whatsoever, no opposition of subject and object, but a tendency to inherent consciousness that can unify harmoniously; what is called nothingness and sincerity points to this realm.

In the everyday life of our distracted self, we cannot affirm this experience. We sometimes have experienced it when, lost in a good book, we find our breathing seems to synchronize with the letters on the page as we become absorbed in reading—but this too is not easily obtained.

Especially as we see today, nerves are frayed by an endless cacophony of sounds and garish colors, and because we must live an unstoppable mechanical life, the spirit is run to waste all the more. In a crisis period in which moral character is broken down day by day, it is essential, I think, to consider the significance of pure experience, particularly concentrating on the spirit.

The exalted place of kendo must first be because of *shinkenmi*. Compared to the naked sword, practicing with the bamboo sword is the same principle to a degree: the point is to aim for an opening, striking with your weapon without interruption—not body to body in confrontation but eye to eye in contact, to give pain that will be felt to the bone. This is not child's play but serious business. One cannot help but achieve a focusing of one's spirit. Here, one path of force surges forth.

A samurai wearing two swords was always able to live this *shinkenmi*. In addition, the sword was not meant for killing but for regular moral instruction, for polishing one's soul, in which the respected consciousness of our ancestors and moral sense shone brightly.

In this regard, today's world is utterly lacking in *shinkenmi*. Presently, I feel that my everyday life is flaccid, in which case restlessness sets in, and one moves on the edge of delusion. At that point, I sometimes pick up the sword and swing it, as if to remember. That is the sword with which I concentrated on breath—the moment of breathing when the timing was right and I struck with the sword—that is the inexhaustible wonder I seek.

Previously, I have explained the realm of pure experience, stating that there is no conflict whatsoever between intellect, emotions, and volition, no opposition between subjects and objects, but of course this is definitely not the lifeless and cold mental state of death. It is, as it were, a mountain stream that is dammed up between rocks and full of sediment, or something like the energy to draw a bow as taut as possible and wait for an opportunity to shoot an arrow. In such a case, infinite power possesses a preternatural tension and overflows.

Ancient Confucians spoke of "the mean of the incipient,"[1] the importance of maintaining a constant state of equilibrium and Laozi's concept of "embracing one

---

1. [e.g., *The Doctrine of the Mean*]

(the Way)";[2] the notion of *mu* (not; nothing; nothingness) among Zen practitioners means nothing other than this. Also in *Daodejing*: "Be in harmony with your spirit, embrace one, the Way, and never let go of it." This, in other words, is the continuation of the pure, and what is most revered in kendo.

The Munen ("without any thoughts") school of swordsmanship and the Sword of the Empty Mind all say, "The person who strikes with the sword is empty, the sword is empty, the opponent to be hit is empty, the mysterious effect of an unfettered heart and mind": the wondrous moral effects of embracing the one, the Way, without separation.[3]

In actuality, in a beginner's mind, after all, one moves separately, with heart-and-mind, sword, and body as things apart. Force just the energy (ki) and the body will not move. Even if the body moves, the sword will play uselessly. Nay, rather it will become a hindrance. Even if one is told, "Hey! Strike here!" the flesh is weak and slow to respond.

When the three elements—*ki, ken, tai*—are united as one, the sound of the bamboo sword striking is different. The cut made by a sword is different. The sound of the bamboo sword used unskillfully is that of the bamboo whisk; used skillfully, the bamboo sword sounds clear. In unskilled hands, the sword will cut in swipes; in the hands of a master, it is like slicing through air. When one reaches the rank of master, one no longer cuts with the sword. One cuts with the soul.

This is the poem composed by the famous Zen master Bukko Kokushi, also known as Mugaku Sogen (Wuxue Zuyuan, 1226–1286), when he was about to be killed at the hands of Yuan soldiers in Wen Zhou:

Cutting the Spring Breeze

乾坤無地卓孤筇
喜得人空法亦空
珍重大元三尺劍
電光影裏斬春風

In heaven and on earth, there is no place to put my walking stick
Happy am I for the Void and the Law of the Void
How valuable the three-foot sword of the great Yuan swordsmen
That cuts the spring breeze like a flash of lightning

So it was with the famous swordsman Yamaoka Tesshū (1836–1888), who was capable of mastering the sublime truth of the sword, and who was said to have

---

2. [*Daodejing* 10]
3. [*Fudōchi shinmyōroku*, by Takuan Sōhō]

teased out the meaning of the last line of the poem, "cuts the spring breeze like a flash of lightning," to require leaving behind the physical sword and entering the philosophical realm of *yūgen*—the subtle and profound. Symbolizing the beauty of kendo, this line contains the exquisite taste of the infinite.

Conversely, from the view of the object, just as one is overwhelmed by external stimuli while still unpolished, when facing off while one's swordsmanship is still at the beginner's mind stage, or facing a master, one can't help but keep the opponent in one's vision. The opponent's form flickers before one's eyes, and his thrusting sword can't help but become an obstacle. Even while thinking, "Now I will strike," one somehow feels drawn into the opponent's sword, and one's body becomes cramped. Once one advances a little in technique, or when facing an opponent who is less skillful than oneself, however, the opponent's form is no longer fixed in one's gaze, and his sword is no worry at all. This is an extremely interesting fact that can be easily experienced.

Taking an example from the old masters, we might recall that Yamaoka Tesshū, even after having matured in the practice of swordsmanship, was for a long time overwhelmed by the swordsmanship of Asari Matashichirō of the Ono-ha Ittō-ryū school and felt powerless before him. Yamaoka strived to devise a way to break Asari's level of swordsmanship, but Asari's specter would appear and, like a great boulder, would not yield to cleaving or breaking apart. In the end, Yamaoka took up the practice of Zen and, one morning after achieving complete understanding, he grabbed his bamboo sword and suddenly the specter disappeared. Even when Yamaoka actually faced off with him, Asari did not appear before his eyes. How can this be so? Here again, the problem is focusing the mind and the experience of surrendering one's whole soul. As I have said many times before, this is a phenomenon most important for human beings and one that must be reached through extraordinary enlightenment. In swordsmanship, one is easily able to peek into this realm.

In association with Yamaoka Tesshū, I most definitely wish to record next the anecdote concerning the spearmanship training of Takahashi Deishū, one of our most respected compatriots in modern times. Takahashi was one of the "Three Shu" (along with Yamaoka Tesshū and Katsu Kaishū), who was born the second son of Yamaoka Ichirōemon Masakuni (Takahashi is his adopted family name), and whose real brother was Yamaoka Ki'ichirō Seizan, genius of spearmanship who died at an early age. Tesshū (born Ono Tetsutarō) was Deishū's most beloved disciple, and Deishū had Tesshū marry his younger sister. Seizan, Deishū's real older brother, was a samurai of genius in both his character and *budō*, something difficult to achieve. Regrettably, he died in the second year of Ansei (1855) at the young age of twenty-seven. Takahashi, who was only twenty-one at that time, had already manifested talent under his brother's training.

Deishū's talent gradually grew more and more solid, and just when his technique had become deeply ingrained, the unexpected loss of his brother gave rise to bitter anguish, all the more acute since his brother was also his honored teacher. Now, taking a breath, striving to reach the peak of his skillfulness, he suddenly lost his teacher, as if he flew over a cliff, and he was perplexed. From then on, he was as one possessed, intent on understanding what constituted the essential core of spearmanship.[4]

It happened one night three years after Seizan died, in the early spring of the second month of the fourth year of Ansei (1857). Seizan appeared before him—it was not a dream, neither was it reality—and spoke the words,

> It has already been three years since I passed from the world. I ascended to the heavenly realm where there is no end of pleasure, but my love for you is earnest and you have been constantly on my mind. Therefore, I have come. I wanted to come and see whether you had made any progress in your skill with the spear.

Takahashi screamed:

> What!? What manner of reason is this that a dead man can once again show his form? You are some kind of sly fox or badger spirit come to deceive me, knowing how much I long for my brother, come here wanting to confuse me.

"No, no," the phantasm interrupted,

> You know not reason that is beyond reason. After life is death. After death is life. Life-death-life-death is an infinite transformation. Good causes bring good effects, bad causes, bad effects—without changing in the least. Because you do not understand this logic, believing only in one temporary body, so you think that I now appear as a fox. I am now in the celestial world; already having obtained a body and will, I can come and go as I please. Therefore, thinking of you, I suddenly appeared here. If I appear as a kind of fox or badger, you will not be able to touch me with the point of your spear.

Finally, in the dream, he stood up and appeared to pick up the spear—without a doubt, it was Deishū's brother Seizan. For a while, the two of them engaged in a heated bout with spears. The outcome for Deishū, who had been no match for Seizan before, placed him eye to eye with Seizan as his equal. But Seizan said, "I think tonight this thing called 'you' is still holding back. The same applies to me also. So, tomorrow night, I shall come again."

---

4. It may be futile to lament so, but of late, a strange "spirit" pops up again and again. A "spirit" like Deishū's that should be respected does not show itself at all these days. The world is a dreary place.

So saying, he ascended to heaven, swathed in clouds, aloof. Takahashi called for his brother as long as he could, but there was no answer. And then from his dream he was torn. His entire body was drenched in sweat.

The following night, Seizan appeared, just as he said he would, at his pillow. "This is the night we fight, getting to the heart of the secret arts." Responding to his brother's voice, Takahashi took his spear, bowed once, and faced off, determined. Ten winning moves makes the victor, but it was clear from the first nine that Deishū had won. Seizan said in a way that sounded joyful, "Well done! How diligently you have trained in the art of the spear. Now you have exceeded my level. That gives me peace of mind. So we must part our ways forever."

After speaking these words, Seizan once more ascended to the heavens, disappearing airily in a cloud. Surprised, Takahashi cried like a madman, "My brother! My brother!" attempting to follow him—and then he was once again torn from his dream.

Deishū sat up in bed and wiped the sweat off his body. Bitter and lonely, he was dumbfounded for a while, and then, perhaps overtaken by strange thoughts, ran to a temple, Bodai-ji, before night gave way to dawn. Seeking the man in his dream, he called out at his brother's grave. Stripping himself to the waist, he was just about to disembowel himself, when someone from the house came and hurriedly stopped him. He suddenly returned to his senses (see chapter 8, "On Takahashi Deishū).

This true story has a real, profound significance, I think, in the training and discipline of the way of martial arts. *Budō*, in this meaning, to take up the sword, to take up the spear so as to create a grander self, is a grueling discipline. It is a heroic struggle to see how far the relative self can be assimilated into the absolute self.

Regarding this subject, Zhuangzi has a fascinating tale in "The Mastery of Nourishing Life," about a cook carving up an ox (*Zhuangzi*, Inner Chapter 3).

A highly skilled cook was carving up an ox when the ruler Wen Hui walked in. With his smooth wielding of the knife, the cook kept up a kind of rhythm, separating the skin, meat, and bones. "It is very valuable if you have such a great skill!" said the thoroughly impressed ruler with a sigh of admiration. The cook replied,

> No, it is not a skill, but rather, I would say, *dao*, a Way, advanced one step further. When I first began to butcher an ox, the carcass got in the way, and I couldn't control my hands. After three years, I could no longer see the ox. Now I do it with the heart and mind. And, I dare say, the hands, feet, ears, and eyes are not involved.

Zhuangzi taught that if you still the turmoil of your body and mind, you can nurture your life.

Without a doubt, based on personal experience, I too deeply believe in this principle. All of the power of life is consciousness—rooted in the unity of moral character. Look at the narrowed eyes of a cat sleeping on a veranda that sparkle at the sound of a clattering mouse. Nothing expresses a person's psychological condition as much as the eyes. When moral character thrives, the eyes always shine. And attached to one's attitude is a kind of will power and dignity.

In observing today's students and young people, perhaps a bias on my part, but I see a lack of brilliance in their eyes, their attitudes wavering, like the proverbial dog in a house of mourning: hungry and neglected. Among the literati as well, there are many of that ilk. If there are no expectations for serious scholarship, there will be no case for resplendent *belles lettres*. Is this not a common evil, particularly of the present?

Weak, materialistic emotions and a sentimental life are natural phenomena of a degenerate age, each and all lacking in *shinkenmi*. Consequently, we the people who have made a lifework of establishing a young Asia, or those who strive to truly realize moral character, we must hold these phenomena in universal contempt.

The sublime truth of the way of kendo is explained in this simple poem: "Beneath sword fighting lies hell / until one is ready to lay down one's life, no opportunity will arise" (*Kendo dōka*).

This has become a well-known phrase, similar in meaning to "nothing ventured, nothing gained." Kendo is a martial art that explicitly first makes man face hell; only then can he grasp true liberation. That is why kendo has gravity and dignity.

It must be recorded for posterity that the spirit of kendo, as we know it, gradually became the foundation of all the arts and letters, and of Eastern thought.

To interpret lightly the meaning of the negation of nothingness in the thought of Laozi and Zhuangzi is a shallow idea. In order to truly gain an awareness of the thought of Laozi and Zhuangzi, it is necessary to study and practice Zen and to accomplish the difficult task of discovering one's most deep-seated inner truth. All *kleśā*, all earthly desires and appetites of the flesh, must be broken down and overcome. Like the literary production on Laozi that was popular for a time, what can be called the thought of Laozi today, if not worked over even more, amounts to nothing more than the currently popular sentimental literary production in a light style.

The *tariki* doctrine is a very high moral standard, and it is outrageous to fancy oneself a *tariki* believer while having pride, covetousness, lasciviousness, and lewdness.

Without the feeling of standing under a naked sword, or of spreading your hands and flying over a cliff, one cannot experience a true articulation of the spirit of the East. Indeed, the spirit of the East is nothing indulgent. Rather, it is something stern. The arts and sciences are a white cloud wandering over a precipitous peak—not a café coughing up the smell of meat and face powder. Without passing over the peak with scratched hands and feet, one cannot gain true joy.

Kendo and Mental Principles
On Miyamoto Musashi (宮本武蔵, 1584–1645)

I. The Foundations of Kendo

A point of pride among the characteristics of the Japanese *Volk* not found in other countries, one among many in various fields of endeavor, is Japanese kendo—the great accomplishment of samurai, an impressive and unparalleled art, a Way. As explained in previous chapters, kendo definitely is not the art or technique of swordplay. Neither is it a means to protect oneself or control one's enemy. Truly, to temper and perfect a person's mind and body with an adamantine sword is to reach a unified state of the Way—a mind free of distraction devoting oneself to the sword.

Through mastery of the sword, samurai can become enlightened to all philosophic principles, be they Confucian, Zen, or Shinto, and grow to embody those principles. Swords are not merely weapons, but rather nothing less than the outward manifestation of an innermost spirit. The subtle and profound way of the sword came into being in Japan from the time of the Sengoku (Warring States) period through the early Tokugawa era. After all, it must be understood that the development of the spiritual life of samurai contributed to the attainment of kendo—the Way of the sword—especially from the Kamakura period onward, over its two thousand-year history.

From time immemorial, the Japanese *Volk* have loved life. Of course, there are no human beings that do not love life; but when observed quietly, the love of life is great in diversity. Even the indulgent life lived blindly is a kind of love of life. Even those who seek a life of pleasure through various sensual stimuli show a kind of love of life.

What is called our love of life, however, is not something blindly sensual, but something having the qualities of purity and beauty. This is the love of life that means shedding attachment to the desires of narrow human beings and living immersed in the flow of life, naturally vigorous and with a selfless, innocent attitude. This love is exhibited, for example, in the Japanese *Volk's* love of plants, flowers, insects, and other forms of nature.

Consequently, a characteristic of the Japanese *Volk* is their great ardor for freedom. A life tied down and bound with the external and the formal is to be abhorred. Samurai and others of the Warring States period were most vigorously spirited by this way of living. Ban Dan'uemon Naoyuki (1567–1615), unable to tolerate the rigidity of being pent up under the service of Katō Yoshiaki (1563–1631), abruptly resigned and became a *rōnin*, leaving behind this verse: "遂不留 江南野水 高飛天 地一閃鴎"[1] (In the end, the goose [Ban], not stopping at the water of the plains [Katō] of Jiangnan, flies high in the sky), meaning, "I am leaving the patronage of Katō and will climb higher." This episode accurately reflects the morale of the samurai of the times.

Shinto, the indigenous spirituality of Japan, resonated with a pure, bright feeling that loves life and respects freedom. For the samurai, the influence of Buddhism—and the inspiration of Zen in particular—gave them a deep sense of the impermanence (*mujō*) of the body, inspiring them to steadfastly lay down their lives for duty and honor, and to live the Way. Ashikaga Takauji (1305–1358), the first Muromachi shogun, was one example of this. He confessed to the *kami* and Buddhas that this world is indeed but a dream and yielded the fame and fortune of the present world to his brother, Tadayoshi, praying fervently that he, Takauji, might live in the Way.

Kusunoki Masatsura (1326–1348) is another example of this attitude. The emperor offered Ben no Naishi's hand in marriage, which he declined, saying, "How could I possibly make a vow in a provisional world where nothing lasts forever?" The actions of Ban Dan'uemon, Gotō Matabei, Sanada Yukimura, and others who joined in the Osaka Siege, without casting an eye toward the enfeoffment that was so much in demand, laid down their lives in the thrill of battle, a source of eternal exultation for Japanese. Their spirits were too high to indulge in the good life with all the comforts of food, clothing, and shelter—the life of the birds and the beasts, absent the Way. Rather, these men lived life to the fullest, in high spirits, and their whole human character was in high tension. There was no reason for living if one's whole soul was not involved in something. They vested their entire soul into a sword called the *sanjaku no shūsui*, a luminous sword three feet in length, secured at the waist—the so-called soul of *bushi*—with which they tested the temper of dignified humanity. To consider kendo as a technique or practice that came about as a result of a necessary means of life or of some kind of tournament is extremely shallow.

---

1. [Yasuoka's text includes the Japanese rendering of Ban's lines: "終に江南野水に住まらず。高く飛ぶ天地一閑鴎".]

II. Levels of Technique

The word "kendo," as explained before, contains a spiritual meaning of profundity and subtlety, but originally it was called the art of war or strategy of war (兵法 *heihō*). The character 兵 originally meant soldier or combatant, indicating a warrior who fought with a weapon; later, it came to denote the weapons and arms themselves. Subsequently, the word took on the meaning of one who uses a weapon to defeat another.

Of course, *heihō*—the art of war—evolved together with the weapons of war. The great name associated with developing *heihō* into an activity of the human spirit was Iishino Chōisai. He is the person who is said to have founded the Shintō-ryū school of kendo, through the divine response to his earnest prayers at the Kashima and Katori shrines. From that time through the Sengoku period, the main *ryū-ha*, or schools, of *heihō* were Aisu Koretaka's Kage-ryū, Kamiizumi Ise-no-Kami's Shinkage-ryū, and Chūjō Hyōgonosuke's Chūjō-ryū. The famous Ittō-ryū grew out of this Chūjō-ryū, while Yagyū-ryū emerged from the Kamiizumi-ryū.

People of these various schools all lived off the art of war. They traveled as much of the country as possible, taking along their family and disciples, during which time they trained diligently and practiced discipline, aspiring to perfect attainment of martial art. This so-called discipline of the samurai, we must not forget, was, together with itinerant Zen monks, the honored self-cultivation and self-discipline of our ancestors.

Just as itinerant monks from Zen temples were respected, the powerful daimyo families of each area greatly esteemed the training and discipline of the samurai. If found agreeable, they were given high salaries and retained. If not, they were rewarded handsomely and sent on their way. These samurai wandered as they pleased. The brave warriors who conquered the castle in the Siege of Osaka did not all necessarily participate because they felt obligated to Toyotomi. For most of them, it was instead the perfect opportunity to exercise samurai training and discipline. Upon the fall of the castle, not a few of them dispersed across the country. The shogunate's fear at the beginning of the Tokugawa period was that these *rōnin* might look for a chance to test their mettle against it for the sake of honor.

Miyamoto Musashi was born in Miyamoto village, in the Yoshino district of Mimasaka Province, in the third month of the twelfth year of Tenshō (1584), during the Sengoku period, which was the most vigorous period of samurai activity. As for his lineage, he was a descendant of the Akamatsu clan from Banshū, who took the family name of Hirata. His grandfather's generation served in the domain of Takeyama Niimi in Mimasaka, and, appointed to an important post by Niimi Sōkan, was newly presented with the family name Niimi (also read Shinmen). His father's generation retired to Miyamoto village and from then on used the name

Miyamoto. Musashi's father, Munisai Miyamoto Takehito Masaie, not surprisingly, was a brave and accomplished samurai. He was usually called Miyamoto Musashi Masana (or Genshin). Following from his father's name, he would have been called Miyamoto Takezō Masana (or Genshin). His childhood name was Bennosuke.

As befits the son of a great samurai, Musashi was a rough and wild child, at times unmanageable. Finally, at the age of nine, he ran away from home, absconding to the temple in Banshū, where his uncle lived. During the time he stayed at the temple he became a gallant and imposing young man, continually developing his skills and discipline in martial art. At the age of thirteen, he toppled the martial artist Arima Kihei of the Shindō-ryū. Then, at sixteen, he had a bout with a samurai named Akiyama from Tajima Province, a samurai of great strength, and defeated him.

The next year, the battle of Sekigahara began. Seeing storm clouds on the horizon, his father must have called him back home. Niimi, the master of the house, departed for the front as a subordinate of Ukita Hideie, one of Toyotomi's Council of Five Elders. Seventeen-year-old Musashi also followed the forces. In the aftermath of defeat, he became a *rōnin* in Kyushu, accompanying the massive dispersal of people from all their domains and clans. After that, at the age of twenty-one, he went to the capital city of Kyoto and engaged in frequent bouts with masters of martial art, never losing a single match. By the age of twenty-eight or twenty-nine, he had engaged in over sixty matches and continued to win them all.

One particularly famous event occurred on the fourth month of the seventeenth year of Keichō (1612) at Buzen Funajima, when he was twenty-nine, where he fought Sasaki Kojirō. Permit me to set the stage as to the gravity of this moment of truth, to see Musashi's disciplined bearing as he stood on the border of life and death, and Sasaki, samurai of honor, about to wipe clean the enmity between them.

In the popular imagination, it is thought that Sasaki, known as Ganryū, "Boulder style," was a coward who fled after attacking Musashi's father in the dark. This is clearly a falsehood, having no basis in reality. Sasaki was the leading disciple of Tomida Seigen, celebrated master of the Chūjō-ryū (Chūjō school) of swordsmanship. After receiving his license to teach, he traveled the country and made a name for himself in the martial arts, eventually founding his own school called Ganryū. Traveling about, he arrived at Buzen Kokura, where he was feted by Lord Hosokawa Tadaoki, and where he trained the lord's vassals.

It just so happened that Miyamoto Musashi, traveling west, ran into him there, and it was arranged that the two great rivals of nature have a duel to test their strength and skill against each other. According to an account of Musashi's life in the *Niten-ki* (*Record of Niten*), he had gone to Kyoto and heard of this renowned Sasaki Kojirō and called on his father's disciple, Nagaoka Sado, an old retainer of Hosokawa's, to arrange a duel.

According to popular legend, Ganryū had a secret technique called *tsubame-gaeshi*, the Swallow's Return Cut, a sword technique to which Sasaki Kojirō was suddenly enlightened one day while watching swallows in flight, sweeping through willow branches. This is an appealing and fascinating tale, but one that Miyamoto Musashi scholars all deny.

Ganryū's secret technique was not the Swallow's Return Cut, but the *tora kiri*—the Tiger Cut—according to *Gekiken Sōdan* (Anthology of swordsmanship). This technique is also called *isshin ittō*, One Heart, One Sword. In this case, the *kamae*, or stance, is grasping the large long sword in both hands and holding it above one's head, advancing in brisk steps, with one's focus on the opponent's nose, and then striking as quick as lightning; or, winning by leaning forward at the time of the strike and raising the shoulders above the place to be hit. It is said that Kotani Shin'uemon of Inshū Tottori was also of this *ryū*, and he thought that calling this technique *tsubame-gaeshi* was purely coincidental but appropriate. Or, perhaps as a matter of personal taste, the swordsman referred to the technique as either *tsubame-gaeshi* or *tora kiri*.

Whichever the case may be, the meeting of the two great rivals finally took place on the thirteenth day of the fourth month of the seventeenth year of Keichō (1612), offshore of Kokura, on the beach of the island of Funajima, under the provisions that both be standing on impartial ground and that no spectators be allowed. Kojirō was to be escorted by Lord Hosokawa Tadaoki's boat and Musashi by Nagaoka Sado Okinaga's boat. Sado was Hosokawa's chief retainer. The fact they selected an island location for the duel and strictly prohibited spectators shows the great care taken in its arrangement.

Musashi being Musashi, thinking that the duel might cause some strange feelings of conflict between Hosokawa, the lord, and Sado, his chief retainer, decided it would be best if he did not ride in the boat escorted by Sado. On the 12th, the day before the duel, he confirmed the particulars, the time he would be departing with Sado, and then disappeared for the night. Then a great consternation arose. There were those who taunted Musashi, saying he had lost his nerve. Sado, too, must have grown uneasy; when he sent a messenger to check on Musashi, he was found down the coast at the checkpoint, sitting calmly at the ferry station. Via the messenger, Musashi sent this letter and his salutations to Sado:

Regarding the matter of tomorrow's duel, I appreciate the profound kindness and graciousness of your offer to have me ferried to Mukōjima (another name for Funajima). However, at this juncture, Kojirō and I are enemies. Thus, if Kojirō is to be brought by Lord Hosokawa's boat and I in yours, this would make you feel awkward relative to your lord. Please do not put yourself to any trouble for my sake. *I wish I could tell this to you directly, but since you had already gone to the trouble of making all the arrange-*

ments, I did not say anything. Now that I am here, I would like to decline the offer. There should not be any impediment in my crossing to Mukōjima from here tomorrow morning. I shall arrive at the appointed hour. Therefore, please understand this matter.—Musashi

Because of Musashi's considerate intentions, delivered in this message, everyone thought his actions reasonable. Likewise, Sasaki Kojirō did not utilize Lord Hosokawa's boat.

The next day, Musashi awoke composed and leisurely finished eating his breakfast, as if the big bout was someone else's affair. He procured a single oar from the master of the house and whittled it down to a four-foot wooden sword. He casually stayed where he was, not budging an inch in response to the urgent demand to ferry across. A single boatman rowed him across to Funajima, arriving at the appointed hour. Disembarking, he hitched up his *hakama*, wore his short sword to his side, held his long wooden sword in his hand, and waded nimbly toward the shore in his bare feet. Wrapping a small towel around his head, he made his way calmly and quietly.

Kojirō, waiting impatiently for some time, approached in a rage. Fixing Musashi in his sight, he castigated him in a loud voice: "You're late! You're late!" But Musashi continued slowly on his way, pretending he hadn't heard a word. Unable to bear it any longer, Kojirō suddenly threw down his scabbard, strode forward, and waited for Musashi to make a move. Musashi sneered and said, "Kojirō, you will lose!"

"What!" said Kojirō, visibly angered.

"Don't you see?" Musashi shot back. "Throwing down your scabbard is proof of your defeat."

Burning with rage, Kojirō slashed out, quick as lightning, with one stroke, the Tiger Cut—but Musashi already had delivered a blow to Kojirō's brow with his wooden sword. As Kojirō was taking a heavy fall he made a swipe at Musashi, tearing open about three inches of the hem of his *hakama*. At the same time, Musashi's sword sliced downward, striking a severe blow to Kojirō's side. Kojirō spat up blood and breathed what seemed to be his last breath. Assessing for a moment whether Kojirō was dead or alive, Musashi soon faced the judges of the duel and, bowing once, left on the boat he had arrived on, returning to Shimonoseki.

Various rumors later circulated that Musashi had not delivered a finishing blow to Kojirō, but in the words of Musashi, "Delivering a finishing blow is the conduct of a sworn enemy. We were merely comparing levels of martial art. There is no reason to deliver a finishing blow when one has already won." His consideration spread throughout the land.

Two years later, the infamous war known as the Siege of Osaka occurred.

Musashi joined in the campaign with Toyotomi against Ieyasu and fought bravely. An inscription on a monument at Kokura reads,

> In the battle of Sesshū Osaka, with Lord Toyotomi Hideyori, Musashi fought valiantly; it is impossible to express his warrior reputation even in words of praise as wide as the sea, flowing like a valley stream, so this brief record is made.

Musashi himself said, "In four of the six battles I have had occasion to join from the time I was a young man, no one was first on the battlefield but I" (*Sakazaki Naizen ate Kōjōsho*). This is the perfect stage, no doubt, for storytellers to let their imaginations run wild.

III. Stages of the Way

For the decade or so prior to these events, Musashi was not seen as one who understood true kendo—in other words, the philosophy of the sword. He explains in the preface to his book, *Gorinsho* (*The Book of Five Rings*):

> From my young years of long ago, I have set my heart and mind on the Way of *heihō*. At thirteen, I had my first duel. At that time, I struck down a formidable martial artist called Arima Kihei of the Shintō-ryū (New Hitting-the-Mark School). At sixteen I defeated a martial artist called Akiyama of Tajima Province. When I was twenty-one, I went to Kyoto, the capital, and met martial artists from all over the country, engaging in numerous duels and never once failing to attain victory.
>
> After that I traveled from province to province, encountering martial artists of various schools. I never lost a match, even though I dueled more than sixty times. This all took place between the ages of thirteen and twenty-eight or twenty-nine.
>
> Having passed the age of thirty, I looked back on the footprints of my past. My victories lay not in having mastered *heihō*. Perhaps it was because I was innately skilled in the Way and had not departed from the laws of heaven, or was it maybe in the deficiencies of the other schools of *heihō*? From then on, I practiced from morning to night to attain still deeper principles and came naturally to a realization of the Way of *heihō*. I had then reached about fifty years of age.

In other words, from the age of thirty, Musashi deepened his knowledge of kendo rather than his knowledge of swordsmanship. At the same time, he progressed beyond one sword and began his own special way of using two swords. This technique originated, apparently, from childhood, learning the use of the *jutte* (a short metal truncheon) from his father.

During the twenty-year period from his thirties to his fiftieth year or thereabouts, coinciding with the early Tokugawa period, Musashi traveled far and wide, from Kinki and Chūgoku, to Bishū, Kantō, and Ōshū.

At Nagoya, he served Tokugawa Yoshinao and manifested samurai valor to the highest degree. During his sojourn, Musashi disseminated the teachings of the school of swordsmanship known as Enmei Niten Ichi-ryū, and trained fellow samurai such as Takemura Masatoshi, Hayashi Suketatsu, Hatta Tomoyoshi, and others.

There was at that time an extraordinary man named Yagyū Hyōgo Toshitoshi (1579–1650), the grandson of Yagyū Munetoshi of the Bishū *han* (domain). When Hyōgo Toshitoshi was twenty-five, he received initiation into the secrets of martial arts from Kamiizumi Ise-no-Kami, and he also studied Zen deeply. By the age of nineteen, he was entreated to serve under Katō Kiyomasa and granted a stipend of 3,000 *koku* of rice. At any rate, it seems he was quite a personage. When Musashi came to Nagoya for a time, he met a distinguished-looking samurai whose bearing and gaze was not that of a usual man. "This is the first time in a while I have seen *a man so full of life*," said Musashi. "You must be the famous Yagyū Hyōgo!" And indeed he was—or so the story goes.

A few years later, Musashi met Miyamoto Iori (Hachigorō), who would later become his adopted son. Miyamoto Iori exhibited military prowess no less than his father. Musashi took Iori under his wing while he was a *rōnin* in Ōshū—and this tale, too, is stranger than fiction.

One year, when Musashi left Hitachi and entered Dewa, approaching Shōhōjihara field, he noticed a child of thirteen or fourteen loitering roadside with a pail he had filled with loaches (a type of fish). Musashi asked if he would part with some. The child said, "You can have them all!" Musashi declined his offer, saying he wanted just enough for his evening meal. But the boy replied, "What a bother—take them all with you!" and handing the pail to Musashi went away.

That night Musashi slept in an inn and the next morning began his trek across the same fields as the day before; but no matter how far he went, the grassy plains stretched endlessly, with nary a house in sight. Daylight was fast fading and Musashi was greatly troubled when, far away in the shadow of the mountain, he saw the flicker of a lamplight. Relieved, he hurried toward the spot, and as he drew near he saw a ramshackle house. A boy emerged and beckoned him inside. Surprisingly, it was the boy who had given him the loaches the day before. The boy invited Musashi to sit by the fire and brewed some coarse tea for him. Something about the boy's appearance and demeanor was out of the ordinary. Not trusting the boy, Musashi inquired into his circumstances. He was a boy from Shōhōji village and had moved to this place in the fields with his father. Eventually, both his mother and father had died, and he lived all alone in the ramshackle house.

The boy offered Musashi some weak boiled rice with millet and urged him to go to sleep. Soon, the boy himself retired to the next room. Musashi, dozing fireside on the floor, was unable to sleep well. Various thoughts ran through his mind—what kind of person is the boy and how can he live alone in this place? Then, in the middle of the night, he heard in the next room the sound of a sword being sharpened.

Is this the house of mountain brigands? He wondered. Thinking to test the brigands' courage, Musashi made a big yawn. Hearing this, the boy asked from the next room if he couldn't sleep. When Musashi answered that a noise like the sound of sword-sharpening kept him awake, the child laughed mockingly and said, "You look like a strong samurai, but you're a coward. Even drawing my sword, what can I, as a little boy, do to you?" Truly, this was a fearless and audacious boy, Musashi thought.

"What are you doing sharpening your sword?" Musashi asked.

"Oh, it's just that my father died yesterday. And I thought I would try to bury him in my mother's grave in yonder mountain. I'm not strong enough to carry his body by myself, so I was going to cut it in half and carry it to the grave in pieces."

Musashi was shocked. "You needn't do such an outrageous thing. I'll help you." And together they buried the body.

Taking stock in this child, training and disciplining him, Musashi personally recommended him to Ogasawara Tadasane, lord of Kokura Domain—this child was Iori. The one who fought in the tournament of champions of all Japan, held at Fukiage Castle on the twenty-second day of the ninth month of the eleventh year of Kan'ei (1634), crossing swords with Araki Mataemon, who was renowned for his *kenpō*, was none other than this man.

Musashi again stayed in the Edo area, where he was said to have given himself over to quiet Zen meditation. His hermitage and the Buddha of his personal protection are said to remain in Fujiwara, Katsushika.

During his stay in Edo, the Tokugawa shogunate regime changed from Ieyasu to Hidetada and then to Iemitsu. Samurai morale gradually lost its vigor and tautness, and all of them tended to be salaried.

The man of trust who was reflected in the eyes of the patriots during this time was none other than the shogun Iemitsu. Iemitsu had also heard of Musashi's great renown and thought he would have a close look at this samurai's prowess. However, at the time the Yagyū-ryū school of swordsmanship had already been embraced by the shogun household, so Musashi deliberately declined Iemitsu's kind request, though graciously. He painted a vivid scene on a screen and presented it to the shogun. In addition to kendo, Musashi had developed a distinctive style in calligraphy, painting, and sculpture.

After his stay in Edo, Musashi went down to Kokura, a place full of memories for him, and for a time was a guest of Ogasawara Tadasane. He also fought in the

Shimabara Rebellion of 1638. After his seven-year sojourn, he left Iori behind and, alone and aloof, went from there to Kumamoto.

Since his duel with Sasaki Kojirō in the Hosokawa Domain of Kumamoto, Musashi had many acquaintances among both the ruling and the ruled, and it was a place where the ethos of the samurai spirit still flourished. Musashi was well-known to Lord Hosokawa Tadatoshi, who welcomed him as a guest and granted him a retinue of seventeen men, along with a stipend of 3,000 *koku* of rice.

During this period, for four or five years from his fifty-seventh year, Musashi was able to cultivate not a few excellent disciples. Outstanding among them were Terao Magonojō, the Dōmoto Menosuke brothers, Furuhashi Sōzaemon, and Tokō Tahei. The lord was another earnest disciple, for whom Musashi was more than a teacher of kendo, including being an expert advisor on war tactics and on political matters in general.

Ogi Kakubei Masakuni states in his *Musashi-ron* (Treatise on Musashi),

> Asked what he thought of Musashi, one man replied, "Niimi Musashi is a renowned master of *heihō*. As a guest he was afforded treatment of the first order and rewarded with 3,000 *koku* of rice. Is this not extraordinary treatment to receive? I answered that there was not another *heihō* master like him in the world. He was a top-ranking samurai of the time, wise, and vested with great integrity. He would be a Myōe or a Takuan [famous Zen monks] in a different guise. Moreover, in the lord's assessment, his talent was formidable, and he was called upon to serve as intimate political advisor. Merely to be a samurai of art and talent would not merit such treatment."

Musashi's later years, after the training and discipline of risking his life in sixty bouts over twenty years and traveling about as a *rōnin* for another twenty years, during which time he mastered the art of the sword and consummated his spiritual understanding, were of unparalleled illustriousness. As he records in his *Gorinsho*, since fifty years of age, "There remains no Way which I must delve into, and I live out my days. Following the principles of *heihō*, I have attained the Way of all arts and skills. In all things, I have no teacher." By the power of his own mental attitude, he manifested marvelous uniqueness in the tea ceremony, calligraphy, painting, sculpture, and *renga* poetry.

In his fifty-eighth year, at the beginning of the second month of the eighteenth year of Kan'ei (1641), at the request of the Lord Hosokawa Tadatoshi, he wrote *Thirty-Five Essential Rules of Heihō* and presented it to him. On the seventeenth of that month, Tadatoshi, his friend for life, died of a sudden illness. Just as the Zhou dynasty musician Haku Ga (Be Ya), upon hearing of the death of his friend, Shō Shiki (Zhong Ziqi), broke his zither and stopped playing forever, Musashi was profoundly moved by the death of his friend.

Musashi, too, was growing old, his hands and feet gradually losing their freedom of movement, and he was aware that his days were numbered. At this point, he decided to create a literary work of his life in order to record for posterity his own valued experience.

Barely a mile to the west of Kumamoto Castle, in a scenic spot of mountains and valleys, is a cave capable of holding a hundred people called Iwatozan Reigandō. Always fond of this lovely spot and its natural beauty, Musashi frequented it to read or to sit in meditation. Sensing the ripening of his ideas, he sequestered himself in this spot, unbeknownst to others, from the beginning of the tenth month of the twentieth year of Kan'ei (1643) and undertook the writing of *Gorinsho*, pouring his heart's blood into the work. In the preface, he states,

Having spent many years cultivating the Way of *heihō* called Niten Ichi-ryū [the School of Two Heavens], I will now attempt to put it into writing for the first time, during these early days of the tenth month of the twentieth year of Kan'ei (1643). I have climbed Mount Iwato in the province of Higo, Kyushu. I bow to heaven, make obeisance to Kannon, and turn toward the Buddha. I am Niimi Musashi Fujiwara Genshin, a warrior born in Harima Province, now sixty years of age.

From my young years of long ago, I have set my heart and mind on the Way of *heihō*. At thirteen, I had my first duel. At that time, I struck down a formidable martial artist called Arima Kihei of the Shintō-ryū. At sixteen, I defeated a martial artist called Akiyama of Tajima Province. When I was twenty-one, I went to Kyoto, the capital, and met martial artists from all over the country, engaging in numerous duels and never once failing to attain victory.

After that I traveled from province to province, encountering martial artists of various schools. I never lost a match even though I dueled more than sixty times. This all took place between the ages of thirteen and twenty-eight or twenty-nine.

Having passed the age of thirty, I looked back on the footprints of my past. My victories lay not in having mastered *heihō*. Perhaps it was because I was innately skilled in the Way and had not departed from the laws of heaven, or was it maybe in the deficiencies of the other schools of *heihō*? From then on, I practiced from morning to night to attain still deeper principles and came naturally to a realization of the Way of *heihō*. I had then reached about fifty years of age.

Having no Way to investigate since then, I passed the time. For me, there was no teacher in anything; I put my stock in the principles of the *heihō*, learning the Way of all arts and skills. Writing this book now, I do not use the old precepts of Buddhist dharma, Confucius, or Taoism, neither the old stories from war chronicles, nor books on military tactics. To reveal my mind about Niten Ichi-ryū and its true meaning, I take up my brush and begin to write, with the Way of heaven and Kannon as mirrors, on the night of the tenth day of the tenth month, at the hour of the tiger [around 4:30 a.m.].

Deeply involved in writing for two years, he realized that the days of illness were growing heavier, and the time of his death was finally approaching. He sent this letter on the thirteenth day of the fourth month of the third year of Shōhō (1646) addressed to Nagaoka Shikibu, the chief retainer of the domain, Nagaoka Kenmotsu, and Sawamura Uemon, and then he entered a state of intense concentration in Reigandō:

> I apologize for having written each of you. Having been ill for a while, I took a turn for the worse this spring and since then have had difficulty, especially using my hands and legs. Before, I had no desire to serve the fiefdom because of illness. Because the late Lord Hosokawa Tadatoshi also had an affinity for *heihō*, I wanted to explain the standards for [Niten] Ichi-ryū to the lord. When he had acquired most martial arts techniques, alas, his death meant the loss of this unparalleled happiness and of my reason for undertaking this work. I received the order to disseminate the essence of *heihō*; however, because of my infirmity, I hope you will understand and accept the writing alone. I have just finished researching the draft, a new standard for *heihō*. I have not used old passages of military law or old phrases of Confucians and Buddhists, only the knowledge of Ichi-ryū, one school, with thoughts on its merits and advantages. I know the Way of all arts and skills; I attained a higher perception of truth but regret that it does not fit the world. Until now, the world thought I made my livelihood by *heihō* alone. The aforementioned items become a burden on true *heihō*. What I say now, in my own case, one person living his last days, is that if I were to follow a master of ancient times, I should convey the secrets of *heihō*. However, I cannot move my hands and legs as I wish. I feel I have only this year to live, but it is difficult to tell. Even if it is one day, I would like to secure my mountain place and stare death in the face. Please intercede at my request with the outside world, as I will be in seclusion. —Musashi

As time passed, rumors of various improprieties in the domain arose. His disciples or friends, because of their strong sense of justice, could not ignore the problem. Nagaoka Shikibu, among others, took action, and badgered Musashi to return home. Finally, he returned to his residence in Chiba Castle and took to his sickbed. With his condition worsening day by day, he quietly wrote by his own hand nineteen precepts of the self-discipline of his life, and then passed away on the twelfth day of the fifth month, as if going to sleep. He was sixty-two years old. His close friends, including Shunzan Oshō (monk) of Taihōji Temple, prayed for the repose of his soul. Following the request of his testament, they buried him in his battle armor in Higashiyuge, Kumamoto.

In what follows, I attempt to investigate the thought, training, and discipline of this great man, as found in his *Gorinsho*, *Jikaisho*, and other works.

IV. Dokkōdō and Gorinsho

Leaving his father's side while still a child, Musashi spent a lifetime—not learning from the most eminent martial artists, not inquiring into Confucianism, not entering a Zen temple—but earnestly pursuing swordsmanship and skirting the border of life and death. Finally, consummating the wonder of mysteries, Niten Miyamoto Musashi forged a free and independent character of truth and dignity. On his deathbed, to leave behind for his disciples, he wrote *The 19 Precepts of the Way of Self-Reliance*. These courageous precepts demand the attention of our insignificant selves:

1. Do not disparage the Ways of generations past.[2]
2. Be fair in all things.
3. Do not seek comforts for yourself.
4. Be free of desires your whole life long.
5. Have no regrets in your personal affairs.
6. Do not envy others' good or evil.
7. In whichever path you walk, do not grieve separation and what's left behind.
8. Do not make excuses for yourself or others.
9. Do not let your affection cause attachments.
10. In all things have no preferences.
11. Have no desire for luxury in your home.
12. Have no fondness for rich food.
13. Don't harm your body through excess.
14. Do not keep old equipment.
15. Do not care for too much equipment, especially weapons.
16. Do not shun death in matters of the Way.
17. Do not seek treasures or fiefdom for your old age.
18. Respect the *kami* and Buddhas, but do not rely on them.
19. Never stray from the Way of martial arts [*dokkōgyō*].

These precepts are the realm of the Way, the Way of "freedom" made possible by Musashi's enlightenment through *heihō*. Freedom is certainly not "disparaging the Ways of generations past." It is not "seeking comforts for yourself." Neither is it indulging in "desires your whole life long." Nor is it letting "affection cause attachments" in your life.

The basis of these precepts is the premise that one lives one's life adher-

---

2. He who wavers within the flow of ever-changing customs and traditions, turning the new into the true, is a superficial person. The master considers the soul of the eternal.

ing to one thing, struggling with the chains of worldly desire. The harder one struggles, the tighter the chain's grip. Freedom, accordingly, breaks the adamantine chains with Herculean strength—one frees oneself from the trap; it is based on one's becoming independent, standing firmly on one's two feet, walking one's path alone.

On whichever path you walk, do not be saddened by separation and what you leave behind. Reconcile yourself to the laws of heaven and follow them faithfully. This is similar in meaning to the Zen concept of following one's fate, opening one's heart and trusting in one's true nature, roaming freely. In this regard, we ourselves are so full of attachments; we should be disgusted with our worldly complaints.

Regarding the precept, "Do not let your affection cause attachments": Is this something heartlessly unachievable for modern man, who eagerly pursues carnal desires, pleasures, and sensual decadence?

"Do not shun death in matters of the Way" and "Respect the *kami* and Buddhas, but do not rely on them" represent the solemn soul of the samurai of great integrity. Modern man has completely annihilated this samurai spirit. All manner of uncertainties, uneasiness, and misapprehensions well up from this point like storm clouds. As stated by the founder of the religious sect, those believers in the infinite hell of Other Power, "who indulge in worldly desires and selfishness, but put their trust in Buddha's great vow, have no understanding of how detestable this world is, or of the evil within themselves." Such people, as well as those who shoulder governing, elevating their own vanity, without talent themselves, must reflect deeply on this.

The final precept, "Never stray from the Way," the so-called Way of *heihō*, I should like to explain a bit more.

Asai Hidehiro, who consummated the tradition of Niten Ichi-ryū during the Tenpō years (1830–1843), wrote in a doctrine of Niten Ichi-ryū, "Musashi's Ichi-ryū governs the spirit (*ki*), mastering its essence. In other words, it is nothing other than the laws of heaven, realizing the morality of *heihō*, the mysterious effect of nature." As such, the Way of *heihō* comes down to spirit, so, using the thirty-five rules of *heihō* that form the foundation of Musashi's *Gorinsho*, I intend to record here the focus of these spiritual laws.

As indicated in the title, *The Book of Five Rings* comprises five books or scrolls: Earth, Water, Fire, Wind, and Void. In the Book of Earth, Musashi states, "In swordsmanship in general, the true Way is difficult to achieve." Just waving a sword about is not a Way. To establish the fundamental concept, he wrote this section as an outline of the Way of *heihō*, as it corresponds with his Ichi-ryū, his individual school. Next, in the Book of Water, his treatment is water as metaphor: Water takes the form of its container, square or round; it can form one drop, and it can form a great ocean. To identify the principles of swordsmanship—if a man can freely defeat one enemy he can defeat all the people in the world—such principles were herein recorded.

In the Book of Fire, Musashi writes, "Fires can be large or small; battle outcomes depend on a burning spirit."

The fourth book, Wind, records matters of other schools, "the other schools in the world of *heihō*." Musashi was certainly a hero who followed the Way of self-reliance, of going alone. He was a man who trod his own path, not narrow-minded and selfish, and not a person who disregarded others. His observations of other schools are individually detailed. One can examine a world of difference between "a master and a *tengu* [braggart]."

In the fifth book, Book of Void, Musashi explains,

> Here nothing would be the beginning and nothing would be the secret essence. Having attained the true Way, leave the true Way behind you; the Way of *heihō* will set you free, the Way of *heihō* will make you a benevolent person. In the fullness of time, know the timing of things, strike naturally and spontaneously, hit naturally and spontaneously. These are all the Way of the Void. I have chronicled this entering of the true Way as the Book of the Void.

For those who practice *heihō*, *The Book of Five Rings* truly delivers, in clear language, an explanation of the Way of *heihō*. There are those who criticize it, saying it departs from the truth, or it is too glib and facile. However, it goes without saying that difficult and profound truths that defy simple thinking and language are, by definition, ineffable. Typically, one conveys the content through the soul to others' souls, or receives it as one by reciting Zen mantra. However, trying to manifest the self-discovered truth through writing requires a great heart of immeasurable compassion.

Before we peruse Miyamoto Musashi's *Gorinsho*, it is necessary once again to think carefully about the aims and objectives behind his writing of this book and how it came to be. Having read his preface and his letter to the daimyo's chief retainer and then having read the first part of the first book, the Book of Earth, we can understand his motivation for writing it.

As I have stated before, the Way of *heihō* forges a noble and free character with weapons, especially the sword of the samurai spirit. In the greater sense, the Way of *heihō* is the great precious thing leading to the Way that governs the world, more than the small sense whereby it defeats one enemy. In an age of vice, *heihō* gradually became something to trade in, a commodity, contrary to Musashi's concept of *heihō*. This, together with the decline of *shidō, the Way of samurai of great integrity*, was Musashi's most direct and intense motivation for writing the book— his righteous indignation toward those circumstances fired by his spirit of the Way.

He disparaged the current of the times this way:

> Looking at the world as I see it, where all artistic accomplishments are turned into
> something to sell, when people think to sell themselves and even invent ways of selling
> their equipage, then appearance and reality, flower and fruit are divided in two, and
> the showy flower of appearances is valued more than the fruit of hard reality. The Way
> of *heihō*, in particular, is dressed up for showy performance; people open one dojo
> then another, seeking profit by those who teach the Way and those who study it. The
> saying, "Unprofessional *heihō* is a source of great damage" has much truth in it, indeed.

For us in today's world, where everything has a price, these are harsh words.

An attempt to give a detailed explanation of *Gorinsho*, properly reflecting Musashi's feeling of righteous indignation, would have to be manifested in a very large volume. However, for an abbreviated version, we can return to the thirty-five articles that Musashi presented to Lord Hosokawa Tadatoshi.

One characteristic of Niten Ichi-ryū is the use of two swords. The reason for using two swords is simply so that one can draw a sword from either side. Usually, the left hand is not as skillful; a soldier gets into deep trouble grasping a weapon with the left hand when riding on horseback, on riverbanks, narrow roads, rocky fields, or in crowds. Learning to use *tachi*, the long sword, one builds strength. At first, wielding it may seem heavy, but later one can use it freely.

After explaining the reason for using two swords, Musashi records his *opinions about the Way of heihō: There are large-scale and individual heihō, and understanding the large and the small (numbers of enemies), the Way of heihō deals with both of them.* As for the body structure of *heihō*, at a glance, each part of the body should come together into an integrated whole. One should give attention evenly from head to toe in equipoise, neither too strong nor too weak, not to make oneself one-sided.

Next is how to grasp the sword. The main point in grasping the sword is pressing with the little finger. There is the Hand of Life and the Hand of Death. When taking a stance, parrying, or checking the opponent's sword, the hand that seizes up and forgets to strike a man down is the Hand of Death. The Hand of Life is the hand that does not stiffen, is relaxed, that seeks an opportunity, attends to changes, and operates at will. So it is with the wrist; one does not overextend the knees or lean into a move too much, but on every occasion, never losing a constant state of focus and presence of mind.

Then, look at the "posture":

> As for the body, the face does not look down, neither does it look up too much; the
> shoulders are not lifted up, neither are they slumped down; the belly is thrust out

without the chest; the hips are not slouched, the knees are not stiffened; the body is erect, with limbs apart from the body, and a wide visual aspect is maintained. The everyday body is the body of *heihō*. The body of *heihō* is a body of usual life. Reflect well on the meaning of this.

When we read this today, is it not, for the most part, like reading the Principles of *Zazen*, the instructions for sitting in Zen meditation? Especially the words, "The everyday body is the body of *heihō*," and "The body of *heihō* is a body of usual life," it must be said, are quite similar to Dōgen's words, the words he heard Master Nyojō say that led to Dōgen's enlightenment: "To learn the way of dharma is casting off the veil from the body and the mind.... Enlightenment is casting off the body and mind; casting off the body and mind is enlightenment."

Once posture is correct, next is footwork. Of course, there are big steps and small steps, fast and slow, but the essential point of footwork is in not losing one's everyday way of walking. The jumping step, the floating step, the fixed step, the drawn-out step, the left-behind step—these are all considered forbidden footwork. However difficult the situation might be, one must walk in the usual manner, as one normally would. He also called this everyday way of walking Yin-yang footwork.

The gaze, or *focus of the eyes*, must be considered carefully. The eyes primarily are focused on the face of the opponent, with the eyes narrowed somewhat more than normal. The eyeball does not move; even if the enemy approaches, one does not shift the eyes to look far away. If so, regardless of what moves the enemy makes, one's vision can see both sides of the opponent. Types of focus are, generally speaking, the perceiving eye, the seeing eye, and the signaling eye. In other words, there is the mind's eye, the physical eye, and the signaling or inviting eye.

The perceiving eye means to illuminate with your mind, which possesses more profound functions than the physical eye. The signaling eye is the manipulating of the physical eye, which functions to mislead the enemy's intentions—this eye has a function of will. The perceiving eye should be strong, the seeing eye weak. Intentions can be seen in the eye, but not in the mind.

The concept of estimating the gap between two martial artists differs greatly among various schools. Establishing or judging the space between oneself and one's enemy is an obsession driven by cowardice. It will be determined naturally as one gets used to combat. Originally, when you took up your sword against an enemy, it was thought that if your sword could touch the enemy, the enemy's could touch you. When one thinks to strike down a man, the self must be forgotten.

Accordingly, in all things, a "*frame of mind*" is essential. It is possible to consider "*frame of will*" (the heart of will) and "*frame of mind*" (the heart of hearts) as two distinct things. The heart of will is the condition of one's will. The heart of hearts is a selfless activity that is a more elevated heart of wholeness. In Confucian terms, this is called the "Mean." Musashi says, "Make the heart/mind like water, a heart/mind that corresponds to changing circumstances."

In the Book of Water, Musashi states,

> In the Way of *heihō*, the heart and mind should never depart from one's everyday heart and mind. Constantly, during *heihō*, keep the heart and mind unchanging, broaden the heart/mind, rectify it; neither tensed nor relaxed, the heart/mind is not biased; center it in your being, make it tremble quietly; keeping that moment of trembling going without stopping requires careful reflection. In quiet times, do not let the heart/mind be quiet; in hurried times, do not let the heart/mind be hurried at all. The body does not tug the heart/mind; the heart/mind does not tug the heart/mind. Guard the heart/mind; do not guard the body. Do not let the heart/mind be not enough; do not let the heart/mind be too much. Even if the top of the heart/mind (the heart of will) is weak on the outside, the bottom of the heart/mind (the heart of hearts) is strong on the inside. Do not let the heart/mind be discerned by others. Those small in stature must know the heart/mind of the large; the large in stature must know the heart/mind of the small. Large or small, one must keep the heart/mind straight and keep oneself free from bias. This is essential.

In addition to the "heart of will" and the "heart of hearts," Musashi also speaks of *zanshin*, the remaining heart/mind, and *hōshin*, the releasing heart/mind. When taking up the sword against an enemy, release the "heart of will" and let the "heart of hearts" remain. When determinedly striking down an enemy, release the heart of hearts and let the heart of will remain.

Musashi next discusses *kamae*—stances or positions. There are five *kamae*: Upper, Middle, Lower, Right Side, and Left Side. Becoming attached to *kamae* is reprehensible. *Kamae* that have a meaning of stillness are for times when no enemy is present. To assume a position (*kamae*) originally meant to have an unmovable heart/mind when challenged by another person. So the way of victory in *heihō*, in whatever one does, is striving to take the initiative. *The heart of assuming a position is the heart of waiting for the enemy's initiative.* Just as rushing water roils when striking a boulder, flying when it reaches a cliff, a *kamae* must be such that free, unobstructed movement is achievable, one in which one anticipates opportunity and attends to changes, one that embodies Center and Void and Spirit.

Musashi also explains the No-Stance Stance. A stance is a physical observation; No Stance a metaphysical observation; one harmonious action that transcends nothingness is the strange truth of *kamae*.

The taking of proper measurements with *a carpenter's chalk line* is yet another analogy Musashi uses. One must make one's own heart and mind straight as the carpenter's line so as to measure the enemy's strengths and weaknesses, tautness and slackness, crookedness and straightness. This wisdom is like the Zen teaching of making one's heart and mind clear as a mirror and quiet as still water. Having a heart and mind like a carpenter's line, one can sense the changing moment; it is termed *"Keiki wo shiru"*—*"Understand the conditions."*

Another important teaching of Musashi is *the Way of the long sword*. All farmers have their way of holding spades and hoes; boatmen know how to ply with sculls and oars. Similarly, without understanding how to wield the long sword, when one tries to strike the enemy one cannot always hit with strength and misses the target. Striking and hitting are two different things. *Heihō* requires training and discipline to make a true strike.

In order to achieve a true strike, it is essential to awaken oneself to the Three Sen—the three ways of preempting. They are:

+ *kakari no sen:* one gets the jump on the enemy, attacking first
+ *machi no sen:* waiting for the enemy to attack first
+ *tai tai no sen:* mutual engagement; both strike at the same time

Kakari no sen is a frontal attack that puts the enemy on the defensive. *Machi no sen* is to squash the enemy at the very moment of his first move. *Tai tai no sen* is for when the enemy attacks forcefully and one attacks quietly but strongly; when the enemy attacks nimbly, one attacks suddenly, following his fervor and striking soundly.

There are "Three Ways of Parrying." This must be considered as a paradox of the above. This is accomplished by *trampling the sword*. When the enemy's sword has come down, trample it, either with your foot or your own sword. And then, if you attack preemptively, you can always win.

Being able to control the "Yin-yang Shadow" is also important. Grasp the enemy's unpreparedness, confuse his spirit; oppress the enemy's outcomes, make him feel anguish. In brief, it is a way of taking the initiative.

Musashi also explains moves known as "Releasing the Bowstring" and the "Combing Lesson." Releasing the Bowstring is used to upset the enemy's timing and make him feel dispirited. The Combing Lesson is to take apart the enemy's intentions, as a comb untangles hair, and demonstrate your realization of how the enemy is going to move, making him feel that there are no countermeasures he can take.

Another important principle is "Knowing the Timing." Generally speaking, *timing* is the secret to all things. Musashi says,

> Although all things have a time or rhythm, without training in timing in *heihō*, especially, one cannot grasp it. Walking on the Way of *heihō*, one encounters timing and

rhythm in shooting an arrow, firing a gun, and riding a horse. Throughout all the arts and skills, timing cannot be gone against. Even emptiness has a rhythm. For a samurai himself, there is a time for completing one's service, a time for remaining quiet; a time for meeting expectations, a time for disregarding expectations. Or, in the Way of the merchant, there is a time for being wealthy, and, once wealthy, a time for losing wealth. Every Way has its own specific timing: a timing for things to flourish, a timing for declining—these must be distinguished carefully.

In *heihō* as well, there are various matters of timing. First, one must know good timing and understand bad timing. There are big, small, fast, and slow timings; among them, knowing the timing for hitting, knowing the timing for pausing, knowing the timing for outmaneuvering—these are the specialty of *heihō*. One is not proficient in *heihō* until he attains an understanding of the timing of outmaneuvering. In a battle of *heihō*, know the timing of the enemy, grasp the timing of not being drawn into the enemy's thinking, and then strike, being spurred by the timing of wisdom and the timing of emptiness.

In these matters of timing, when considered from the perspective of their function, we encounter a number of strokes: the One Well-Timed Blow, the Timing of the Second Bounce, the No-Design No-Concept Stroke, the Flowing Water Stroke, and many others. The One Well-Timed Stroke is to strike the enemy's *mu*—nothingness or Void—with your *mu*, all at once. Your *mu* is the culmination of nothingness, whereas the enemy's is the *mu* of futility. Whatever the enemy attempts to do—to draw his sword, release his sword, or to hit—you must find the gap and strike him quickly, before he has time to think.

The Timing of the Second Bounce is being aware of the enemy's tension when the enemy feels one is about to strike him, then throwing the enemy's timing off, like releasing a bowstring and striking him swiftly at the moment he feels dispirited.

The No-Design No-Concept Stroke is for when one is mutually engaged with the enemy, both thinking to strike at the same time. Usually, both sides hesitate but, preemptively, strike freely and forcefully with perfect serenity of mind, like a strong wind crossing the void.

The Flowing Water Stroke is for, when struggling with the enemy during the encounter, you notice his hurriedness to draw or release, and you strike with a large and strong stroke, like flowing water, as an infinitely pushing flow.

One must also bear in mind the "Stroke of the Situational Demands." At the enemy's sword, one wields one's sword to return the blow, to parry at times, to hit at times. Whether you swing, parry, or hit, do not think about doing it in a certain way. Hitting or parrying all depends on the occasional demands of the enemy's sword. Do not lose the stroke that is the mind of everyday action. This will become clear, even if inferred from the principle of a *kamae*—posture.

The point is that timing is a pivot of the free and unobstructed activity of a clear mind. Do not let your eyes wander over quick moves that are mere forms. Musashi's explanations are the immeasurable taste of wonder.

> The idea of *hayaki*—too fast—is that by not being synchronous with rhythm between the timing, too fast becomes too slow. One who becomes proficient in the Way does not appear to be fast. There are people who are fast runners, for example, who travel forty or fifty *ri*. But they do not run fast from morning to night. Those who cannot walk fast, even if they seem to run all day, show no measureable progress. In the Way of dance, when a poor singer follows the lead of a skilled singer, the tempo will lag, making them rush to catch up. Also, when the Noh piece "Old Pine" is played on the drums, it is a quiet song, but, again, an unskilled player will slow it down and so speed it up. "Takasago," on the other hand, has a brisk tempo, but it is bad to perform it too fast. "He who hurries, stumbles," as the saying goes, and he will not get there on time. Of course, being too slow is also bad. A skilled person's performance appears relaxed but never misses a beat. One who is disciplined in all things never appears rushed. Principles of the Way can be known from these examples.

"Holding Down the Pillow" is yet another move Musashi explains. When you sense that the enemy is about to make a strike, hold him down with your sword, your body, or your mind at the very moment he thinks to hit. This is the same as what is called "Managing the Yin-Yang Shadow." Once these moves are mastered, the "General and Soldier Lesson" is realized: one can make the enemy do one's bidding, as a general commands his soldiers' actions.

Musashi repeatedly describes another principle of Niten Ichi-ryū: "A Body Like a Rock." In *The 35 Principles*, he says,

> "A Body Like a Rock" means to be immovable, having developed a strong and great heart and mind. Such a body naturally possesses infinite reason, and all sentient living things avoid "A Body Like a Rock." It is difficult even for insentient plants and trees to put down roots on a rock. Falling rain and the blowing wind are the same. Examine "A Body Like a Rock" closely.

This is the consummation of martial art training for one to attain infinite power, to become mighty and immovable. In the words of Sō Kokuhan (Zeng Guofan), "The body is like a stable three-legged cauldron; the spirits are like the rising sun."

However one attempts to explain the warp and woof of consummate understanding, if one wants to uncover the truth, call it void, call it nothingness. It is said, "the most profound emptiness you, yourself, must develop through dedicated spiritual improvement." As Musashi writes in *Gorinsho*,

Speaking of the Void, here nothing would be the beginning and nothing would be the secret essence. Having attained the true Way, leave the true Way behind you; the Way of *heihō* will set you free, the Way of *heihō* will make you a benevolent person. In the fullness of time, know the timing of things, strike naturally and spontaneously, hit naturally and spontaneously. These are all the Way of the Void.

Accordingly, Musashi progressed from swordsmanship and entered the Way of *heihō*. On the Way, he did not fear death. On the Way, he continuously shed most earthly desires and lived more than fifty years of his life, by which time he was finally able to refine his mind and body to an unparalleled, resplendent freedom. Through his example, I am able to appreciate the model of a true Japanese samurai. In addition, for people today, he is surely, I believe, a giant who pioneered a path that should be taken. Investigating his spiritual training and discipline, taking note of his life, even the decadent people of today must feel an urge to commit themselves to self-improvement.

Life today is too caught up in frivolity. There is no polishing of the self, including the spirit. This, I believe, is a calamity.

15   Womanhood in Japan

All the virtues heretofore expounded that ought to be attained through deep self-reflection by Japanese men must also be fully understood by Japanese women. This is like unto the leaves of trees, changing in hue with the arrival of autumn, the oneness of nature. In the words of the great teacher, Sekitō Kisen (Shitou Xiqian, 700?–790, Chinese Chan Buddhist), men and women are as "two branches" of the same "tree of life."

Needless to say, branches develop from the tree—or spiritual source—and grow to completion; so it is with people, who can feel a sense of humanity all the more through having man and woman. The more masculine the man and the more feminine the woman, the more exquisite human beings become. The cold, grey world where men become like women and women become like men is most desolate and intolerable.

Such a world is a signal of the ruination of "the life" of human beings. The more masculine women become, the more difficult to appreciate the true meaning of man; the more feminine men become, the more difficult to appreciate the refinement of woman. For example, when man is truly masculine, the truly feminine of woman is then comprehensible.

For some parts of society, the demonstration of a masculine sense is taken to mean wild actions and authoritative control. A consistent feminine sense is understood as unable to oppose whatever men do and to thrive in the domestic environment merely caring for the male. Many are those who speak ill of the conventions and customs of Japanese women, advocating equality of the sexes and rejecting the stubborn traditional mindset that men should always be masculine and women feminine. But this thinking is problematic and needs consideration. As to what meaning explanations of the unconsciousness of Japanese women may have, it is confusing in the abstract among the masses and especially among groups of women.

Accepting the misconceptions of natural science, they follow the shadow of empty, general concepts and cannot embrace the subtleties, appearances, and nature of reality. And, because they are unable to extract themselves from a materialistic view, forms are broken down, and it is impossible to experience life directly. The majority of men and women purported to have received today's new education, having no calm, meditative thought whatsoever, chatter on indiscriminately about the conventions of women's lives, taking the superficial aspects only—is this not exposing their own lack of shamelessness?

Indeed, conventional women's lives must have contained many unreasonable elements. Many unforgiveable acts of rudeness, too, must have been committed toward women by the men whom they served. In building a just world of the future, we of course are obligated to point out this unreasonable behavior and correct it.

In doing so, however, disdaining them as if the women of ancient Japan had no correct life at all and speaking ill of Japanese men as if they were entirely lacking in moral sense toward women is nothing other than a frenzied state of forgetting ourselves. In particular, Bushido is reviled in open society today. I cannot help but think that such an uncritical attitude is strange.

As to how women of old conducted themselves and what kind of moral thinking they possessed, this has a deep significance that is certainly not permitted by today's trifling arguments. Bushido did not view women as slaves, but instead we can see an attempt to demand a thoroughly moral character in women. Seen from this perspective, I would here like to propound two or three fundamental problems that challenge the moral consciousness of contemporary women.

Moderns shed their previous lives of blindly following only what they were taught, an unavoidable function of the Enlightenment, recognizing and understanding phenomena with *Verstand*: one method of reasoning and subjective thinking. This was met with astonishment and pride. And thinking that the greatest life was as a machine operated by reason through the laws of natural science, they triumphed in gaining knowledge, merely analyzing and synthesizing things and events. They possessed a vain, general knowledge but did not consider deeply the true meaning of things. Furthermore, they had no cultivation or enhancement of moral character. Even if they had a clever knowledge of superficial things, they had no pure deeds or intuitions by which they could experience the true life of things.

Women of the future absolutely must disenthrall themselves from this sort of knowledge that is praise-seeking and ostentatious. Knowledge is certainly not something that has intrinsic worth. The truly valuable is creative moral character building. It is love. And—as regards the creative power of women from ancient times—is woman not a caring bodhisattva of love?

True knowledge must be, in all actuality, love. No matter if one can speak English or French, no matter how much one may know the names of philosophers and artists and their achievements, it does nothing whatever to increase the value of moral character. In a word, knowledge lies in how deeply and widely the conduct of moral character can reach through knowledge of these things. A mother who sits quietly and sews her daughter's kimono would have a far deeper knowledge of life than the daughter who digests novels and chatters on about the human condition.

Everyone, perhaps, has heard that the essence of life, especially of a woman's life, must be found in love. However, it is necessary to be conscious, without partiality, of the meaning of this love.

Love is wholly a function of the fusion of self and other. It is shedding the narrow, vulgar, material self and invoking ideals that try to live in the great world of moral character. Love, therefore, always makes the person selfless. A woman, however deep her desires may be, will give all she has, without knowing it, for her lover. Even a cold-hearted miser will not begrudge carrying things to the teacher for the sake of a child. A loyal subject would not regret giving his own life for his master.

In this way, since love is the engine that drives the ideal self, love inevitably leads to self-reflection; there is no stopping the yearning of human beings for the value of moral character. When a woman is in love, why does she become chaste in her dress? As the saying goes, "For whom are you wearing makeup?". Clearly, love makes the woman introspective and greatly stimulates her desire to become more beautiful and to be a better person—even if only a little bit more. Consequently, love naturally brings with it "shyness" (charming shyness). Meeting her lover, the innocent woman is mostly bewildered by the joy of receiving the one she hoped for and the feelings of being awakened to her own inexperience. Charming shyness has to be the most attractive sign of a woman's purity.

Women today, however, are shameless. They are much criticized for being arrogant. The arrogant conduct of a woman makes a hundred years of memories fade in one morning. That is because it exposes the absence of a woman's most valued introspection.

In this way, love makes a woman moderate, and at the same time, love makes it impossible not to entreat her lover to become more and more of a better person. The breakdown of the lover's moral character, the person on whom she staked her life, is at the same time the death of the woman who loves him. These, I think, are the essential demands of love.

There are examples from olden times too many to enumerate of wives and mothers committing suicide or becoming nuns because of fathers' or sons' improper conduct against a *bushi*. The code was "for embarrassing his lord, the minister must die." To give an example from recent times, a famous literary man and a woman reporter committed a double love suicide and left their bodies exposed to the world. But had the husband of the woman been a true *bushi*, he most likely would have committed *seppuku* or become a *rōnin* cenobite.

Love (*ai*), pure love, is effort; romantic love (*koi*), of course, is also effort; that is a marriage—accordingly, it is a sacred relationship between husband and wife.

Nevertheless, impulsive emotions are mistaken for love. If we consider the relation between husband and wife as being comprised merely of a shameless life of likes and dislikes, then we scorn the sacred moral effort of love. This is not what human beings should do. When a child shows bad behavior, a parent's love becomes most serious. It is then one must speak of the priceless essence of love. When a husband neglects his wife and leaves home, the wife, for the first time, is engaged in a test of love.

The unswerving determination of a woman of virtue is truly something to be prized. When a woman takes a lover immediately upon learning that her husband has taken a lover, staining her own conduct, such relations are the making of the animal realm. When a man who already has a wife causes disorder by being tempted by another woman, this is an even more shameless thing than the woman's infidelity—so it has been noisily debated since ancient times. Nay, whether a man is married or even single, one whose all is stolen away because of love and who neglects to do his duty has lost his presence of mind.

A woman's immorality is also the husband's shame. Under these circumstances, the way that a *bushi* is supposed to manage is to save his honor. Saving one's honor is, in other words, taking the most moral stance. In some cases, he would sever relations (divorce) without saying anything, leaving it to their free conduct. In other cases, there might be self-immolation. In any event, love in all things must be dignified. The kind of disgraceful behavior today, hiding under the good name of the doctrine of the supremacy of love, is—in reality—a bestial depravity. In such circumstances, how can the freedom of sublime moral character be recognized?

True consciousness must first be firmly realized as what is most precious in life. This fundamental problem can be clearly seen by looking at people who are said to be conscious, who have received a new education. Instead, an exceptionally large number of educated women demand human value in knowledge, status, assets, and capability. As Japanese novelist Natsume Sōseki (1867–1916) said, "In the real world, unless a man employs all his skills to grasp the authority or assets that are visible to the naked eye, he is not thought a man." Many are the educated women who believe so. Clever conversation and fashionable clothing are remarkably influential regarding these "enlightened women."

To borrow the words of a mystic, these women stop at cogitation and are lacking in meditation and contemplation. Therefore, they cannot possibly perceive the true value of character. The true value of character requires one to have introspection that is absolutely pure. Only when a woman is pure, can she love a man of valor, an estimable man of character. There is no likelihood that a woman who does not understand a man's spirit can have true love.

That *bushi* thought love base or vile is a complete falsehood. Love itself was not thought base or vile, but only love that was not part of the Way—a love toward something of no true value. When a cherished daughter secretly loved a man, and he was revered as an illustrious *bushi*, her father would speak of the discovery, slapping his knee, "Well done! That is my daughter!" The love of the daughter became the father's love. Isn't this spirit of love something to be joyful about? A bitter smile, instead, cannot be forbidden toward the wretchedness of the numerous ladies of today who happily give themselves to superficial and frivolous but stylish gentlemen and successful men of the world, smelling of money-lust.

Previously I have propounded on love that is both introspective, contemplative, and also a moral endeavor. Love's introspection, before long, will make a woman "modest." All people, through introspection, have engendered feelings of modesty. The feelings of reverence that manifest themselves in the body are, in another words, propriety and courtesy. This is what we call "*tsutsumashii*" (humble and modest). Accordingly, the moral endeavor that possesses the necessary roots in introspection must follow these feelings of reverence. A woman who possesses honor and fidelity that cannot be taken away is necessarily *tsutsumashii*. Moreover, she is kind and gentle.

Love is power. And because love makes a person selfless, the woman of love does not fear self-sacrifice through the life of love. Even when dealing with emergency circumstances, she does not panic. She has already achieved the final resolution.

For example, during the earthquake of 1923, when a rumor about attack by Koreans began to spread, young women broke into an ugly panic, whereas older women exhibiting great fortitude were exceedingly numerous. What must be called calm courage and great valor always springs from the sincerity of selflessness.

To my eyes, men and women educated today have very little "modesty" as such. Rarely does one meet a person whose body is ready to match the course of action of daily life. Everyone moves as if there were no bones in their arms and legs, lacking bodily firmness. Their way of walking is slovenly, their eyes sullied with lust and glistening for the voluptuous, their talent exposing the frivolous, affecting the coquetry of a prostitute—all the thought and life that is born of such an existence has, for all of them, no sincerity.

Now, the issues of women's participation in government and employment are creating a clamor. Thinking people must all give this serious consideration. There is a terribly foolish notion that women have no value without employment of some type, or that women working in order to have economic independence, or to participate in government—no, even leaving domestic duties to a housekeeper—is more valuable than living in the home.

As mentioned before, because people do not know the true meaning of life, the first principle is always found in a life of sincerity. Employment and political enfranchisement are the inevitable problems of secondary or tertiary importance.

There is no distinction of rank whatsoever between a wife working in the society called the household and a man working in the society of employment. The value they desire is determined solely by their moral character. "The wife lives in the home to slavishly serve the husband" and other such explanations are a prejudiced opinion that makes sense only in the vile house of a kept mistress. Were we to solve the inequalities of the working woman and the housewife, we would have to admit that people living on this earth naturally depend on slavery and would have to escape from this planet.

People today again need to reflect deeply on women's virtues. Forgetting the self and having tender affection for others and the light of intellect that spreads from there, paying scrupulous heed, having humility that listens to the good words of modesty, labor that does not begrudge loved ones, refined education—these are women's virtues, held by wives, mothers, and sisters. Such is the happy home that makes the Japanese *Volk* the envy of the world.

Afterword to the 2005 Japanese Edition

On the occasion of the publication of a new edition of *Nihon seishin no kenkyū* (*The Japanese Ethos*), one of Yasuoka Masahiro-sensei's major works, I had the pleasure of assisting with the Notes and Commentary.

The first edition, published in 1924, was a voluminous book extending to four hundred pages and forty-six printings. The revised, expanded edition, published in 1937, grew to a more than three-hundred-page octavo volume. Although the work was a collection of essays penned by Yasuoka-sensei in his twenties, on the eve of his university graduation while immersed in his studies and research, its impact, both in terms of quantity and quality, was overwhelming. Rich in persuasiveness on the one hand, the book was also difficult to comprehend.

As he stated in the introduction to the first edition, "I recollect I suffered over this small work, a record of an impassioned soul that grasped the essence of the Japanese spirit through my innermost self as daybreak disperses the shadow of darkness and confusion," the exuberant Yasuoka-sensei created the book from his whole body and soul. This book, together with *Ōyōmei kenkyū* (*A Study of Wang Yangming*), published in 1922, the year he graduated from university, had already, in his early twenties, established his reputation as a thinker.

All the more now that eighty years' time has passed, interpreting this great work—overwhelming as it is in quality and quantity—is not an easy task. The revised, expanded edition of 1937 was already a complete structure; proof of this is Yasuoka-sensei's argument, based on the teachings of the ancient and modern classics and histories of China, Japan, and the West, beginning with the four categories of Chinese learning: classics, histories, masters, and anthologies. Even returning to and understanding his sources and traditions require Herculean effort. So this time, for the Revised Edition, we decided to include notes and commentary on terminology, sources, and traditions. Throughout this project, we again had nothing but admiration for the mastery of the mysteries and secrets that is wide-ranging in Yasuoka-sensei's scholarship, making adequate notes and commentary nearly impossible.

However, relying on the reader's capacity and desire for wisdom that sincerely seeks to realize the brightness of the passion and soul of Yasuoka's education and learning, I hoped only for the inadequate Notes and Commentary to be supplemented.

The era of this work was a time when the world lurched in upheaval from the complications of nationalism and internationalism, the Russian Revolution, the Communist Internationale (Comintern) and other political movements, the advance and suppression of Asian nationalism, and the testing of a new world order by the League of Nations, immediately after World War I. The state of Japan's nationalism was being examined anew, and within it, an exploration of Japanese national identity, a divining of its essence, was being undertaken.

Nationalism and its diverse equivalents (*minzokushugi, kokuminshugi, kokkashugi*) have three indispensable aspects: (1) a tradition linked to the past; (2) current interest (national interest); and (3) the role, mission, and vision that should be achieved in the world in the future. In addition, the common understanding of the national individuality and characteristics that govern these three sides is identity—what can be said to form the core of nationalism.

Nihon seishin no kenkyū, covering these three dimensions as well as identity, the state of nationalism in Japan, how it ought to be, and with its full explanations, came to indicate a clear course for Japan during the turmoil of the Taishō (1912–1926) and Shōwa (1926–1989) eras. In other words, this book served as a forerunner to Shōwa nationalism, eventually assuming a pivotal role. The appreciation of this book and expectations of it were consequences of this.

Yasuoka-sensei said,

> Those who argue for a new emerging Asia are prone to assay Oriental thought lightly, relative to Western thought. However,…the problem is surely that unless Oriental thought is contemplated deeply, together with possessing an adequate understanding of Western thought, there can be no argument. It is human thought that is equal. First, grasping the kernel of problems such as human existence, the basis of reality, human ideals, et cetera, then one must consider deeply the characteristics of Oriental and Western thought, otherwise one cannot conduct Oriental thought that must truly embody a new emerging Asia.

This statement by Yasuoka-sensei, within his "fundamental attitude in a self-conscious world," indicates an Asianist stance, as it were, in the burgeoning "emerging Asia debate" concerning national mission and vision.

Since the Meiji era (1868–1912), Japanese nationalism—because its world recognition was based on a structure of oppositions, "East and West" and "Europe and Asia"—posed the big question of how both sides would cope. How to deal with these oppositions was divided largely into two currents: (1) the "out of Asia debate," inclined toward Europe; and (2) the "emerging Asia debate" and its Asianism. It is well-known that in Japan's modernization across all fields, the former has become the main current and the latter, a tributary. And, from the Taishō era, a third way of thinking arose: the "East-West civilization fusion debate," but still putting forward the argument that promoting the fusion of both civilizations was Japan's destiny. First centering on the "out of Asia debate," the "emerging Asia debate" was handled subordinately.

Given this historical background, what Yasuoka-sensei advocated in *Nihon seishin no kenkyū* was a consideration of East-West civilization fusion centered on the "emerging Asia debate" and an Asianism based on the Japanese ethos. His recollections can be seen as a testament to this.

> The peoples of Asia…when first trying to concretely realize a noble life in Asia, a land suited to Mahayana Buddhism, there began a sublime significance….Thus, the responsibility of the Japanese people is of unparalleled importance….I have no other reason for writing this book.

The day will come when the historical reputation of the Shōwa era—which endured sixty-four years as a period of upheaval and sudden change that included all the important events of human experience—will be settled. Yasuoka-sensei, his education, and learning, looked up to as a fatherly master and teacher of a lifetime, overcoming these upheavals and sudden changes to the end, will be regarded as a central figure providing leadership for the Japanese ethos during the Shōwa period. If one considers the Japanese ethos during the Shōwa period from the viewpoint of nationalism within these circumstances, *Nihon seishin no kenkyū* and its supplementary volume, *Nihon seishin tsūgi* (*Principles of Japanese Ethos*), come into focus.

In *Nihon seishin tsūgi*, published in 1936, Yasuoka-sensei states,

> Japan is now advancing in world affairs at the fastest pace in recorded history, truly eventful both domestically and internationally,…I have argued for the true significance of the Japanese ethos amid today's noisy Asianism and Westernism, making clear the way of Shinto, Confucian, and Buddhist negotiation and development, important in the history of the Japanese heart and mind and in the history of life.

It is said that Nitobe Inazō's *Bushido* is read widely. Sixty years after the war, there are among those reexamining Shōwa history from the viewpoint of nationalism—a taboo under the occupation policy—many readers who will turn to the new edition of *Nihon seishin no kenkyū*. This, by itself, makes our efforts worthwhile.

Arai Katsura
Chief and Deputy Director
Kyōgaku Institute, an Incorporated Foundation

Glossary

Bakumatsu	the final years of the Tokugawa era, between the opening of the country to foreign trade in 1853 and the Meiji Restoration in 1867
bu (武)	martial arts
budō (武道)	the way of martial arts
bushi (武士)	samurai warrior
Bushido (武士道)	the way of the samurai
heihō (兵法)	art of war, strategy of war
kai no ben (華夷の弁)	argument between civilized and uncivilized countries
kendo (剣道)	the way of the sword
kenpō (剣法)	swordsmanship
kleśā	in Buddhism, polluting thoughts and emotions that cause suffering
kōzen no ki (浩然の気)	a great and magnanimous spirit
kunshi (君子)	person of virtue
Other Power	salvation in the Pure Land through the power of Amida Buddha (*tariki*), as opposed to self power or individual effort (*jiriki*)
rōnin (浪人)	masterless samurai
shi (士)	samurai of great integrity
shidō (士道)	the way of the samurai
shishi (志士)	warriors of high ideals engaged in a noble cause

Index

About the Author

Crowned by a letter of condolence from Emperor Hirohito, Yasuoka Masahiro's funeral in January 1984, a month after his private services, was attended by every living Japanese prime minister and top business and political leaders from Japan, Korea, and Taiwan. The funeral services were overseen by Kishi Nobusuke, a former prime minister, and public eulogies were led by then-current Prime Minister Nakasone Yasuhiro. As a private scholar-advisor to many of those in attendance, Yasuoka had a major influence on modern Japanese history.

Yasuoka Masahiro (1898–1983), a dominant philosopher and intellectual beacon during Japan's transition into the modern era, was born in Osaka in 1898. He was born into the Hotta family, which traced its samurai lineage to the 14th century. Just 30 years after the Meiji Restoration, it was a time when Japan was increasingly turning its eyes towards Western civilization, and away from the samurai way of life and spirit.

Just as any samurai from the days of old would have done, Yasuoka practiced kendo (Japanese sword fighting) and studied Chinese classics from a very young age. He graduated from Tokyo Imperial University in 1922 as a political science major. There, he had studied all of the Western disciplines which flowed into Japan in those days, but his attitude towards these ideas, as he aptly expressed in a college essay, remained: "It is not how new it is, but how true it is that matters."

After graduating from college, Yasuoka published *A Study of Wang Yangming* (王陽明研究), and in 1923, while still in his early 20s, compiled his essays, and published *The Japanese Ethos: A Study of National Character*, the following year. These two books quickly established Yasuoka's fame as a scholar, and he attracted a strong following of top political and business leaders, bureaucrats, and court officials.

His great passion being to educate others, Yasuoka never sought the political spotlight, choosing to remain relatively unknown to the broader public. Instead, he established Toyo Shisō Kenkyūjo (Institute for the Study of Eastern Thought) in 1922, Kinkei Gakuin (Kinkei School) in 1927, and Nihon Nōshi Gakkō (Japan

Agricultural Leader School) in 1931, all devoted to educating young leaders and spreading self-cultivation through Eastern thought. In 1947, after World War II, he established the Shiyu Society (師友会), an institution dedicated to educating the general public, young and old. The mission of the school was encapsulated in their motto: 一燈照遇　万燈照国, which translates: "Even if the beginning is a small light shining from a corner, if those lights are gathered to hundreds, and thousands, it becomes a light shining all over the country."

At the same time, he led numerous study groups with business and political leaders, teaching them the "Great Leader's Way": lessons on how to cultivate moral character and become a "great man." He also became a private scholar-advisor to prime ministers, and other top political and business leaders. His list of distinguished students includes Yoshida Shigeru (1878–1967), who led the post-war Japanese congress twice, and, though twenty-years Yasuoka's senior, reverently referred to Yasuoka as "Old Master" (老先生), and Satō Eisaku (1901–1975), a three-term prime minister and recipient of the Nobel Peace Prize, who relied on Yasuoka to review every official speech he made. It is also a well-known fact that Emperor Hirohito's surrender speech at the end of World War II was edited by Yasuoka, and "Heisei," the name of the era of Emperor Akihito, originated from him.

Today, Yasuoka's legacy lives on through the books about him and his writings, which continue to be published more than 25 years after his death. As one critic, Fumiko Halloran, astutely noted several years ago, "The legend of Yasuoka is still alive."

Additional information about Yasuoka Masahiro may be obtained from:

Kyōgaku Institute
671 Sugaya, Ranzan Machi,
Hiki Gun, Saitama, 355-0221, Japan
Tel: (81)0493-62-3375
E-mail: kyogaku@kyogaku.or.jp

Kansai Shiyu Society
4-7-15 5th fl, Minami Senba,
Chuo-Ku, Osaka, 542-0081, Japan
Tel: (81)06-6244-3326
Fax: (81)06-6244-3327
E-mail: siyukai@guitar.ocn.ne.jp

About the Jacket Artist: Masanori Minami

Masanori Minami was born in Osaka in 1951. At the age of 9, he lost both his arms in a tragic accident, and, at age 15, he was chosen to be the last student of Junkyō Ōishi, a nun in the city of Kyoto, who is known as the "Helen Keller of Japan." Junkyō had also lost both her arms and, under her tutelage, Masanori learned classical Japanese-style painting.

In 1967, Masanori first submitted his work to the Sakai Municipal Exhibition in Osaka. He won, and has received the awards every year since. In 1975, he was accepted as a member of the Association of Mouth and Foot Painting Artists, and in 1999, he received a distinguished service medal from the Soroptimist International Society. Besides art, Masanori is involved with a volunteer group that builds schools in Nepal. So far, he has participated in the building of three schools. He also visits jails and youth correctional centers in Japan as a mentor/speaker.

Production Notes for Yasuoka/ *The Japanese Ethos*
Cover design by Julie Matsuo-Chun
Composition by Wanda China with display type in Franklin Gothic and text in Adobe
Jenson Pro and MS Mincho
Printing and binding by Sheridan Books, Inc.
Printed on 60 lb. House White Opaque, 500 ppi